THE

ROMAN ARMY

THE GREATEST WAR MACHINE
OF THE ANCIENT WORLD

THE

ROMAN ARMY

THE GREATEST WAR MACHINE OF THE ANCIENT WORLD

EDITED BY CHRIS McNAB

OSPREY
PUBLISHING

First published in Great Britain in 2010 by Osprey Publishing,
This revised edition published 2013 by Osprey Publishing.
Midland House, West Way, Botley, Oxford OX2 0PH, UK
6th Floor, Rizzoli Building, 31 W. 57th St., New York, NY 10019, USA
Email: info@ospreypublishing.com

Osprey Publishing is part of the Osprey Group.

Previously published as BTO 27, Nic Fields, *The Roman Army of the Punic Wars 264–146 BC* (2007); BTO 34, Nic Fields, *The Roman Army: the Civil Wars 88–31 BC* (2008); BTO 37, Nic Fields, *The Roman Army of the Principate 27 BC–AD 117* (2009); CAM 36, Mark Healy, *Cannae 216 BC* (1994); CAM 84, Simon MacDowall, *Adrianople AD 378* (2001); CAM 174, Si Sheppard, *Pharsalus 48 BC* (2006); ELI 121, Duncan B. Campbell, *Ancient Siege Warfare* (2005); ELI 126, Duncan B. Campbell, *Siege Warfare in the Roman World* (2005); ELI 155, Ross Cowan, *Roman Battle Tactics* (2007); ESP 6, Kate Gilliver, Arian Goldsworthy & Michael Whitby, *Rome at War: Caesar and His Legacy* (2005); ESS 16, Nigel Bagnall, *The Punic Wars 264–146 BC* (2002); FOR 43, Duncan B. Campbell, *Roman Legionary Fortresses 27 BC–AD 378* (2006); MAA 46, Michael Simkins, *The Roman Army from Caesar to Trajan* (1984); MAA 83, Michael Simkins, *The Roman Army from Hadrian to Constantine* (1979); MAA 121, Terence Wise, *Armies of the Carthaginian Wars 265–146 BC* (1982); MAA 247, David Nicolle, *Romano-Byzantine Armies 4th–9th Centuries* (1992); MAA 283, Nicholas Sekunda and Simon Northwood, *Early Roman Armies* (1995); MAA 291, Nicholas Sekunda, *Republican Roman Army 200–104 BC* (1996); MAA 390, Graham Sumner, *Roman Military Clothing (2) AD 200–400* (2003); MAA 425, Raffaele D'Amato, *Roman Military Clothing (3) AD 400–640* (2005); NGV 89, Duncan B. Campbell, *Greek and Roman Artillery 399 BC–AD 363* (2003); WAR 9, Simon MacDowall, *Late Roman Infantryman AD 236–565* (1994); WAR 15, Simon MacDowall, *Late Roman Cavalryman AD 236–565* (1995); WAR 71, Ross Cowan, *Roman Legionary BC–AD 69* (2003); WAR 72, Ross Cowan, *Imperial Roman Legionary AD 161–284* (2003); and WAR 101, Nic Fields, *Roman Auxiliary Cavalryman AD 14–193* (2006).

A CIP catalogue record for this book is available from the British Library.

ISBN: 978 1 78200 942 9

Page layout by Myriam Bell Design, France
Maps, artwork and diagrams by Brian Delf, Gerry Embleton, Adam Hook, Christa Hook, Richard Hook, Angus McBride, Graham Sumner, The Map Studio Ltd., and Boundford.
Index by Alan Thatcher
Typeset in Perpetua and Optima
Originated by PPS Grasmere Ltd, Leeds, UK
Printed in China through World Print Ltd.

13 14 15 16 17 10 9 8 7 6 5 4 3 2 1

The Woodland Trust
Osprey Publishing is supporting the Woodland Trust, the UK's leading woodland conservation charity, by funding the dedication of trees.

www.ospreypublishing.com

Front Cover: 'Vercingetorix Throws Down His Arms at the Feet of Julius Caesar' by Lionel Noel Royer, (Corbis)
Back Cover: Two Roman soldiers armed with helmet, shield and *pilum*. They show the classic fighting stance of a legionary. (AKG Berlin / Erich Lessing)
Title Page: Detail from Trajan's Column (akg-images)

CONTENTS

CHRONOLOGY

753 BC	Traditional date for the foundation of Rome.
***c.*616–578 BC**	Reign of Tarquinius Priscus.
***c.*578–534 BC**	Reign of Servius Tullius.
***c.*534–510 BC**	Reign of Tarquinius Superbus.
510 BC	Expulsion of Tarquinius Superbus, and the establishment of the Roman Republic.
494 BC	The protest of the plebeians and the establishment of the plebeian tribunate.
437–426 BC	The Roman-Fidenaen War.
406–396 BC	Rome defeats Etruscan city of Veii.
390 BC	Gallic sack of Rome.
113–101 BC	Invasions of Gaul and Italy by Cimbri and Teutones (Germanic tribes).
106 BC	Birth of Cnaeus Pompey and Marcus Tullius Cicero.
100 BC	Birth of Julius Caesar.
91–89 BC	The Social War, a widespread rebellion of Rome's Italian allies, defeated only after heavy Roman losses; Roman citizenship is extended to nearly all the peoples of Italy.
88 BC	Marius attempts to take the eastern command away from Lucius Cornelius Sulla; Sulla marches with his army on Rome, the first time any Roman commander has done this.
87 BC	Marius and his ally Cinna seize power in Rome, massacring their opponents; Marius dies of natural causes.
83–80 BC	Sulla lands in Italy and is joined by Pompey; Sulla defeats his opponents and wins the civil war; Sulla becomes dictator, publishes proscriptions, and attempts to reform the state, rebuilding the Senate's authority.
79 BC	Sulla retires.
78 BC	One of the consuls, Lepidus, stages a coup; the Senate uses Pompey to defeat him.

73–71 BC	An escaped gladiator called Spartacus rebels and forms a huge army of slaves; he defeats successive Roman armies and devastates much of Italy before he is finally defeated by Marcus Licinius Crassus.
71 BC	Rivalry between the Aedui and Arverni leads to the Sequani, Arvernian allies, hiring German mercenaries and together they defeat the Aedui; Pompey and Crassus camp with their armies outside Rome and demand the right to stand for election to the consulship.
70 BC	Consulship of Pompey and Crassus.
67 BC	Pompey given extraordinary command against the pirates.
66 & 62 BC	The Allobroges revolt, mainly due to poor Roman administration.
66 BC	Pompey given extraordinary command against Mithradates of Pontus.
63 BC	The consul Cicero defeats the attempted coup of Catiline.
62 BC	Pompey returns from the east but fails to secure land for his veterans or the ratification of his Eastern Settlement.
61 BC	Caesar becomes propraetorian governor of Further Spain; Aedui request help from Rome, Rome declines to assist but the Senate formally confirms Roman support for them; the Helvetii prepare to migrate to western France.
60 BC	Caesar returns and forms the 'First Triumvirate' with Pompey and Crassus.
59 BC	Consulship of Caesar and Bibulus; Caesar is appointed governor of northern Italy (Cisalpine Gaul) and Dalmatia for five years from 58 BC; Southern France (Transalpine Gaul) is added to Caesar's jurisdiction after the sudden death of the governor.
58 BC	The plebian tribune Clodius forces Cicero into exile; Caesar takes up his governorship; in late June Caesar defeats the migrating Helvetii at Bibracte and orders them home; in mid-September Caesar defeats Ariovistus.
57 BC	Serious rioting in Rome; Pompey called upon to supervise corn supply; Caesar campaigns against the Belgae; late in the year, Galba is defeated in the Alps.
56 BC	Crisis in the triumvirate averted by meeting of Pompey, Crassus and Caesar at Luca, Caesar's command is extended for a further five years; Roman naval defeat of Veneti; Roman legate Sabinus defeats tribes of Normandy; Roman legate Crassus reduces Aquitania (south-west France); the Menapii and Morini (Belgian coast and Rhine delta) successfully resist Roman incursions.
55 BC	Second consulship of Pompey and Crassus; German tribes cross the Rhine and are massacred by Caesar; the Romans bridge the Rhine; first Roman invasion of Britain.

54 BC	Serious rioting in Rome; death of Julia, Pompey's wife and Caesar's daughter; Crassus invades Parthia; Morini submits to Rome, possibly intimidated by the presence of the Roman fleet in the English Channel; attacks on Roman winter camps in Gaul; second Roman invasion of Britain.
53 BC	Crassus is defeated and killed by Parthians at Carrhae; Caesar leads punitive campaigns against Belgic tribes.
52 BC	Milo's gang kills Clodius; Gallic revolt: siege of Alesia and the surrender of Vercingetorix.
51 BC	Repeated attacks on Caesar's position in the Senate; Pompey passes law requiring a five-year interval between holding a magistracy and being appointed to a province; Cicero sent to Cilicia; Gallic revolt: blockade and surrender of Uxellodunum (in Lot, south-west France).
50 BC	Curio acts on Caesar's behalf in the Senate; Cato and other prominent senators struggle to ensure that Caesar will not be permitted to stand for the consulship without laying down his command of the army; Pompey's position unclear for much of the year; minor Roman campaigns in central Gaul.
49 BC	The tribunes flee from Rome; Caesar crosses the Rubicon and civil war begins; Pompey chased out of Italy, and sails with most of his troops from Brundisium to Macedonia; Caesar defeats Afranius and Petreius in Spain; Curio defeated and killed in Africa.
48 BC	Caesar crosses to Macedonia, prolonged stalemate at Dyrrhachium eventually broken when Caesar retreats; Pompey brought to battle at Pharsalus and utterly defeated; Pompey flees to Egypt and is murdered; Caesar pursues him and is besieged in Alexandria; beginning of affair between Caesar and Cleopatra.
47 BC	Caesar is able to break the siege of Alexandria after reinforcements arrive, and defeats the Egyptian army; later in the year he moves to Asia and defeats Pharnaces at Zela; Caesar returns to Rome and prepares to campaign against the Pompeian army mustering in Africa under Scipio, Cato and Juba.
46 BC	African war ended by Caesar's victory at Thapsus; Cato and Juba commit suicide, and Scipio is drowned; Caesar returns to Rome and celebrates triumphs, but departs for Spain in the autumn.
45 BC	Spanish War ended by Caesar's victory at Munda; Labienus, Pompey's eldest son, killed; Caesar returns to Rome and establishes dictatorship.
44 BC	Caesar is murdered on 15 March by a conspiracy led by Brutus and Cassius; Octavian arrives in Rome and rallies support from Caesar's veterans; Antony given command in Cisalpine Gaul.
43 BC	Octavian initially fights Antony on the Senate's behalf, but later in the year they, with Lepidus, form the 'Second Triumvirate', they capture

	Rome and reintroduce the proscriptions, executing large numbers of prominent Romans, including Cicero.
42 BC	Brutus and Cassius defeated at Philippi.
41 BC	Antony visits Cleopatra in Alexandria and their affair becomes publicly known.
40 BC	Antony marries Octavia.
40–36 BC	Antony's Parthian War.
38 BC	Sextus Pompeius wins naval victories over Octavian.
37 BC	Antony publicly 'marries' Cleopatra.
36 BC	Sextus Pompeius defeated at Naulochus near Sicily.
32 BC	Octavia openly divorced by Antony; Open civil war between Antony and Octavian.
31 BC	Octavian defeats Antony at Actium; Antony and Cleopatra escape, but commit suicide; Octavian becomes undisputed master of the Roman world.
27 BC	Octavian takes name Augustus and restores Republic; provinces shared between Senate and Augustus.
27–24 BC	Campaigns in Gaul and Spain.
20 BC	Parthians return captured Roman standards.
12–9 BC	Campaigns in Balkans.
12 BC–AD 6	Campaigns in Germany.
AD 6–9	Suppression of provincial revolts.
AD 9	Varian disaster in the Teutoburger forest in Germany.
AD 14	Death of Augustus; legions revolt in Pannonia and on the Rhine.
AD 17–24	Campaigns against Tacfarinas in Africa.
AD 40–44	Conquest of Mauretania.
AD 43	Claudius begins invasion of Britain.
AD 58–63	Campaigns against Parthia.
AD 60/1	Revolt of Boudicca in Britain.
AD 66	Start of Jewish Revolt.
AD 68–9	The Year of the Four Emperors; civil war breaks out after Nero's suicide.
AD 69	Vespasian's victory ends civil war.
AD 70	Capture of Jerusalem and destruction of the Temple.
AD 83–97	Domitian campaigns against Dacians on the Danube and Chatti on the Rhine.
AD 98	Accession of Trajan.
AD 101–6	Dacian Wars.

AD 106	Annexation of Arabia.
AD 113–17	Campaigns against Parthians.
AD 115–17	Jewish revolt.
AD 117	Accession of Hadrian; evacuation of eastern conquests.
AD 122–6	Construction of Hadrian's Wall in northern Britain.
AD 132–5	Bar Kochva revolt in Judaea.
AD 142	Construction of Antonine Wall in northern Britain.
AD 161	Accession of Marcus Aurelius; Parthians invade Syria and Armenia.
AD 162–6	Lucius Verus campaigns against Parthians.
AD 166	German tribes cross upper Danube.
AD 167–80	German wars of Marcus Aurelius.
AD 180	Accession of Commodus; peace with Quadi and Marcomanni.
AD 192	Assassination of Commodus.
AD 192–3	Year of the Five Emperors: civil war.
AD 193	Septimius Severus defeats Pescennius Niger in the east.
AD 194–5	Severus campaigns against Parthians.
AD 197	Severus defeats Clodius Albinus in Gaul.
AD 197–200	Further campaigns of Severus against Parthians.
AD 208–11	Severus campaigns with sons Caracalla and Geta in northern Britain.
AD 211	Accession of Caracalla.
AD 213–14	Caracalla campaigns on Danube.
AD 215–17	Caracalla campaigns in the east.
AD 217	Assassination of Caracalla.
AD 222	Accession of Severus Alexander.
AD 226	Sassanid Ardashir overthrows Parthian dynasty.
AD 231–2	Severus Alexander campaigns against Sassanids.
AD 234–5	Severus Alexander campaigns against German tribes.
AD 235	Assassination of Severus Alexander by troops.
AD 243/4	Gordian defeated by Shapur I of Persia.
AD 251	Death of Decius in battle against Goths.
AD 260	Defeat and capture of Valerian by Persians; Franks invade Gaul; Alamanni invade Italy; revolts in Balkans.
AD 261–68	Odaenathus of Palmyra takes control of eastern provinces.
AD 262–67	Goths invade Asia Minor.
AD 271	Aurelian withdraws Romans from Dacia; circuit of walls built for Rome.

AD 272	Aurelian defeats Palmyra.
AD 275	Murder of Aurelian.
AD 284	Accession of Diocletian.
AD 293	Tetrarchy. Diocletian appoints Maximian as co-Augustus and Constantius and Galerius as Caesars.
AD 305	Abdication of Diocletian and Maximian.
AD 312	Constantine captures Rome after battle of Milvian Bridge.
AD 324	Constantine defeats Licinius and becomes sole emperor.
AD 337	Death of Constantine at the start of the campaign against Persia.
AD 353	Constantius II defeats usurper Magnentius and reunifies Empire.
AD 355	Julian co-opted by Constantius as Caesar.
AD 357	Julian defeats Alamanni at Strasburg.
AD 361	Death of Constantius.
AD 363	Julian's invasion of Persia and death.
AD 376	Goths cross the Danube.
AD 378	Defeat and death of Valens at Adrianople (Edirne).
AD 382	Theodosius settles Goths in Balkans as federates.
AD 394	Theodosius defeats usurper Eugenius and reunifies Empire.
AD 395	Death of Theodosius; Empire divided between Arcadius and Honorius.
AD 406	German tribes breach Rhine frontier.
AD 408	Stilicho executed.
AD 410	Sack of Rome by Alaric and Visigoths.
AD 418	Establishment of Visigoths in Aquitania.
AD 429	Vandals cross into Africa.
AD 445	Attila becomes sole ruler of Huns.
AD 451	Attila invades Gaul; defeated at Catalaunian Plains (near Troyes).
AD 453	Death of Attila.
AD 455	Vandals sack Rome.
AD 476	Odoacer deposes Romulus Augustulus, the last of the Western Roman Empire.
AD 493	Theoderic captures Ravenna and kills Odoacer.
AD 502	Kavadh invades eastern provinces and captures Amida (Diyarbakir).
AD 505	Truce on eastern frontier; Construction of Dara starts.
AD 507	Clovis and Franks defeat Visigoths at Vouillé.
AD 527	Renewed warfare in east; accession of Justinian.

INTRODUCTION

THE ROMAN EMPEROR Severus Alexander (r. 222–35) is said to have had the motto 'One need not fear a soldier, if he is properly clothed, fully armed, has a stout pair of boots, a full belly, and something in his money-belt.' Within Severus' statement lurks the prospect that the Roman soldier, depending on the ambitions of his leadership, could be as much a threat to Rome's internal governance as it was to its external enemies. Yet, particularly with the establishment of the Augustan principate in 27 BC, the Roman Army and its allies were stable and powerful enough to create one of the most sizeable and durable empires in all history.

We must not mythologize the material that made up the Roman Army. Unsurprisingly, military service seems to have been most attractive as a career to the poorest of men. For such men the army offered a roof over their head, food in their bellies, and an annual income. Overall a soldier's life was more secure than that of an itinerant labourer. Naturally, there was a harsher side to a military career. Service, depending on the period in history, could last for a single bloody campaign or for decades. During that time a soldier ran the risk of being killed or crippled by battle or disease. On an everyday basis he was subject to the army's brutal discipline, with both corporal and capital punishment being imposed for misdemeanours. Training was aggressive and frighteningly realistic.

The product, however, was a formidably well-organized army as cruel as it was disciplined. With this tool Rome could fully express its imperial ambitions.

Imperialism implies a conscious desire to conquer, and if it is to carry weight in the historical balance, it must lead to some spectacular and abiding achievement. The expression *pax Romana*, adopted from the elder Pliny, was used by that polymath incidentally, in describing plants 'now available to the botanist from all the corners of the world, thanks to the boundless majesty of Roman peace' (*Historia Naturalis*, 27.1.3). But *pax Romana* should not be sneered at, especially if we consider the terrible plight of our own world today. Despite notable exceptions, the Empire and its armed frontiers were relatively quiet for two centuries. This was something new, and as yet to be repeated, for the human condition.

In its broad outline, the manifest destiny of Rome was devastatingly simple. The mood of the time, if correctly reflected in the literature of the day, leans unmistakably toward irresistible expansion beyond the confines of Italy on the grounds of mission, decreed fortune and divine will. We can credit the progressive but eccentric Claudius with a concept of the unity of the Empire, an Empire in which the conquered, whatever their race, profited as much as the conquerors from *pax Romana*. However, bigotry and understanding are strange bedfellows at the best of times, and within the Empire, despite the wisdom of Emperors such as Claudius in taking the longer view, there was a permanent division between the conquered and their conquerors. For in truth world dominion rested on Rome's military arm, whose strength and length were not indefinite. Moreover, with its laws against the bearing of arms, *pax Romana* would eventually create a state whose citizens would forget how to fight. For returning to the point made above, in fact on the field of battle Rome had no secret weapon. It prevailed not through technical superiority but by the fruit of iron discipline, dogged pertinacity, exceptional organization and sanguine reputation. The Roman Army was always at its best in set-piece, face-to-face encounters, and in that way it conquered much of the known world.

This book is not a history of the Roman Republic and Empire, although we will make some in-depth studies of particular campaigns, periods and battles. (The chonology on pp.6–11 serves to provide the broader historical framework to the book.) Rather it is a study of how the Roman war machine evolved from the foundation of Rome in the 8th century BC to the fall of the Western Roman Empire in the 5th century AD, with a glimpse beyond to the enduring Byzantine Empire. As we shall see, the story is one of how much hardened men can achieve when their efforts are disciplined and focused in the service of the state.

THE EARLY REPUBLICAN ARMY,

753–146 BC

INTRODUCTION: THE FIRST ROMAN ARMIES

THE EARLIEST PRESERVED MILITARY REMAINS from Rome date from the 8th and 9th centuries BC. At this time, the huts of the village which would eventually become the Eternal City lay on the Capitoline Hill, while the necropolis of the settlement was situated on the Esquiline Hill. A number of early tombs there were excavated in 1885 during construction work on a housing project. Of these tombs, some are clearly 'warrior-burials', while others contain assorted weapons. It is from these finds that we can begin to form an impression of the earliest Roman warriors, while early textual sources provide some indication of the Roman military structure.

The earliest reliable information concerning the size and organization of the fledgling Roman Army describes how it was recruited from three 'tribes'. Roman society was at some early stage divided into three tribes and thirty *curiae*. The word *curia* is generally derived from *co-viria*, that is, 'an assembly of armed men'. The *curiae* formed the voting units of the earliest Roman assembly, the *comitia curiata*. Each *curia* was formed from a number of families (*gentes*) and ten of these *curiae* formed a tribe (*tribus*).

Each tribe seems to have been commanded by a *tribunes militum* and to have contributed 1,000 men (i.e. 100 from each *curia*) to a Roman military force. This led the Roman antiquarian Varro to speculate that *miles* (the Latin for 'soldier') was derived from *mille* (the Latin for 'a thousand'): 'soldiers are *milites* because at first the legion was made of three thousand and each of the individual tribes of Tities, Ramnes and Luceres sent a thousand soldiers' (*De Lingua Latina*, V:XVI). Although Varro's etymology is probably incorrect (the true etymology of *miles* is unknown), the fact that he was able to suggest such an interpretation demonstrates that the principle of having a thousand men to the legion was already well established when he wrote.

The horsemen in this tribal organization are said to have been divided into three groups, each of 100 men. Livy and Cicero tell us that these groups had the names *Ramnes*, *Tities* and *Luceres*, names which Varro said also applied to whole tribes. This confusion should not worry us unduly – the longer survival of this early cavalry organization meant that these names were later associated only with the cavalry. It is unclear whether these cavalrymen are the same as the 300 *celeres* (literally 'the swift') who were supposedly instituted by Rome's first and legendary king, Romulus, as a bodyguard (see Livy, Festus, and Servius).

Previous page:
Hannibal in Italy, attributed to Jocopp Ripanda. One of three frescos in the 'Hall of Hannibal' in the Palazzo dei Conservatori of the Capitoline Museum in Rome. (© Gianni Dagli Orti, Corbis)

THE EARLIEST ROMAN WARRIORS, *c.*700 BC
Had Romulus (left) and Remus (right) existed, they may have looked like these two figures, based on 8th-century finds. In the foreground lies an Estruscan warrior. (© Richard Hook, Osprey Publishing)

Exactly what these 'horsemen' were is unclear. True cavalry may not have existed at this time, and we can perhaps compare them to warriors in archaic Greece. Here the title of *hippies* was given to elite bands of hoplites who no longer used horses in battle but had originally used chariots and horses as a means of travelling to the battlefield and

EARLY MILITARY ARTEFACTS

Only two helmets have emerged from early Rome, and both are of the 'Calotte' type, though it is possible that other helmet types were used too. The standard form of body-protection was the pectora' or breastplate, of which three have survived. They are rectangular in shape, with incurving sides, a little less than 20cm wide and a little more than 20cm long. Presumably they were worn with the long side running vertically, although this is not certain. The smaller sides are pierced with holes for the attachment of a leather backing and straps to hold the pectoral in place. The pectorals are decorated with bands of geometric ornamentation round the edge, and five bosses, one in the centre and one in each of the four corners.

One large ornamental bronze shield has survived. This shield is entirely Etruscan in style, and may well have been manufactured in one of the major manufacturing centres of Etruria, such as Tarquinii. We should also note, however, that an iron boss found separately might have come from a wooden shield. Two sizes of sword have been recovered: short swords about 44cm long, and long swords about 70cm long. Sword blades at this time were generally bronze, but iron examples are occasionally found. Numerous spear-heads have been found in the Esquiline tombs, sometimes of iron, sometimes of bronze. They have leaf-shaped blades and typically a multi-faceted central section, sometimes decorated with a geometric pattern.

an indication of their social status. Thus the Roman *equites* of the 5th century BC may have no more been horsemen than the Spartan *hippies* of the same period.

Tradition claims that the tribal system was introduced by Romulus in the 8th century BC, but modern historians are unanimous in concluding that this cannot be the case. The three tribal names (*Tities*, *Ramnes* and *Luceres*) are clearly Etruscan. Consequently the system of three tribes and 30 *curiae* was introduced under the direct influence of the Etruscans, probably towards the end of the 7th century BC. This raises the much larger problem of which method of warfare and equipment was used by the three tribes. It is possible that hoplite tactics and equipment were introduced in Rome at the same time as the tribal system, i.e. a little before 600 BC; but it is more probable that Servius Tullius introduced them some half-century later.

This 'Calotte' helmet from Esquiline Tomb 94, now in the Capitoline Museum, had been dated to the first half of the 7th century BC. This early photograph demonstrates the fragmentary state of the skull: it is possible that the helmet originally had a number of plumes and other fittings which were not recovered during the excavation. (N. Sekunda & S. Northwood)

THE HOPLITE ARMY

Hoplite tactics were developed in Greece *c.*675 BC and reached Etruria *c.*600 BC, where their use is confirmed in a wide variety of contemporary artwork. Dionysius of Halicarnassus reports how the Etruscan towns of

ROME, 6TH CENTURY BC

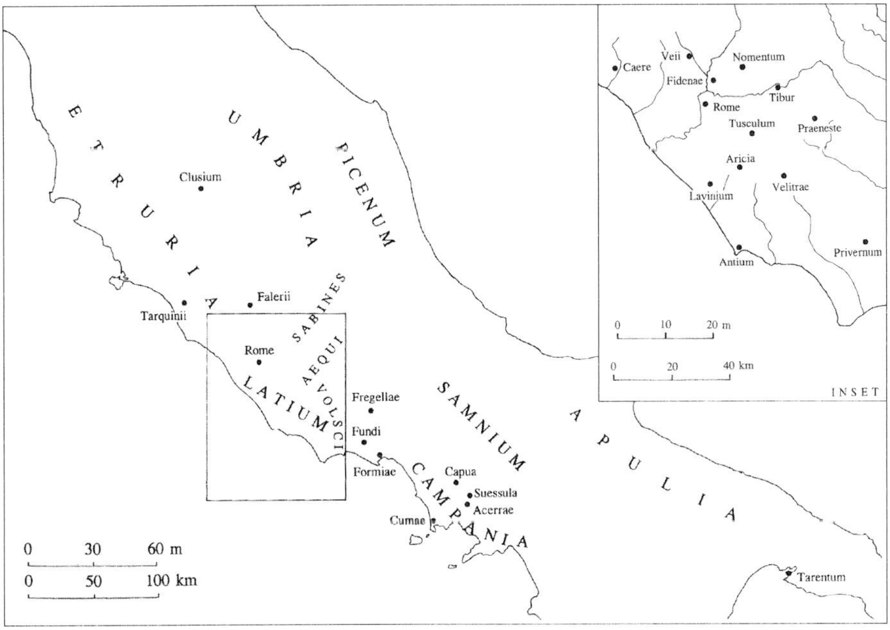

Falerii and Fescennium preserved hoplite equipment, despite being colonized by Romans: 'Falerii and Fescennium were even down to my day inhabited by Romans ... in these cities there survived many ancient customs which the Greeks had once used, such as their type of weaponry: Argolic shields and spears' (*Roman Antiquities*, 1:21).

From Etruria this new form of warfare spread to Rome and to the other Latin tribes. This fact is well established in the ancient tradition: 'In ancient times, when the Romans used rectangular shields, the Etruscans fought in phalanx using bronze shields, but having compelled the Romans to adopt the same equipment they were themselves defeated' (Diodorus Siculus, *The Library of History*). 'The Romans took close battle formation from the Etruscans, who used to attack in a phalanx' (Athenaeus, VI, p.273). 'The Etruscans did not fight in maniples but made war on us armed with bronze shields in a phalanx; we were re-armed and adopting the equipment of the enemy we formed up against them; and in this way we were able to conquer even those most accustomed to fighting in phalanx' (Anon, *Ineditum Vaticanum*). Even Livy knew this, remarking that before the introduction of military pay, the Romans had employed the round shield in a Macedonian-style phalanx.

The introduction of the hoplite tactics to Rome is associated in Roman historical tradition with the penultimate king of Rome, Servius Tullius (traditional dates 578–534 BC). Servius was said to have introduced a sweeping reform that changed the prevailing social order, divided by the *gens* and *curia* we have already described. The most important innovation was that citizenship by race was replaced by a rule based on residence, thus increasing the pool of military manpower. These newly defined citizens were subject to the census in which their wealth was assessed, and this in turn provided the basis for an army where the wealthy were obliged to serve and provide their own military equipment.

Those obligated to serve armed as hoplites were said to be part of the *classis*; and those who were not sufficiently wealthy (perhaps the majority) were termed *infra classem* and may have served only as light armed troops (see Aulus Gellius, and Festus). That the *classis* was indeed a hoplite formation is confirmed by Festus, who comments that an army, known in his day as an *exercitus*, had in ancient times been called *classis clipeata* (i.e. the *classis* armed with the hoplite shield, *clipeus* being the Latin term for the hoplite shield).

A number of indications make it clear that the Servian political assembly, based on the division *classis* and *infra classem*, arose from a military reform. In later times the developed form of the citizen assembly still met outside the *pomerium* (the sacred boundary of the city of Rome) on the Campus Martius, a field dedicated to Mars, the Roman god of war. The asssembly could only be convened by a magistrate holding *imperium* (the authority required for military command). It was summoned by a trumpet blast (*classicum canere*) with red flags flying on the Janiculum and the Arx when assembled, and the formulae used to summon it included phrases like *exercitum imperare* (to command the army) and *exercitum urbanum convocare* (to summon the urban army). The fact that this 'Servian' system was entirely unsuitable for recruitment of a manipular army (see below) confirms its predominantly hoplite character.

LIVY'S ACCOUNT OF THE REFORMS

Anyone who reads the full historical accounts of early Rome written by Livy and Dionysius will note that they describe the Servian reform somewhat differently from the simple division of *classis* and *infra classem* outlined above. Livy's account runs as follows:

> The population was divided into classes and centuries and the following arrangement, suitable for both peace and war, was made based upon the census. I) Of those who had a census rating of 100,000 *asses* or more he made 80 centuries, 40 of seniors and 40 of juniors, all of whom were called the first class. [An *as* was a small copper coin, worth ⅒th of the silver *denarius*.] The seniors were to be ready to guard the city, and the juniors to wage war abroad. The armour which these had to provide consisted of helmet, round shield, greaves, and breast-plate (all of these items made of bronze), to protect the body; their offensive weapons were the spear and the sword. To this class were added two centuries of engineers who served without arms and whose duty was to construct siege

HORATIUS AT THE BRIDGE, 508 BC

This plate illustrates the story of how Horatius Cocles (centre) along with two others held off an Estruscan army attempting to take over Rome; the bridge was eventually demolished and Horatius leapt into the river and swam to safety. The figure on the left illustrates the typical uniform and equipment of a Roman hoplite, while the figure on the right is the Latin equivalent. (© Richard Hook, Osprey Publishing)

engines in time of war. II) The second class was drawn from those assessed between 75,000 and 100,000 *asses*, and from these 20 centuries (juniors and seniors) were formed. Their prescribed armour was the same as the first class except for the breastplate and the rectangular shield in place of the round one. III) He determined that the census rating of the third class should be 50,000 *asses*; the same number of centuries was made and the same arrangement by ages; nor was there any change in their arms except that greaves were omitted. IV) In the fourth class the census rating was 25,000 *asses*; the same number of centuries were formed but their equipment was changed: nothing was given them but a spear and a javelin. V) The fifth class was made larger with 30 centuries, and these carried slings with stones for missiles. Amongst this class were also the horn-blowers and trumpeters who were placed in two centuries. This class was assessed at 11,000 *asses*. VI) The lesser census rating contained all the rest of the population, and of these one century was formed which was exempt from military service.

(Livy, *History of Rome*, 1.42.5–43.8)

Livy's account is largely paralleled in the description given by Dionysius in his *Roman Antiquities* (4.16.1–18.2). In Dionysius, however, the fourth class is equipped with shields, swords and spears where Livy gives just spears and javelins; and Dionysius' fifth class is given javelins in addition to the slings in Livy. Dionysius adds the two centuries of artisans to the second class, not to the first class as in Livy, and he adds the centuries of musicians to the fourth class rather than to the fifth class. Finally he gives the census rating of the fifth class as a minimum of 12½ *minae* (equal to 12,500 *asses*) rather than 11,000 *asses* as in Livy.

The descriptions of the Servian army in Dionysius and Livy clearly assume that each of the census classes formed a line in the military formation. Thus the hoplites constituted the first line with the second, third and fourth classes drawn up behind in that order, each with lighter equipment than the previous line. Finally the fifth class acted as skirmishers outside the line of battle. Such a formation contradicts our own description of the Servian army previously discussed, an army composed entirely of hoplites all from a single *classis* supported perhaps by light-armed troops from the *infra classem*. In this case we must examine the descriptions in Dionysius and Livy more closely and show why the five class multi-equipped army cannot truly represent conditions in 6th-century Rome.

The Servian 40-century legion, drawn from an assembly with three distinctions of wealth, is itself a development from the original legion which, as we have seen, had only one census class. It is therefore most likely that in its earliest form the Servian army consisted of just one class of hoplites and that classes two to five did not exist. The original Roman phalanx therefore consisted of one *classis* of 40 centuries of 'juniors' (i.e. 4,000 men) equipped in full hoplite panoply, with light-armed troops drawn from the *infra classem* who were not as yet organized into classes. At some point a further 20 centuries were added (i.e. classes II and III) to make the total 60 centuries. As the organization of

Etruscan statuette of a warrior on a candelabrum from the 'Circolo del Tritone', Vetulonia, now in Florence. The decoration on the back of the shield indicated that the warrior carries a more robust version of the Estruscan parade shield, which was actually used in combat. The fact that the warrior carries the shield suspended from his shoulders, presumably to allow him to throw his spear, shows that the attachments on the back of the parade shield were designed for attachment to straps. He also carries a mace in his left hand. (N. Sekunda & S. Northwood)

the army expanded with the addition of the extra census classes, the original *classis* of 40 centuries was preserved as the first class in the descriptions by Livy and Dionysius.

What then is the correct chronology of the development from a legion drawn from a single hoplite class of 40 centuries to one of 60 centuries from an assembly divided into three census classes? Though we can offer no conclusive proof, the most appropriate time for this expansion seems to be the end of the 5th century BC. Rome had embarked on a ten-year war with Veii (traditionally 406–396 BC) which, when placed alongside the commitments generated by membership of the Latin League, must have greatly stretched her military resources. It was then that military pay was introduced for the first time (Livy, *History of Rome*), a development that looks very much like a measure intended to ease the burden on less-wealthy citizens newly brought into the army.

Given that the primary evidence is so difficult to interpret, it is hardly surprising that other historians have adopted alternative views regarding the development of the early Roman Army. Yet the most dependable evidence seems to suggest the following three principles: hoplite tactics were introduced into Rome, via Etruria, in the mid 6th century BC; the earliest Roman hoplite army was composed of 40 centuries of hoplites; at some point before the creation of an additional legion, the 40 centuries were augmented by a further 20 centuries. Some suggest that this took place before the collapse of the Roman monarchy (traditionally 509 BC) but *c.*400 BC seems a more likely date.

These two terracottas from Veii, produced at the beginning of the 5th century BC, show a pair of naked young men engaged in a war dance. As in ancient Greece, the war dance was a survival of pre-hoplite warfare; its steps were designed to train the young warrior in the moves employed in single combat. (Museo Nazionale di Villa Giulia, Rome)

EARLY CAVALRY

The first plausible evidence for the establishment of a force of true cavalry in Rome comes in 403 BC, during the final and decisive struggle with Veii. As has already been noted, this war saw the introduction of military pay and probably also the expansion of the infantry legion. Livy records that 403 BC was the first year in which cavalrymen served on their own horses and that they were then rewarded by the introduction of pay for the cavalry. Such volunteers serving on their own mounts were called *equites equo privato* or *equites suis merentes*. We presume that the original *equites equo privato* were by and large recruited from the 'leading citizens' of the *sex suffragia*, which was by this time

ANTESIGNANI IN COMBAT WITH ACHAEAN CAVALRY, 146 BC
The Elite Roman footsoldiers (*antesignani*) are equipped with small swords and shields in place of their full legionary equipment. They attack both riders and steeds, striking up at the bellies of the horses and at the legs of the riders. The Achaean cavalryman is based on a statue of Polybius and a polychrome terracotta from Corinth. (© Angus McBride, Osprey Publishing)

SAMNITE WARRIORS, *c.*293 BC
This plate attempts a reconstruction of the dress that might have been worn by the Samnite army at the battle of Aquilonia in 293 BC. The central figure illustrates the appearance of a soldier of the legio linteata. Note how the Samnite tunic was extremely short and curved at the bottom. (© Richard Hook, Osprey Publishing)

a political grouping rather than a military organization. The establishment of the *equites equo publico* (cavalry with horses provided by the state) enabled all 600 to serve as cavalry. The expansion of the *equites equo publico* to a strength of 1,800 probably only occurred towards the end of the 4th century BC (see below). In the Second Punic War, when the number of *equites equo publico* was insufficient to provide the cavalry complement of a vastly increased number of legions, the institution of *equites equo privato* had to be relied on once again.

THE EXPANSION OF ROMAN MILITARY STRENGTH

By the end of the 4th century BC, the Roman Army definitely comprised four legions. Unfortunately there is no specific ancient testimony telling us exactly when and how new legions came into being. Instead we have to proceed using a mixture of guesswork, assessment of probabilities, and inference. The type of problem confronting us should be clear when we recognize that an increase in the number of Roman legions could be the result of two quite different processes. On the one hand, existing manpower could have been split into a larger number of units (i.e. a purely organizational development involving no increase in manpower). On the other, it could be the case that new units were created by means of increased conscription. It is quite possible, moreover, that both processes operated but at different stages of development. What follows is an outline of the most likely pattern of development in the 4th century BC.

THE INFANTRY

We have already attempted to show that the Roman Army *c.*400 BC consisted of a single legion of 6,000 men. In 366 BC, however, after many years of electing military tribunes with consular power as the main officers of state, Rome resumed the election of just two annual consuls. It is likely that as a response the legion was split into two. At this time Rome cannot have been in a position to recruit extra troops from thin air; manpower must therefore have remained the same and was now divided into two legions each of 3,000 men. Yet we know from Livy that by 311 BC Rome had four legions. He comments that this year saw 'the election by the people of 16 military tribunes for distribution amongst four legions, whereas these had previously been almost exclusively in the gift of the dictators and consuls' (*History of Rome*, 27:36) and the implication is that the existence of four legions was a recent development. These legions were undoubtedly formations organized around the unit known as a maniple (Latin: *manipulus*; pl. *manipuli*) and, if we follow Polybius' description of the manipular legion, consisted of 3,000 heavy infantry and 1,200 light-armed infantry. The total force was therefore 12,000 heavy infantry and 4,800 light troops: more than double that available in 366 BC.

These moulded representations of mounted hoplites from Roman temples are hardly evidence for the adoption of hoplite tactics by the Roman Army, rather than simply hoplite equipment. Furthermore, many moulds used in Rome were also used in other towns in Latium and southern Etruria. Consequently we have no idea whether these moulds were even manufactured in Rome. (N. Sekunda & S. Northwood)

Such a large increase becomes understandable when we consider Rome's success in the 4th century BC, particularly her defeat of the Latins and the conditions of the peace made in 338 BC. Rome imposed terms on her defeated enemies that significantly increased the pool of citizen manpower. Not only were the towns of Lanuvium, Aricia, Nomentum, Pedum, Velitrae and Antium all given full Roman citizenship, but a new type of citizenship was also introduced. This was the *civitas sine suffragio* (citizenship without the vote), a status whereby the holder was liable for taxation and military service but could not participate in Roman political assemblies or hold office. This status was given to the important Campanian towns of Capua, Suessula and Cumae (plus Acerrae in 332 BC), and the Volscian towns of Fundi and Formiae (and Privernum in 329 BC).

These citizenship grants in themselves hugely increased available manpower, but Rome pursued another policy that must also have had the same effect. This was the appropriation of some of the land of a number of defeated opponents. Land confiscation allowed the resettlement of Romans citizens – citizens who previously may have been too poor to be liable to military service under the Servian system. But now, with their new land, they would become sufficiently wealthy to qualify for military service.

Thus even without the creation of *civitas sine suffragio* Rome would probably have increased her available manpower. But with all these measures combined, the increase must have been remarkable. The census records for the 4th century BC are generally considered to be very unreliable, and we are therefore unable to quantify this increase precisely. However, we can at least note that because of expansion in the mid-4th century BC, the area of land occupied by Romans citizens increased from about 1,500 square kilometres to about 5,500 square kilometres. And we should not forget that allied communities possessing treaties with Rome also had to supply their own contingents for Rome's wars.

LEGIONARY BLAZON

Pliny, after telling us that Marius gave the Romans legions their eagle standards during his second consulship in 104 BC, mentions that previously the legions carried eagle standards as their first badge, but that in addition they carried four others; wolves, minotaurs, horses and boars in front of the various *ordines*. *Ordo* usually means 'rank' and so the natural interpretation of Pliny's words would be that these standards would be carried in front of the various ranks of the manipular army: that is the *triarii, principes* and *hastati.* There is an obvious problem that four standards do not go into three ranks, so it seems reasonable to assume that Pliny has misunderstood his source, presumably one of the antiquarians. Given that there were traditionally four legions from the closing decades of the fourth century onwards, it is tempting to assume that Pliny's source was describing the four legionary standards.

The wolf, together with the woodpecker, was the animal sacred to Mars (Plutarch, *Life of Romulus,* 4). The significance of the boar is less certain, but it was perhaps originally the symbol of Quirinus, the Sabine equivalent of Mars, who had continued to have a special cult existence in Rome after the amalgamation of the two founding communities around 600 BC. In Greek iconography the minotaur is shown as a bull-headed human, and, indeed, such a beast is shown on an early moulded relief from Rome. The human-headed bull is, however, much more common, especially on Sicilian and Italian coins, where it is usually interpreted as representing some or other river-god. The human-headed bull was also the symbol of the Campanians. This is presumably the minotaur referred to by Pliny's source. Thus it may be suggested that one of the four legions of the late 4th century was formed from Campanians to whom Roman citizenship had been extended, hence they took as their badge the former national symbol of Campania. The horse also appears on Italian coins issued by a large number of towns – we note that citizenship was extended to both Latin and Volscian communities at about the same time as it was to the Campanians, and it may be that these communities made up the fourth legion.

THE CAVALRY

We have already suggested that the Roman Army of the late 5th century BC had a maximum of six centuries of cavalry, and these were represented in the electoral assembly by the *sex suffragia*. We have also seen that the further 12 centuries of the electoral assembly, which brought the total up to 18, were a later addition. It is interesting, therefore, that the 12 additional centuries amount to the total cavalry component of a four-legion manipular army (see Polybius). It seems very likely therefore that the introduction of the four-legion army was accompanied by an overhaul of the cavalry in which 1,200 new *equites equo publico* were created, 300 per legion. The existing force represented in the *sex suffragia* must have been relegated to a ceremonial and electoral role only. A hint of this large increase in cavalry resources can be found in the *Ineditum Vaticanum* whose author greatly stressed Rome's need to augment her cavalry forces in order to face the Samnites (quoted below).

FOUR STANDARD BEARERS OF THE FOUR REPUBLICAN LEGIONS

Pliny tells us that Marius gave the Roman legions their legal standards during his second consulship in 104 BC. Prior to that the eagle had been their first badge along with four others: the wolf, the minotaur, the horse and the boar. (© Angus McBride, Osprey Publishing)

The expansion of the strength of the *equites equo publico* to 1,800 seems not to have been the only increase in Roman cavalry resources. In 340 BC, 1,600 Capuan *equites* were granted Roman citizenship for their loyalty to Rome at a time when the rest of Capua had deserted to Rome's enemies. In addition, the Capuans were forced to provide each cavalryman with 450 *denarii* to pay for the upkeep of their horses (Livy).

Opposite:
Fragments of the Sassi Caduti temple at Falerii Veteres, showing an armoured warrior with a curved sabre. The use of auxiliary thigh and arm protectors died out in Greece in the 6th century BC, but they continued to be popular in Etruria. The sculpture dates to the beginning of the 5th century BC. (Museo Nazionale di Villa Giulia, Rome)

MANIPULAR ARMIES

THE ROMANS ADOPTED THE MANIPULAR LEGION either just before or during their wars with the Samnites (the First Samnite War began in 343 BC, and ran until 341 BC). Yet despite being tactically more flexible, the early manipular legion retained many of the aspects of the hoplite phalanx from which it developed. Thus the Roman Army of the next 200 years remained a provisional militia, and the census recorded those citizens with sufficient property to make them eligible to serve the state.

Originally the term *legio* (legion) meant levy, and obviously referred to the entire citizen force raised by Rome in one year. However, as the number of citizens regularly enrolled for military service increased, the legion became the most important subdivision of the army. By the 3rd century BC, the legion consisted of five elements – namely the heavy infantry *hastate* ('spearmen'), *principes* ('chief men') and *triarii* ('third-rank men'), the light infantry *velites*, and the cavalry *equites* – each equipped differently and having specific places in the legion's tactical formation (see below). The legion's principal strength was the 30 maniples of its heavy infantry, the *velites* and *equites* acted in support of these. These tactical units were deployed in three successive, relatively shallow lines of ten maniples each. It was a force designed for large-scale battles, for standing in the open, moving straight forward and smashing its way through any opposition.

We have two accounts of the manipular legion's organization. First Livy, writing more than three centuries after the event, describes the legion of the mid-4th century BC. Second, the Greek historian Polybius, living and writing in Rome at the time, describes the legion of the mid-2nd century BC. The transition between the Livian and Polybian legion is somewhat obscure, but it is clear that some of the details Polybius describes apply to the legions of the Second Punic War.

In his account of the year 340 BC, after the close of the First Samnite War and as a preamble to the conflict against Rome's erstwhile Latin allies, Livy (*History of Rome*, 8.8.3–8) offers a brief description of Roman manipular military organization. The legions were now split into distinct battlelines. Behind a screen of lightly armed troops (*leves*), the first line contained maniples of *hastati*, the second line was made up of maniples of *principes* and the third line, made up of the oldest and more mature men, consisted of maniples of *triarii*. One significant problem with Livy's account, however, is the fact that he has 15 maniples in each of the three lines as opposed to Polybius' ten maniples. Other groups, whom Livy calls *rorarii* and *accensi*, were lightly equipped and formed a final reserve in the rear. It is from the definitions compiled by Varro (*De Lingua*

Latina, 7.57–58) that we can identify the *rorarii* as lightly armed troops and, here he cites the lost *De Re Militari* of Cato the Censor, the *accensi* as military servants.

Despite its anomalies, Livy's account is pleasingly close to that given by Polybius and almost certainly derives from it. It therefore has little independent value and, if we choose to accept the evidence of Dionysius of Halikarnassos, Livy places the manipular system too far back in time. Dionysius (*Roman Antiquities*, 20.11) says the heavy 'cavalry spear', that is to say the long thrusting-spear of the hoplite, was still employed in battle by the *principes* during the Pyrrhic War (280–275 BC). It seems, therefore, that the transformation from hoplite phalanx to manipular legion was a slow and gradual one, which for Livy was over and done with by the early 4th century BC. For the organization of the legion, *terra firma* is reached only with Polybius himself.

Polybius breaks off his narrative of the Second Punic War (218–201 BC) at the nadir of Rome's fortunes, following the three defeats of the Trebbia, Trasimene and Cannae, and turns to an extended digression on the Roman constitution and army. For us the account of the latter is of inestimable value, not least in that a contemporary writes the detailed description, himself a former cavalry commander (*hipparchos*) in the Achaean League, who had seen the Roman Army in action against his fellow countrymen during the Third Macedonian War (171–167 BC) and had perhaps observed its levying and training during his internment in Rome (167–150 BC).

All citizens between 17 and 46 years of age who satisfied the property criteria, namely those who owned property above the value of 11,000 *asses*, were required by the

THE *DILECTUS*

At the *dilectus*, the citizen-volunteers were arranged by height and age into some semblance of soldierly order. They were then brought forward four at a time to be selected for service in one of the four consular legions being raised that year. The junior tribunes of each legion took it in turns to have first choice, thus ensuring an even distribution of experience and quality throughout the four units. The new recruits then swore an oath of obedience (*sacramentum dicere*), linking them in a special way with the state, their commander and their fellow citizen-soldiers. This military oath developed over time, apparently being formalized only in 216 BC just before the battle of Cannae, presumably in response to the disasters at the Trebbia and Trasimene when morale had reached rock bottom and a formal oath was seen as a way of remedying this. According to Livy this formal oath took the following form: 'Never to leave the ranks because of fear or to run away, but only to retrieve or grab a weapon, to kill an enemy or to rescue a comrade' (*History of Rome*, 22.38.2–5). So as to speed up the process it was sworn in full by one man, with the phrase *idem in me* ('the same for me') being sufficient for the rest. The recruits were given a date and muster point, and then dismissed to their homes.

ROMAN LEGIONARIES IN SPAIN
The oblong shield shown on the sculpture of Minerva from Tarragona has been used for the *hastatus* (left) and the *triarius* (centre). Polybius (*The Histories*, 6. 22) informs us that the *velites* (right) wore a 'simple helmet', which they sometimes covered with the skin of a wolf or some other animal. (© Angus McBride, Osprey Publishing)

Senate to attend a selection process (*dilectus*) on the Capitol. Although Polybius' passage (6.19.2) is slightly defective here, citizens were liable for 16 years' service as a legionary and ten years as an *eques*. These figures represent the maximum that a man could be called upon to serve. In the 2nd century BC, a man was normally expected to serve up to six years in a continuous posting, after which he expected to be released from his military oath. Thereafter he was liable for call-out, as an *evocatus* (a soldier who had completed his service and obtained a discharge), up to the maximum of 16 campaigns or years. Some men might serve for a single year at a time, and be obliged to come forward again at the next *dilectus*, until their full six-year period was completed.

MANIPULAR ORGANIZATION AND WEAPONS

Originally the term *manipulus* meant 'a handful'. Then, as in the early days a pole with a handful of hay twisted round it was used as a standard, *manipulus* came to signify this, and hence a unit of soldiers belonging to the same standard. The legion itself consisted of 1,200 *hastati* in ten maniples of 120, 1,200 *principes* organized in the same way, and 600 *triarii* also in ten maniples. According to Livy, the *hastati* were also men in the flower of youth, the *principes* in the prime of manhood and the *triarii* seasoned veterans.

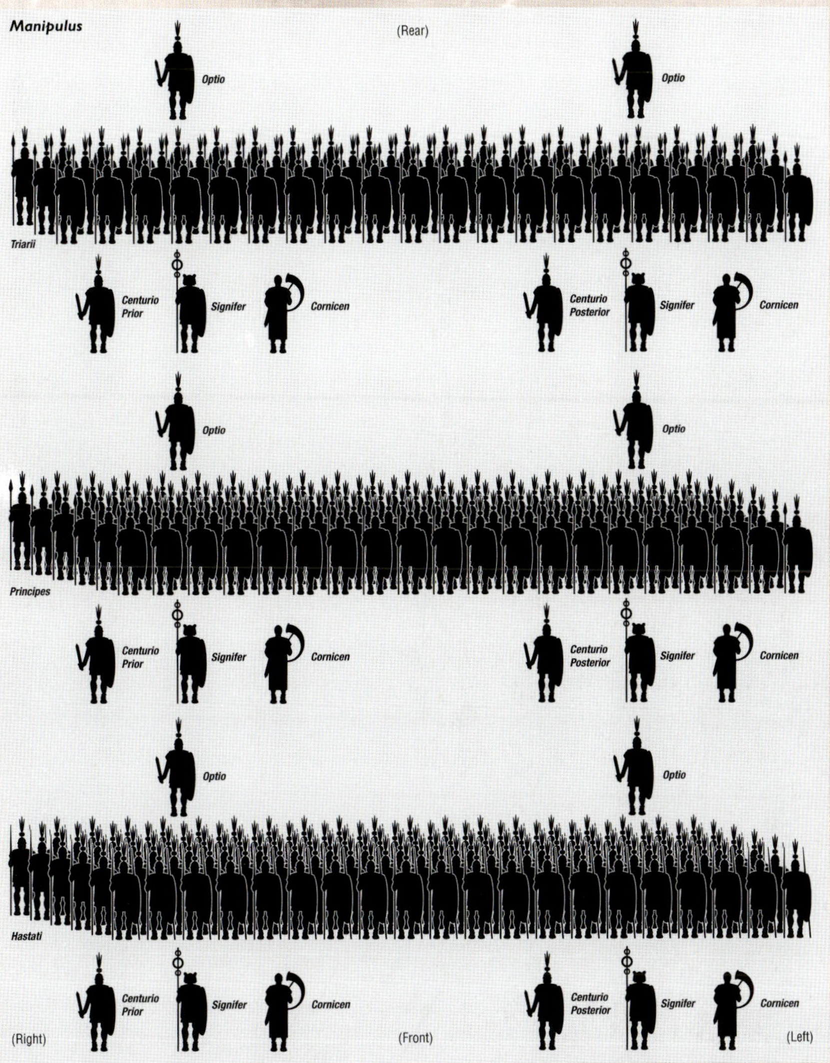

Whereas both *hastati* and *principes* normally had 120 legionaries to a *manipulus*, the *triarii* mustered only 60. A *manipulus* would deploy six (*hastati, principes*) or three (*triarii*) deep, and, according to Polybius, in order to give each man room to use his weapons he would have a frontage of six Roman feet (1.8m) as well as an equivalent depth. On the other hand, Vegetius claims the individual legionaries occupy a frontage of three Roman feet (0.9m) with a depth of six Roman feet (1.8m) between ranks. This close-order formation gives a *manipulus* a frontage of approximately 18m and a depth of 12m (*hastati, principes*) or 6m (*triarii*).

The same order for the three lines appears in both Livy and Polybius' narrative, as well as in other antiquarian sources (Varro, *De Lingua Latina*, 5.89 and Ovid, *Fasti*, 3.128–132), and is implied by the order of seniority amongst centurions of the imperial army, where *pilus* was the most senior followed by the *princeps* and then the *hastatus*.

These two bone plaques from Palestrina, dating to the 4th century BC, belong to a series of *laminae* of different sizes, which probably once formed the veneer of a magistrate's seat of office (*sella curulis*). This pair of hoplite warriors wear the dress and equipment typical of Latin hoplites of the period: crested Italo-Attic helmets, muscle-cuirasses and greaves, together with a short tunic and cloak. (Museo Nazionale di Villa Giulia, Rome, Inv nos. 13236, 13237. Courtesy of Montvert Publications)

Polybius puts the nominal strength of a legion at 4,200 legionaries. However, in times of particular crisis when larger legions were raised, as was the case at Cannae, this might be increased to as many as 5,000. Polybius says that when this happened the number of *triarii* remained the same at 600, but the number of *hastati*, *principes* and *velites*, the less-experienced legionaries, increased from the usual 1,200. As a result, the size of a maniple of *hastati* or *principes* could increase from 120 to 160 men when the legion was first formed and before any campaign losses had occurred.

Of the 4,200 legionaries in a legion, 3,000 were heavy infantry. The *hastati* and *principes* carried the Italic oval *scutum* shield, the famous short Iberian sword (*gladius Hispaniensis*), and two sorts of *pila* spear, heavy and light. The *triarii* were similarly equipped, except they carried a long thrusting-spear (*hasta*) instead of the *pilum*. This 2m-long weapon survives from the era when the Roman Army was a hoplite force. The *hasta* was perhaps obsolete in Polybius' day, though probably still in use during the Gallic tumultus of 223 BC, when they are, for the only time, mentioned in action (Polybius, *The Histories*, 2.33.4), while the annalistic tradition does not notice them at all.

In the Livian legion there is no reference to the *pilum*, which, if Livy's account is accepted, may not yet have been introduced. The earliest reference to the *pilum* belongs to 293 BC during the Third Samnite War, though the earliest authentic use of this weapon may belong to 251 BC. The *pilum* was probably adopted from Iberian mercenaries fighting for Carthage in the First Punic War.

Polybius distinguishes two types of *pilum* (*hyssos* in Greek) – 'thick' and 'thin' – saying each man had both types. Surviving examples from Numantia (near Burgos, Spain), the site of a Roman siege (134–133 BC), confirm two basic types of construction. Both have a small pyramid-shaped point at the end of a narrow soft-iron shank, fitted to a wooden shaft some 1.4m in length. One type has the shank socketed, while the other has a wide flat iron tang riveted to a thickened section of the wooden shaft. The last type is probably Polybius' 'thick' *pilum*, referring to the broad joint of iron and wood. This broad section can be either square or round in section, and is strengthened by a small iron ferrule. The iron shank varies in length, with many examples averaging around 70cm.

All of the weapon's weight was concentrated behind the small pyramid-shaped tip, giving it great penetrative power. The length of the iron shank gave it the reach to punch through an enemy's shield and go on to wound his body, but even if it failed to do so and merely stuck in the shield it was very difficult to pull free and might force the opponent to discard his weighted-down shield and fight unprotected. A useful side effect of this 'armour-piercing' weapon was that the narrow shank would often bend on impact, ensuring that the enemy could not throw it back. The maximum range of the *pilum* was some 30m, but its effective range was most probably half that. Throwing a *pilum* at close range would have improved both accuracy and armour penetration.

A later lexicographer says the *gladius Hispaniensis* was adopted from the Iberians (or Celtiberians) at the time of the Second Punic War, but it is possible that this weapon, along with the *pilum*, was adopted from Iberian mercenaries serving Carthage during the First Punic War. It was certainly in use by 197 BC, when Livy describes the Macedonians' shock at the terrible wounds it inflicted.

The Iberians used a short, but deadly, sword. This was either the *falcata*, a curved single-bladed weapon derived from the Greek *kopis*, or the cut-and-thrust sword, a straight-bladed weapon from which the *gladius* was derived. The earliest Roman specimens date to the turn of the 1st century BC ('Mainz' type), but a 4th-century sword of similar shape has been found in Spain at the cemetery of Los Cogotes (Avila). The Roman blade could be as much as 64–69cm in length and 4.8–6cm wide and waisted in the centre. It was a fine piece of 'blister steel' with a triangular point between 9.6 and 20cm long with honed-down razor-sharp edges, and was designed to puncture armour. It had a comfortable bone handgrip grooved to fit the fingers, and a large spherical pommel, usually of wood or ivory, to help with counter-balance. Extant examples weigh between 1.2 and 1.6kg. The legionary also carried a dagger, *pugio*. The dagger was the ultimate weapon of last resort, but it was probably more often employed in the day-to-day tasks of living on campaign. Like the *gladius*, the Roman dagger was borrowed from the Iberians and then developed.

Polybius says all soldiers wore a bronze pectoral to protect the heart and chest, although those who could afford it instead wore an iron mail shirt (*lorica hamata*). He also adds that a bronze helmet was worn, without describing it, but the Attic, Montefortino and Etrusco-Corinthian styles were all popular in Italy at this time and were probably all used, as they certainly all were by later Roman troops. Polybius says that helmets were crested with a circle of feathers and three upright black or crimson feathers a cubit (46cm) tall, so exaggerating the wearer's height. Interestingly, Polybius clearly refers to only one greave being worn, and Arrian (*Tactica*, 3.5), writing around three centuries

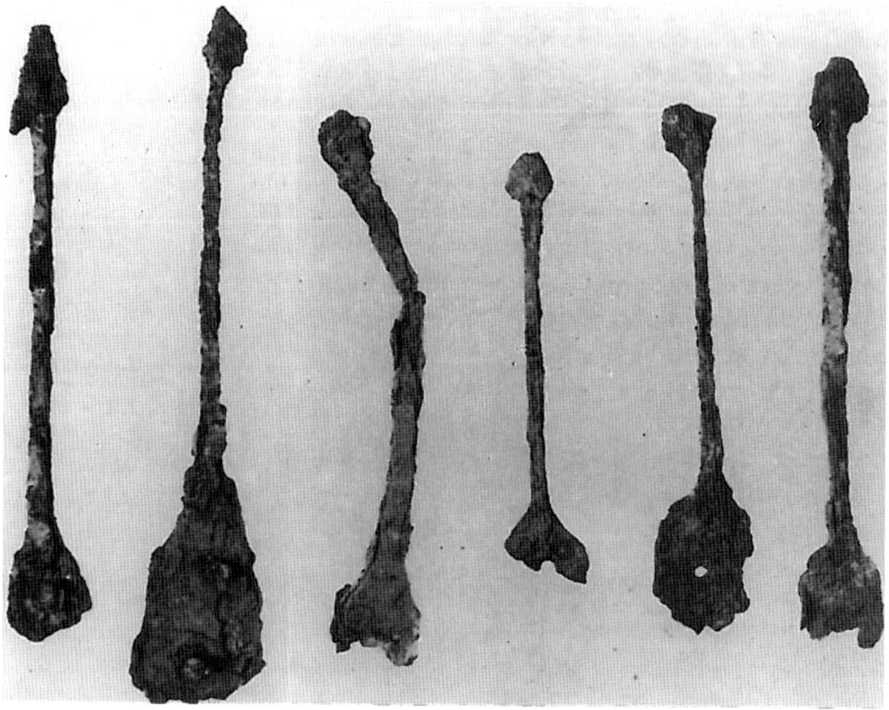

About 60 iron *pilum* heads have been recovered from Telamon, perhaps from a monument commemorating the Roman victory against the Gauls in 225 BC. The temple was built about 300 BC and was destroyed by Sulla's troops in 82 BC. They are certainly Republican in date. (After von Vacano, 1988, abb. 5, taf. xi)

later, confirms this, saying the ancient Romans used to wear one greave only, on the leading leg, the left. No doubt many of those who could afford it would actually have a pair of bronze greaves covering the leg from ankle to knee.

To complete his defensive equipment, each soldier carried a body shield (*scutum*). Polybius describes the *scutum* in detail, and his account is confirmed by the remarkable discovery of a shield of this type at Kasr-el-Harit in the Fayûm, Egypt. The *scutum* was oval in shape, some 1.2m in length and 60cm in width. It was constructed from three layers of birch plywood, each laid at right angles to the next, and covered with canvas and then calfskin. It was thicker in the centre and flexible at the edges, making it very resilient to blows, and the top and bottom edges were reinforced with bronze or iron edging to prevent splitting. Nailed to the front and running vertically from top to bottom was a wooden spine (*spina*). Good protection came at a price, for the *scutum* was heavy, around 10kg, and in battle its entire weight was borne by the left arm as the soldier held the horizontal handgrip behind the bronze or iron boss (*umbo*), which reinforced the central spine of the shield.

Finally, lest we forget, these short-term citizen-soldiers provided their own equipment and therefore we should expect considerably more variation in clothing, armour and weapons than the legionaries of the later professional imperial legions.

Beyond the heavy infantry, the remaining 1,200 men of the legion, the youngest and poorest, served as light infantry and were known as *velites* or 'cloak-wearers', that is, they lacked any body armour. However, it is important to remember that the distinction between what Greek and Roman sources call 'heavy' and 'light' infantry, was not so much that the latter were more lightly equipped than the former, but that heavy infantry were trained to fight together in formation, whereas light infantry were trained to fight as skirmishers.

According to Livy (*History of Rome*, 26.4.9), the *velites* were formally created as a force in 211 BC, leading to suggestions that they replaced the less well-armed and efficient *leves* (or *rorarii*). However, this single passage in Livy is fraught with problems, and he does mention them (21.55.11) at the battle of Trebia in 218 BC. It is more likely that the terms were synonymous, although perhaps *velites* came into common usage at a later period.

Light infantry were divided for administrative purpose amongst the heavy infantry of the maniples, each maniple being allocated the same number of *velites*. As for the *hastati* and *principes*, at times of crisis the number of *velites* might be increased.

Each legion also had a small cavalry force of 300 men organized in ten *turmae* of 30 troopers each. The military tribunes appointed three *decuriones* ('leaders of ten') to each *turma*, of whom the senior commanded with the rank of *praefectus*. Each *decurio* chose an *optio* as his second-in-command and rear-rank officer. This organization suggests that the *turma* was divided into three files of ten, each led by a *decurio* and closed by an *optio*. These files were clearly not independent tactical subunits, for the *turma* was evidently intended to operate as a single entity, as indicated by the seniority of one *decurio* over his two colleagues.

CITIZEN-MILITIA

It is important to note that the legions in the early Republic were not the long-lived institutions of the later professional army and appear to have been re-numbered each year. It is extremely rare for our sources to explain in detail when legions were raised, disbanded, destroyed or incorporated into other units. The weakness of the consular system was that every time the legions were discharged and a new army raised, the whole process had to start again from scratch. Few units would have developed a lasting sense of *esprit de corps* or identity.

Taking the Polybian *drachma* as the equivalent of the *denarius*, the legionary received an allowance (stipendium) of one *denarius* every three days (120 *denarii* per annum), the payment going towards the cost of his rations, clothes and extra equipment. Centurions received double that rate, while the *equites* received even more, one *denarius* per diem, from which to meet the cost of maintaining their mounts. Miserly as it was, the actual amount of money was not meant to be a substitute for normal living expenses. It was well below the wages of an unskilled labourer, who commanded about 12 *asses* per diem (432 *denarii* per annum) in this period. But merely counting how many *asses* soldiers receive misses the point. Roman society had never been broken into the three Indo-European categories, often hereditary, of military, religious and economic groups, as was common in similar civilizations. Thus throughout the Republican period the soldiers fighting for Rome were its own citizens for whom defence of the state was regarded, by the Senate at least, as a duty, a responsibility and a privilege.

When a man came forward voluntarily, he would presumably be accepted gladly, unless, of course, the volunteer was too old, too unfit or under-aged. But there was always a measure of compulsion, and in a loose sense service in the legions of the middle Republic can be likened to 'national service' in many Western democracies in the mid-20th century: an obligation on every fit male to contribute to his country's defence. At first, service in the Roman Army entailed a citizen being away from his home – usually a farmstead – for a few weeks or months over the summer. But the need to fight overseas in Iberia and to leave troops to form permanent garrisons in the newly won provinces of Sicily and Sardinia in the 2nd century BC meant that men were away from home for longer periods. This interruption to normal life could easily spell ruin to the soldier-farmers who had traditionally made up the bulk of citizens eligible for military call-up. Hopkins (*Conquerors and Slaves*, p.35) estimates that in 225 BC legionaries comprised 17 per cent of all the adult male citizens, and in 213 BC, at the height of the Second Punic War, 29 per cent. Inevitably what had previously been seen as a duty and voluntary obligation took on a somewhat different character.

SOCII MILITARY ORGANIZATION

As well as citizens, Rome called on allied troops, at first from its Latin neighbours and then from all Italy. Essentially, when they painfully struggled to obtain the mastery of the peninsula, the Romans had two ways of dealing with peoples who opposed them.

If the enemy resisted them outright, so that the Romans had to take the city by storm, then the whole community might be enslaved and their city destroyed. But if they submitted to the commander of the besieging force in good time – normally before the first siege machines had been brought against their walls – then a different custom prevailed. They were expected to surrender unconditionally and, according to Roman law, once they had done so the enemy were said to have made a *deditio*. At this juncture the enemy were classed as *dediticii*, having, as it was said publicly, 'sought the protection of the honour of the Roman people' (*in fidem populi Romani se dedere*). They then had to await the decision of the Senate on their fate.

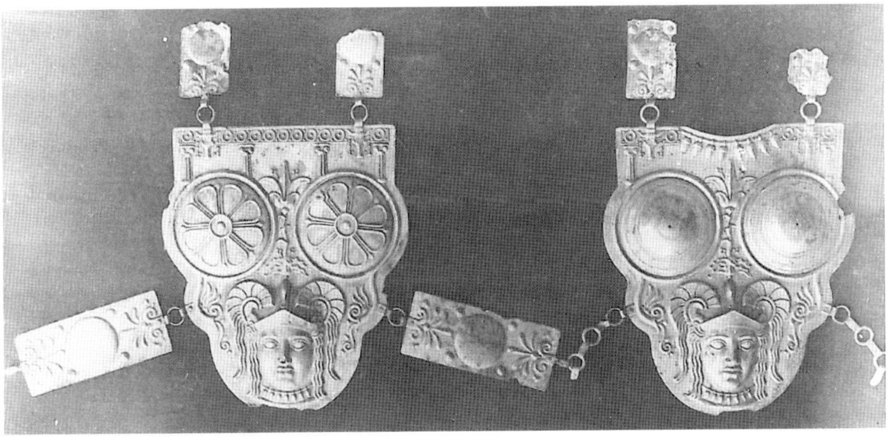

This famous pectoral, of the *trilobate* variety, was found in North Africa, where it had evidently been brought by an Italian mercenary in Carthaginian service. Colour photographs of the cuirass show it to be plated in white metal, either silver or tin, which suggests the possibility that it was an heirloom. The principal decorative feature is a head of Minerva wearing a triple-crested helmet, which follows Greek representations of Athena Promachos dating to the late 4th century BC. (Musée National de Bardo, Tunis)

The Senate, in the light of experience acquired through many struggles and difficulties, would invariably choose the better course of action and bind the Latin and Italian communities to Rome by a long series of bilateral treaties, a multi-tiered system of control that respected the time-honoured principle of *divide et impera* (divide and rule). These treaties normally specified that an allied community must contribute a specific number of troops, as determined by the Roman people (*populus Romanus*), to aid the Romans in times of war, and in return allowed them a share in any booty. Otherwise the ally paid no tribute to Rome and remained free to pursue its own cultural agenda. The durability and success of the arrangement is famous. The precise obligations of the community under the treaty varied according to the conditions in which the treaty was made. A few were entirely voluntary agreements, but most were compulsory, resulting from a *deditio* in time of war.

The allies (*socii*) were divided into two broad groups: Latins and Italians. The *socii nominis Latini* (lit. 'allies of the Latin name'), included a handful of old communities that had not been granted citizenship after Rome's defeat of its insurgent allies in 338 BC, as well as 30 Latin colonies, such as Placentia (Piacenza), Cremona and Brundisium, strategically sited throughout Italy. Their main duty was to supply troops to Rome; according to Polybius (*The Histories*, 2.24), these communities were capable of producing 80,000 infantry and 5,000 cavalry between them. The other allies were Italians of various nations – in the same passage Polybius mentions Sabini and Etruscans from central Italy, Umbri and Sarsinati from the Apennines, Veneti and Cenomani from Gallia Cisalpina, Iapygii and Messapii from Apulia, and Samnites, Lucani, Marsi, Marrucini, Frentani and Vestini from the southern Apennines. Together these allies could provide a further 260,000 infantry and 34,000 cavalry. All allies were theoretically obliged to help Rome with their total manpower, but in practice their obligations may have been defined by what was known as the *formula togatorum* (lit. 'list of adult males'), a kind of sliding scale

ALA

A Latin or Italian *ala* (wing; pl. *alae*), accompanied each Roman legion, theoretically with the same number of allied infantry as citizen infantry, along with three times as many allied cavalry as citizen cavalry. In practice, there were often more allies than Romans in any campaign force – 20,000 allied infantry to 16,000 Roman legionaries at Trebbia, for example. Roman officers called *praefecti sociorum*, apparently three to an *ala*, commanded the allies. Appointed by the consuls, the prefects' role was probably similar to that of the military tribunes in a legion. At lower levels the allies evidently provided their own officers.

requiring so many men for the number of citizen-soldiers raised in any year (see Brunt, *Italian Manpower 225 BC–AD 14*, pp.545–48).

Many of the Latin colonists were in fact descended from Roman citizens, men who had accepted Latin status in place of Roman citizenship in order to make a fresh start. Thus the culture of these colonies was virtually identical to that of Rome, with the same gods, similar institutions and certain rights in Roman law. On the other hand, Rome's Italian allies were a diverse lot, being politically, geographically, ethnically, culturally and often linguistically distinct. They were in theory independent, although in practice Rome was clearly the dominant partner in the alliances. The Senate's capability to intervene in the dealings of the *socii* arose out of its role in foreign affairs, and in particular its duty to secure the confederation and ensure the supremacy of Rome.

An elite force of *extraordinarii* was selected from the best of the allied troops, one-third of the cavalry and one-fifth of the infantry, who camped near the consul's tent (*praetorium*) and were at his immediate disposal. Apart from these chosen troops, each allied unit was composed of men from one town, canton or nation, and would take the standard oath before setting out to join the assembled citizen forces under their own commander and paymaster.

Although Polybius assumes the infantry camped in *manipuli*, the *cohors* (cohort) was a standard unit for tactics well before the Romans employed it, and at least as early as the Second Punic War. It may originally have been a Samnite unit, so some allies may have used it before their incorporation into the Roman Army. Allied *cohortes* of 460, 500 and 600 men are recorded, and the variation in size probably reflects the differing sizes of each community's population. Maniples probably existed as subunits within the cohort, with ten cohorts drawn from different communities placed together to form an *ala*.

As already noted, the allied cavalry force was generally two or three times larger than that of the citizen cavalry force. These horsemen were organized in *turmae* of probably the

Attached to each *legio* was a small cavalry detachment some 300 strong and divided into ten tactical subunits known as *turmae*. With a nominal strength of 30 troopers, each *turma* was organized, probably for administrative purposes only, as three smaller subunits, each one commanded by a *decurio* with an *optio* acting as his second-in-command. The senior of the three *decuriones*, a *praefectus*, also held overall responsibility for the *turma* as a whole.

same strength as the Romans, and were presumably also from the wealthiest strata of society. This is certainly suggested by Livy's references to 300 young men of the noblest Campanian families serving in Sicily, and to the young noblemen from Tarentum who served at the battles of Trasimene and Cannae. The cavalry were commanded, at least from the 2nd century BC, by Roman *praefecti equitum*, presumably with local *decuriones* and *optiones* at *turma* level. Like their citizen counterparts, as well as having a higher social status, allied horsemen were much better paid than those serving as foot soldiers.

THE PUNIC WARS: THE ROMANS ARE TESTED

The Punic Wars (264–146 BC) would tax Roman military talents for more than a century. They would see Rome's armies suffer both total victory and horrifying defeat, and therefore provide a sound case study for our study of the early Republican military machine.

The source of the wars was simply imperial expansion. With the defeat of Taras (Tarentum to the Romans, now Taranto in southern Italy) in 272 BC, according to Florus, 'all Italy enjoyed peace' (*Epitome of Roman History*, 1.14.1). Peace, however, would be short-lived, as the Romans were about to cross to Sicily, which was the first country beyond the shores of Italy on which they set foot, and cross swords with a potential rival in the western Mediterranean, the old Phoenician colony of Carthage.

THE FIRST PUNIC WAR, 264–241 BC

The fire that had been slowly smouldering for some time was kindled into flame in an unexpected manner. After the death of Agathokles of Syracuse (289 BC), a band of his Campanian mercenaries found themselves without employment. Instead of returning home, they decided to seize the *polis* of Messana (Messina), facing across the narrow straits to the toe of Italy, from its Greek inhabitants and to live as an independent community of brigands. Their position was further strengthened by a similar seizure of Rhegium (Reggio di Calabria), across the straits in Italy, by a force of Roman troops made up of Campanian 'citizens without the vote' (Polybius, *The Histories*, 1.7.6). Calling themselves the Mamertini or 'sons of Mamers', the Oscan version of the war-god Mars, they harried north-eastern Sicily until finally defeated by Hieron, the new tyrant of Syracuse. Thereupon some of them turned to the Carthaginians and offered to put themselves and Messana in their hands (265 BC). At the same time, however, another faction amongst the Mamertini had sent envoys to Rome seeking protection as Campani and so as a kindred people, and they likewise proposed to surrender Messana. The acceptance of this appeal by the Senate was the spark for war. The immediate cause of the First Punic War is thus clear. The fundamental causes of the First Punic War, however, are not so sharply defined.

For once we have, in Polybius' account (*The Histories*, 1.10.1–11.2), some of the opinions that were supposed to have been aired in the Senate at the time. It seems in

Polybius' view the overriding consideration in the minds of those senators who advocated acceptance of the appeal, was fear lest the island pass finally under Punic control and 'allow the Carthaginians as it were to build a bridge for crossing to Italy' (1.10.9). Roman fears, though perhaps groundless, may have been quite genuine. It should also be noted that the acceptance of the Mamertini appeal did not mark any new departure in Roman foreign policy: it had long been characteristic of the Senate to accept such appeals, naturally when it suited. The Carthaginians, for their part, could have avoided war had they been prepared to accept a *fait accompli* in Messana, but they must have calculated that if the Romans were allowed to interfere there, this might lead to further encroachment elsewhere in Sicily. At the same time, they had every reason to expect success: their navy could dominate the waters around Sicily and control of the island was ultimately bound to depend on seapower. It appears that the prime reason for the war was the mutual fear in both Rome and Carthage of the other's growing power, each believing their only long-term security lay in weakening the other's power.

After the decision had been taken to aid the Mamertini, the problem facing Appius Claudius, the commander of the Roman expedition, was that his two legions were some 644km north of their port of embarkation at Rhegium and the necessary shipping, all of which belonged to the allies, had to be assembled. Appreciating that any delay would cost him the element of surprise, Claudius despatched a smaller force, which managed to cross the Straits undetected and quickly secure Messana, allowing the Carthaginian garrison to leave unmolested. However, Hanno, the unfortunate Carthaginian commander, was subsequently crucified for his lack of resolution.

Appius Claudius was later able to make a night crossing with his main force without being intercepted. Once ashore, Claudius found himself confronted by the Carthaginians under Hanno and the Syracusans under Hieron. These two former opponents failed to coordinate, let alone concentrate, their respective forces, so were defeated separately, though not decisively. Both were able to withdraw, Hanno into some neighbouring Carthaginian cities and Hieron into Syracuse, which became the Romans' next objective.

With two new consuls and reinforced by a further two legions, the Romans' determination and overwhelming force quickly persuaded 67 Syracusan and Punic cities to reach an accommodation with Rome; shortly afterwards Hieron too entered into an alliance. Meanwhile, the Carthaginians had been raising a mercenary army, mainly from Spain, and when their training had been completed they were transported to the fortified city of Agrigentum on Sicily's south coast. Here the Carthaginians were besieged, but managed to slip out through the Roman lines during the night, leaving the hapless population to be butchered. Until the capture of Agrigentum, the Romans had drawn a distinction between the garrisons of foreign cities and the civilian population, but with the ferocious reprisals that had now been taken, a warning example was set. The effects

Infantrymen from the Aemilius Pauleus Monument, erected after the battle of Pydna in 168 BC. The Roman forces raised for the Third Macedonian War included 2,000 Ligurians. The two figures on the right, from a part of the frieze showing the start of the battle, wear muscle-cuirasses with large rolled-over rims at the bottom and could represent the Ligurian infantry who were involved in the opening skirmish. (After Kähler, pls. 14, 6)

of this new policy are not clear; some inland cities went over to the Romans, but those on the coast that could be sustained by the Carthaginian fleet stood firm.

Note that there was no long-term Roman strategic objective for becoming involved in Sicily; more an uncertain drift towards total conquest. Nevertheless, for the first three years of the war the field commanders were quite clear as to their operational objectives: the occupation of Messana, the subjugation of Syracuse and the reduction of Agrigentum. These precise aims had enabled them to achieve a concentration of force and to take and hold the offensive.

In 261 BC, however, the situation was reversed. There was now an unequivocal strategic objective to clear the Carthaginians from Sicily. Roman strength lay in the set-piece battle, the decisive clash of opposing armies that settled the issue one way or another, but Hamilcar, the Carthaginian commander who had replaced Hanno, was not to be drawn. Instead he used the flexibility within his fleet to dominate the seaboard and its cities. The fighting then became diffuse and reactive as city after city flared into revolt or declared for Carthage. The problem facing the Romans was that even if they were to seek a conclusive action by first concentrating against the main Carthaginian base at Lilybaeum on the west coast, they would be unable to reduce it by siege unless they were able to prevent reinforcements and provisions coming in by sea. Meanwhile, they would incur the risk of being cut off from their own supplies, as had nearly occurred at Agrigentum. An entirely land-based strategy could not break this stalemate and the need for a Roman fleet was self-evident.

THE MARITIME DIMENSION, 260–256 BC

The Romans hastily constructed a fleet, and to compensate for their inferior seamanship raised *corvi* – essentially a plank that could link ships together at sea – on the prows of their ships to enable the legionaries to swarm aboard opponents' vessels. It was in 260 BC at Mylae (Milazzo), on the north coast near Messana, that this development was first seen in action, when 130 Carthaginian ships closed with a superior Roman fleet of 145 vessels and lost nearly half their total strength in the encounter. The victory at Mylae presented the Romans with two strategic options: either they could continue the Sicilian campaign, or they could go on the defensive in Sicily and assault the African mainland with a view to destroying Carthage. They decided on the former, maintaining a consistent strategic objective but one which required a change of operational tactics.

Though the Romans had energetically sought to enlarge their fleet, like their army, it was still not sufficiently powerful to deal with widely spread objectives. Yet in 258 BC, this is exactly what they attempted to do. Instead of concentrating their resources and mounting combined land and sea operations against the coastal cities in Sicily, thereby cutting supply lines to Carthage, or alternatively, ending the politically embarrassing raids against the Italian seaboard by subjugating Sardinia and Corsica, the Romans attempted to conduct both campaigns at once. The result was that, although the Romans won another naval victory and had some successes in Corsica, they were too weak to exploit their achievements and in Sicily they suffered a severe reverse when Hamilcar suddenly took the offensive. The prevailing stalemate led to growing disenchantment and then to an alternative strategy: to carry the war to North Africa. In so doing they set the scene for one of the largest naval battles in history.

In the summer of 256 BC, a Roman fleet of 330 ships set sail southward for Phintias, a substantial port on the southern coast lying under Mount Ecnomus, where two legions were waiting to embark. Meanwhile the Carthaginian fleet, which was about the same warship strength, sailed from Lilybaeum, and following the shoreline, encountered the Romans as they set sail for Africa. As they approached each other, the Carthaginians

Although Carthage could still field a sizeable navy in 218 BC, it was the reality of a numerically superior Roman fleet that prevented Hannibal from considering an amphibious descent on the Italian coast. This relief of a Roman trireme dates from the 1st century BC but retains the characteristics of its Punic War forebears in the prominent ram and prow, and naval infantry carried to board enemy vessels. From the Temple of Fortuna at Praeneste. (Mark Healy)

turned and feigned flight. The Romans then hastened in pursuit but in doing so, became separated from the squadron of ships towing the transports. At a signal from Hamilcar, the Carthaginian commander, the 'fleeing' Carthaginian ships turned on their pursuers, while other Carthaginian squadrons manouevred in from different angles. For a while both navies held their own, but eventually, despite their brilliant initial tactics, the Carthaginian squadrons were forced to flee in earnest. Once again the *corvi* had proved their usefulness, and although nearly as many Roman ships were sunk as Carthaginian, 24 and 30 respectively, 64 Carthaginian ships were captured. The Romans were now free to cross over to Africa.

THE AFRICAN CAMPAIGN, 256–255 BC

The Carthaginians did not have enough troops in Africa to do more than defend Carthage, so they withdrew into the city, leaving the Romans to establish themselves ashore without hindrance some 64km along the coast to the east. The Romans had probably assessed that Carthage, like the fortified coastal cities of Sicily, could only be taken if blockaded from both land and sea. Winter, however, was now approaching and it would have been too late to undertake such an enterprise. There was also a logistical problem with the fleet: if it were to remain in North Africa the Romans faced the task of feeding some 75,000 rowers, who greatly outnumbered the soldiers. It is hardly surprising then that when orders arrived from Rome, only 40 warships were to remain, with 15,000 infantry and 500 cavalry. The others, including all the transports, were to return to Rome. Loading on board the 20,000 slaves that had been rounded up, together with booty, one consul went on his way leaving the other, Marcus Atilius Regulus, the co-victor of Ecnomus, with two legions and sufficient ships to keep communications with Rome open.

After recalling 5,000 infantry and 500 cavalry from Sicily, the Carthaginians felt strong enough to try to prevent the Romans ranging unopposed through the countryside, plundering at will. The Carthaginian foray, however, was swiftly defeated and this encouraged the Romans to advance their forward base to Tunis, a few kilometres south-west of Carthage.

Fame and a triumph now lay within Regulus' grasp; all that was required of him was the reduction of Carthage, apparently tottering on the brink of starvation. This feat was not, however, to prove so easy. Responding to a Carthaginian appeal to the Greeks, Xanthipus, a Spartan general who had received the rigorous training associated with his countrymen, had arrived at the head of a substantial number of Greek mercenaries and quickly appreciated that it was Carthaginian generalship that was at fault, not the mercenary soldiers. Having put things right, in the spring of 255 BC Xanthipus marched out of the city with some 12,000 infantry, 4,000 cavalry and an unspecified number of elephants. In the ensuing battle, the Romans were routed by the elephants, which smashed into the legionaries. Despite heavy losses, the Romans fought on until assailed by the Numidian cavalry from the rear. Only 2,000 of the Romans escaped and some 500 prisoners were taken, including Regulus himself.

When news of the defeat reached Rome, plans had to be radically recast. Abandoning all hope of laying siege to Carthage, an expedition would be mounted instead to rescue any survivors. The strategic aim of the war would then revert to the securing of Sicily. In the early summer, 350 Roman ships sailed to the tip of Cape Bon, a peninsula in north-east Tunis. There they encountered and defeated the Carthaginian fleet, which thereafter made no effort to intervene. The Romans were then free to rescue their surviving legionaries unmolested in a thoroughly successful operation. However, they foolishly provoked the weather gods by a display of hubris. Scorning the advice of the pilots to steer to the west of Sicily to avoid the sudden summer storms that frequently arose off the southern coast, the Romans met with disaster. Off Camarina, towards the south-eastern extremity of the island, the fleet was struck by a savage storm and all but 80 ships were lost, together with their crews and the soldiers they were transporting. Altogether some 100,000 men may have been drowned. A stupendous effort would now be required to replace their losses. Remarkably, the Romans achieved this challenge within seven or eight months. The Carthaginians also had to replace substantial losses, as well as contend with widespread uprisings throughout their African possessions. Punic primacy and overlordship had been challenged. It would have to be re-established before Carthage could confidently resume the struggle.

THE RETURN TO SICILY, 254–241 BC

In the spring of 254 BC, the new consuls left Italy with two fresh armies and 220 new ships, bound for Messana. There they joined up with the survivors from the disastrous storm off Camarina. Once preparations had been completed, the 300-strong fleet sailed round Cape Pelorias along the north coast, while the legions marched to Drepana, embarked and then sailed to Panormous (Palermo), one of the largest and richest Carthaginian coastal cities, with a good harbour providing safe, spacious anchorage. The Roman soldiers landed under the outer walls that encircled the town, breached these defences and set about butchering its inhabitants, a sight that must have encouraged those sheltering behind the city's inner defences to surrender and face slavery.

ROMAN *HASTATUS* OR *PRINCEPS* (CENTRE)

The mail shoulder guard worn over the mail shirt would have been backed by leather to maintain their shape and position: they are obviously based on the design on the Greek linen cuirass. The helmet is of the Montefortino type, which was mass-produced and is considered inferior in quality to the type shown on the *triarius*. The *pilum* is based on a surviving example, the thickness at the joint between the iron and wood being caused by a plate at the base of the head through which securing rivets passed.

ROMAN *VELES* (RIGHT)

Supplied by the poorer citizens, this arm of the Roman Army was completely unarmoured, with only agility and a light shield for defence. A simple 'bascinet' type of helmet of bronze or leather may have been worn by some *velites*. The javelins were about 1.7m long.

ROMAN *TRIARIUS* (LEFT)

Our figure is based on the earliest surviving sculptures showing legionaries: the alter of Ahenobarbus, and a monument erected at Delphi by Aemilius Paullus to celebrate his victory at Pydna in 168 BC. We know small square breast-plates were worn prior to the Punic Wars, and Polybius claims they were still in use in his day, but it seems reasonably certain that by the First Punic War all legionaries except the *velites* were protected by the same type of defences – a mail shirt of iron and a large oval shield. Both Polybius and Arrian state that a greave was also worn on the leading (left) leg.
(© Richard Hook, Osprey Publishing)

The fall of Panormous induced a number of other cities to throw in their lot with Rome, leaving the Carthaginians mainly confined to the west of the island. But in 253 BC, the Romans lost sight of their strategic objective. The two new consuls travelled through Sicily and crossed over to North Africa, not to threaten Carthage but to raid the Libyan coastline some 320km to the south. The Romans probably wished to sustain the unrest amongst the Libyans, but this division of their resources proved ineffectual. Having been fortunate not to lose their fleet off the Libyan coast when it was ignominiously stranded on an ebb tide, the Romans were caught in a storm on the passage back and lost 150 of their 200 ships.

For the next two years Roman resolution seemed to falter. The land campaign was conducted in a desultory manner and the lost ships were only partially replaced. The Carthaginians, on the other hand, had quelled the dissident Libyans and sent reinforcements to Sicily under Hasdrubal, the son of Hanno, who had served with Xanthipus. For two years he dominated the countryside around Lilybaeum, but he was eventually defeated in a messy battle near Panormous from which he managed to escape. He was later recalled to Carthage and, like his father, summarily executed; being a Carthaginian general was no sinecure.

Though the Romans finally received naval reinforcements and troops for the investment of Lilybaeum, they were unable to prevent the Carthaginian garrison being supplied from the sea, while on land they faced a Herculean task. Although they had four legions available, the city lay on a promontory and was secured by a massive wall and a deep ditch that required the erection of siege fortifications. Not long after these had been completed, a violent wind blew down some of the Roman towers protecting their works, and this encouraged the Carthaginians to sally forth and set them ablaze. Following this reverse in fortunes, the Romans gave up trying to take the city by storm and settled down to starve the garrison into submission. Eight years later, when the First Punic War ended, Lilybaeum remained unconquered.

The Romans' next move was to try to destroy the Carthaginian fleet sheltering at Drepana, just north of Lilybaeum, but a Roman fleet of 120 ships under Publius Claudius Pulcher was virtually destroyed, though Pulcher managed to escape with about 30 ships. While these dramatic events had been unfolding, at the other end of the island a massive Roman fleet consisting of 120 warships and 800 transports had sailed from Messana and, after rounding Cape Pachynus (Cape Passero), found itself facing the Carthaginian fleet. Before any serious fighting could begin, the Carthaginians, recognizing the signs of a pending storm, broke off the engagement and took shelter in the lee of the cape, where they were able to ride out the rough weather. The Roman fleet never had a chance to escape, and so was driven on to the rocky shore and almost annihilated.

Roman fortunes were at a low ebb but the Carthaginians were not faring much better. Success at sea had been nullified by failure on land and most importantly, following the ousting of the war party by the great landowners, attention was diverted from Sicily to interests nearer home. On the positive side, Hamilcar Barca, Hannibal's father, a skilful and energetic commander, had been despatched to Sicily, but he did not have the resources to do more than conduct a guerrilla war while the Carthaginian fleet was withdrawn.

After four years of inconclusive fighting, the Roman Senate decided to make a supreme effort to end the costly and unrewarding conflict. In 243 BC, a new fleet was constructed, which set sail the following year to seal off Lilybaeum from the sea. Only late in the day did the Carthaginians recognize the danger and return to Sicilian waters to confront the Romans in the naval battle that was to decide the war. It was not an engagement marked by audacious manoeuvre: the two fleets lined up and clashed head on to fight it out until. After losing more than 50 ships, the Carthaginians conceded defeat and retired to Carthage.

Deserted and with no hope of further support, Hamilcar Barca was left to negotiate the best peace terms he could with Lutatius Catulus, the Roman commander. In the event both commanders showed themselves to be reasonable in their demands, and a treaty was concluded whereby the Carthaginians would retain their arms but withdraw from Sicily and pay a substantial war indemnity. After 24 years of fluctuating fortunes, with a heavy cost in lives and resources, the war had ended, but it was not to bring peace to either side.

STRIFE BETWEEN WARS, 241–218 BC

Almost as soon as the treaty between Catulus and Hamilcar Barca had been signed, both Carthage and Rome found themselves engaged in bitter fighting against other opponents. For Carthage it was first against her mutinous mercenaries and then the conquering of Spain. Yet these events would once again bring Rome and Carthage into war. In 237 BC, the Mercenary War ended, Hamilcar Barca was determined to restore Carthage to her former eminence and avenge the humiliation suffered in Sicily. Appreciating, however, that oligarchic interests in Carthage could prevail and blight his intentions, he decided to establish his own powerbase and make himself independent of Carthaginian vacillation. He would conquer Spain and exploit her riches and raise a mercenary army whose allegiance was tied to him personally, ultimately enabling him to challenge Rome.

As Carthage no longer had an effective navy, Hamilcar had no alternative but to march along the African coast to the Straits of Gibraltar, with a few supply ships keeping pace with him. In 237 BC he ferried his army across the straits and having done so, proclaimed that he ruled by divine power. This soon transformed simple clan and tribal superstitions into a mystical theology centred on the Barcic family, and a dynastic religion was born that tied the loyalty of the army to him and his relations, while debarring ambitious aspirants from Carthage.

Having established his authority, Hamilcar began his campaign of conquest by securing southern Spain, with its high-quality silver mines, before advancing along the eastern coast. He had hardly achieved these objectives when in 229 BC, while negotiating with a tribal king, he was caught off-guard. In attempting to escape across a swollen river, he was swept from his horse and drowned. He was succeeded by his son-in-law Hasdrubal (known as Hasdrubal the Fair), who, having ruthlessly avenged Hamilcar's death, extended Carthaginian domination northwards before founding New Carthage (Carthago Nova), modern-day Cartagena, on the east coast. This location gave him possession of a magnificent harbour and further rich silver mines in the surrounding hills. News of these developments reached Rome, but preoccupation with the Gallic invasion meant that the Romans could do little more than draw up a treaty confirming Carthaginian possessions to the south of the Ebro.

In 220 BC, Hasdrubal was assassinated in his palace by a Celt whose chieftain had been crucified for plotting against the emperor king. When called upon to elect a successor, the army unanimously voted for the 25-year-old Hannibal, who promptly began to extend Carthaginian territory into the north-western highlands of Spain. When news of Hannibal's Spanish expansion was delivered to Rome, envoys were despatched who, though convinced that Hannibal was intent upon war, never imagined that this would be fought anywhere but in Spain. Once again Roman attention was focused elsewhere, this time on Illyria, which enabled Hannibal to consolidate his hold on Spain

Many types of *hastae* were in use during the Republican period. This relief shows a group of Roman marines equipped with shields and Montefortino helmets. (German Archaeological Institute, Rome)

with the capture of the important town of Saguntum after an eight-month siege. Lying some 400km north of New Carthage, Saguntum may not have been a formal ally of Rome – the treaty had not as yet been ratified – but as it lay well within the Romans' sphere of influence, its capture and sacking was an irrevocable step towards war.

THE SECOND PUNIC WAR, 218–201 BC

In the spring of 218 BC Hannibal, leaving his brother Hasdrubal Barca in charge of affairs in Spain, set out from New Carthage on a campaign that was to last for 17 years. The plan to march overland had almost certainly been developed by his father, who, having been precipitously abandoned in Sicily as a result of political irresolution and an incompetent fleet, was determined that henceforth he would be master of his own destiny.

After crossing the Ebro, Hannibal was stoutly opposed by tribes who were friendly with Rome, and by the time he had crossed the Pyrenees his army numbered 50,000 infantry and 5,000 cavalry, with losses of 40,000 and 3,000 respectively since setting out from New Carthage. Not all of these were battle casualties, since a substantial number of Spanish mercenaries had been sent back home (which probably means they deserted). From the Pyrenees to the Rhône, some 257km, progress was rapid, since all Hannibal required of the tribes he encountered was freedom of passage and the purchase of provisions. It seems that they were only too willing to help and speed him on his way. From the Rhône, however, Hannibal encountered two significant obstacles – hostile Gallic tribes and the Alpine mountain range. Both took their toll. Fifteen days after he had set off to cross the Alps, Hannibal at last reached the fertile expanse of the plains but only 12,000 Africans, 8,000 Spaniards and 4,000 cavalry had survived, about a quarter of the number that had marched out of New Carthage some six months earlier.

The cohesive power of Rome lay in its army, so Hannibal's operational aim was to inflict such defeats on the army that the subjugated states would be encouraged to rise in revolt. Hannibal would have to avoid being drawn into positional warfare that would permit the Romans to concentrate overwhelmingly against him. Hannibal therefore adopted manoeuvre-based tactics to bring the Romans to battle on ground and at a time of his own choosing. Hannibal undoubtedly respected the prowess of the Roman soldier in close combat, but the orderly progression of rigidly linear deployment upon which the Romans relied could be broken using surprise and flexibility – two vital elements of Hannibal's tactical thinking behind which always lay the aim of encirclement.

In October 218 BC, Hannibal rested his army after crossing the Alps, then seized Taurasia (Turin) and defeated Publius Cornelius Scipio and his fellow consul on the Trebia, a tributary of the Po. These two deft and determined successes won over most of the Cisalpine Gauls, who until then had been divided in their support for the Carthaginians. The following spring Hannibal marched south through Etruria, burning and devastating the countryside, keeping Cortona and the hills surrounding it to his left and making as though to pass Lake Trasimene to his right. Consul Gaius Flaminius now set off in pursuit, without waiting for his fellow consul to join him.

When Hannibal reached Lake Trasimene, after following the northern shoreline, he set an ambush along a strip of land between the defile of Borghetto and Tuoro. Here, facing the lake, a semicircle of hills forms a natural amphitheatre. Hannibal positioned his Spanish and Libyan infantry conspicuously on the ridge to the west of Tuoro, while the Balearic slingers and his light infantry concealed themselves on the high ground facing the lake. Similarly, the cavalry and Gauls were hidden in folds in the ground running down to the Borghetto defile. In this way the entire area encircled by the hills was dominated by the Carthaginians.

Flaminius reached Lake Trasimene late in the evening, and at dawn the legions started to move forward through the defile across the valley floor. Seeing Hannibal's troops drawn up in battle in front of them, the Romans deployed into line until the bulk of the two legions had passed through the Borghetto defile. Suddenly assaulted by the light infantry and Balearic slingers on their left flank and the Numidian cavalry to their rear, blocked in front and hemmed in by the lake to their right, most of the Romans died where they stood. Others were either weighed down by their armour and drowned, or were dispatched by the Numidians, who rode out into the lake after them. Though some 6,000 managed to fight their way out of the trap, at least 15,000 are estimated to have died, amongst them Flaminius. The Romans' woes were not yet over, however. Servilius, who was belatedly hurrying down the Via Flaminia, was intercepted by a mixed force commanded by Maharbal, the Numidian cavalry commander, and routed. Half the men of the two legions were killed and the remainder taken prisoner.

When the magnitude of the defeat reached Rome, the city was thrown into a state of near-despair, with the crowds thronging the public places as the wildest rumours spread. Thoroughly alarmed, the Senate appointed an aristocrat, Fabius Maximus, as dictator with full *imperium*, which meant that, unlike the consuls, he did not have to consult the Senate about his plans. At the head of four legions Fabius marched down the Via Appia and closed up to Hannibal, but he had no intention of accepting battle in circumstances of Hannibal's choosing. Instead he would hover, threatening and harrying Hannibal, but keeping to the high ground to nullify the superiority of the Numidian cavalry in particular. He earned himself the title *Cunctator*, or 'The Delayer'.

His was a difficult course to pursue, not least because it left Hannibal free to burn and plunder at will while the Romans looked on, apparently too timid to intervene.

Saguntum from the east. It was Hannibal's siege of this city, lasting eight months, which provoked the Second Punic War. The medieval walls and castle probably follow the lines of the ancient walls and citadel. (Spanish National Tourist Office)

LAKE TRASIMENE, JUNE 217 BC

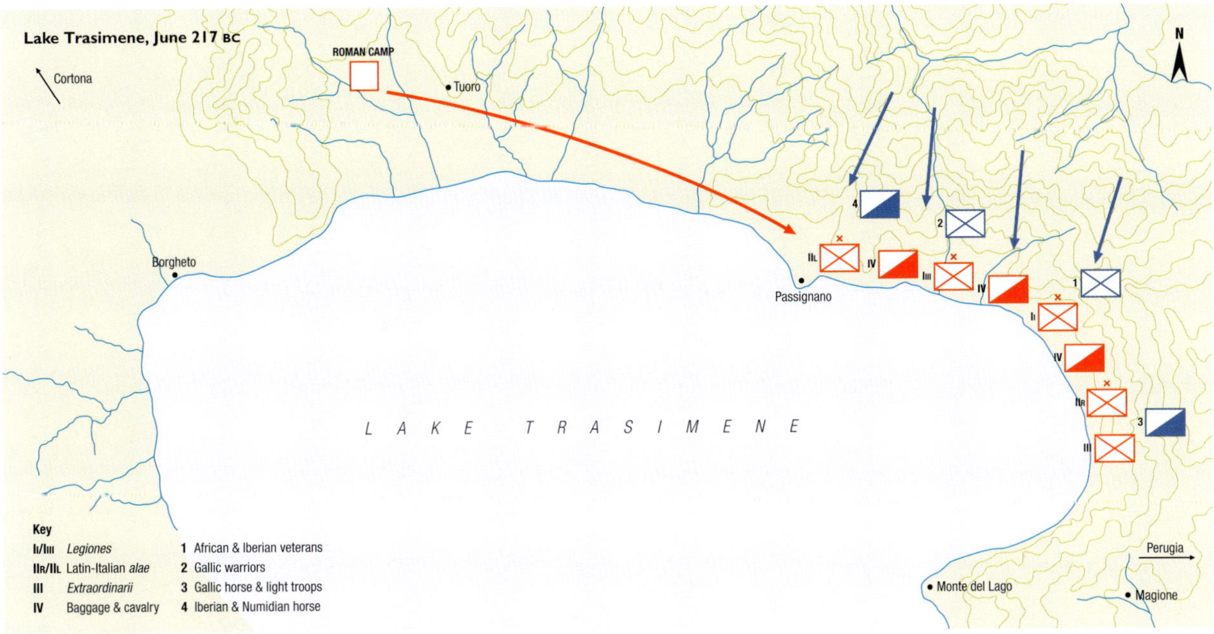

Such a policy could not endure. The allies could not be expected to remain loyal under such circumstances and internal political pressures for resolute action were too strong. In 216 BC, at the end of Fabius' year as dictator, he was replaced by two consuls, Gaius Terentius Varro and Lucius Aemilius Paullus.

The Senate decided that Hannibal must be brought to battle, so four new legions were mobilized and ordered to join the four already shadowing Hannibal in Apulia; concentrated together they would then crush him, in accordance with traditional military thinking. So it was that the fatal day arrived and it was Varro who exercised command at Cannae when, at first light, he moved the Roman Army across the River Aufidus on to the east bank. What followed was one of the greatest defeats in Roman history.

BATTLE: CANNAE, A LESSON IN ANNIHILATION, 216 BC

MILITARY HISTORIANS REGARD the battle of Cannae as a classic example of a successful double-envelopment manoeuvre. Still studied in Western military academies, Cannae is a lesson in annihilation striven after by many military commanders. For instance, Count Alfred von Schlieffen, the architect of the plan used for the German invasion of France in August 1914, was obsessed with Hannibal's victory, studying the battle time and time again for inspiration as he painstakingly drafted and re-drafted his grand design. The resultant plan bore only a superficial similarity to Hannibal's tactics at Cannae and was conceived on an infinitely grander scale.

Senior officer, possibly a tribune, from the Altar of Domitius Ahenobarbus. (N. Sekunda)

Faced by a vastly more numerous force, Hannibal decided, in effect, to use the very strength of the Roman infantry to defeat it, deliberately inviting it to press home its attack on the centre of his line. His African veterans would serve as the jaws of the trap, the Gallic and Iberian warriors as the bait. Finally, Hannibal took equal care with the deployment of his cavalry; it too would play an integral part in the entrapment of the Romans. Instead of distributing his cavalry equally between the wings, he placed more cavalry on the left against the river there. This virtually guaranteed a breakthrough against the numerically far inferior Roman cavalry, and his cavalry would then be available for further manoeuvres. The smaller body of cavalry on the open flank, away from the river Aufidus, where the more numerous Italian cavalry was stationed, would be expected to hold them in play for as long as possible. The Carthaginian dispositions at Cannae, made in full view of the enemy and on a treeless space, actually constituted an ambush. Not only was this a beautifully thought-out, audacious scheme, but it showed Hannibal's absolute confidence in the fighting abilities of all the contingents of his army.

The Roman legions, supported by the allied *alae*, were drawn up in their customary three lines behind a forward

GAIUS TERENTIUS VARRO

The consular elections of 216 BC were held amid scenes of savage bickering and popular demand for strong measures against the Punic invaders (Livy, *History of Rome*, 22.33.9–34.1). It is therefore no surprise that when the first elections were finally held, the sole candidate to be elected was Gaius Terentius Varro, a strong advocate of meeting Hannibal in battle. Varro's subsequent defeat has made him the scapegoat of most ancient writers, who have eagerly seized upon suggestions that he was a gutter demagogue, a butcher's son and a dangerous fool (Livy, Plutarch, Appian). These writers have chosen to ignore the Roman senatorial system and seem not to have investigated Varro's previous career too closely. As Lazenby (*Hannibal's War*, p.74) rightly remarks, it would have been impossible for a butcher's son to be elected to the consulship, and the worst that can be said of Varro in this respect is that he was a *novus homo* (the first in his family to serve in the Senate) rather than from an old established gens. He had in fact already served as quaestor (222 BC), aedile (221 BC) and praetor (218 BC), and thus had climbed the established career ladder, the *cursus honorum*. Like all those seeking political careers, Varro would have first served in the army at the age of 17. It is also possible that Varro had seen active service in Illyria (219 BC). The picture we are usually given of the vain, arrogant bully who could harangue a meeting but not command an army is therefore somewhat wide of the mark. It would seem that Varro, while certainly no military genius, was no worse a commander than his predecessors, notably the unconventional Gaius Flaminius. However, Livy (*History of Rome*, 22.61.15) was quite right to point out that if Varro had been Carthaginian, he would probably have been crucified. Yet even after the catastrophic defeat at Cannae, he subsequently commanded an army in Etruria (208 BC, 207 BC).

screen of skirmishers. However, not only were the maniples deployed closer together than usual but their frontage was reduced and their depth increased. The Roman tactics were to try and smash through the Punic line by sheer weight of numbers as had happened at the Trebia. With this reversion to the principle of sheer mass, flexibility and manoeuvrability were renounced and the rigidity of the phalanx was reinstated. Commanding the centre was Regulus, the *consul suffectus* (a replacement consul who served for the remainder of a deceased or dismissed consul's term) of 217 BC, and Servilius, Flaminius' original colleague. The 2,400 citizen cavalry was stationed on the right flank by the Aufidus and commanded by the consul Paullus, whilst his colleague Varro, who was also in overall command, took charge of the left with the 3,600 allied cavalry.

Meanwhile the Carthaginian centre formed up in a single convex line, also screened to its front by skirmishers, composed of the Gallic and Iberian war-bands. Hannibal himself, with his brother Mago, took up position here. The African veterans, divided into two phalanxes – the hoplite rather than the Macedonian version – were deployed on the wings of this thin crescent-shaped line. However, now dressed and armed with equipment stripped from the dead of the Trebia and Lake Trasimene, they looked to the entire world like Roman legionaries. Hannibal's Gallic and Iberian horse, probably 6,500 strong and led by Hasdrubal (one of Hannibal's Carthaginian lieutenants), was stationed on his left wing by the Aufidus, the Numidians on his right, led by either Hanno son of Bomilcar or Maharbal son of Himilco, the cavalry leader from the battle of Lake Trasimene.

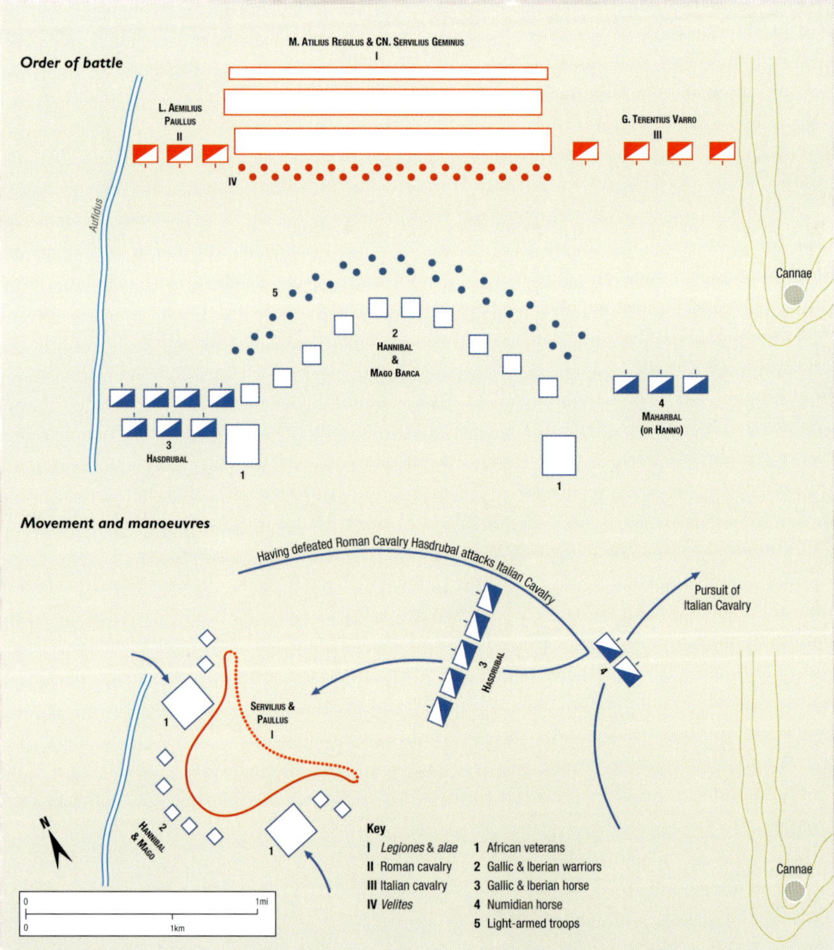

CANNAE, AUGUST 216 BC

The town of Cannae, Apulia, lay on the right bank of the Aufidus some 8km from the Adriatic Sea, the hill upon which it sat was the last spur of generally rising ground in that direction. Below Cannae the river runs through mainly flat, treeless country, but that on the left bank is noticeably more so than that on the right. The left bank, in fact, is perfect cavalry country, whereas on the right bank, though the ground is mostly level, it rises slowly but steadily from the sea to reach the ridge by Cannae.

Hannibal launched the Gallic and Iberian cavalry head-on – the latter were certainly trained and equipped to fight en masse – thereby routing the heavily outnumbered Roman cavalry. Instead of being dissipated in useless pursuit, the victors swung behind the advancing Roman juggernaut to fall on the rear of the Italian cavalry, who had been held in play by the skirmishing Numidian horse. The legionaries gradually pushed back the Gallic and Iberian war-bands, but avoided the Africans, who swung inwards to attack the flanks. The Gallic and Iberian horse left the Numidians to pursue the now fleeing Italian cavalry, and fell on the rear of the legionaries, thus drawing pressure off the Gallic and Iberian warriors and effectively surrounding the Roman centre. This, the final phase of the battle, was not to be an affair of tactical sophistication, but of prolonged butchery. The eventual outcome was a massacre and, in Livy's dramatic rhetoric, the carnage was 'a shocking spectacle even to an enemy's eyes' (*The History of Rome*, 22.51.5).

In a single day some 48,200 Romans were killed, 4,500 were captured on the battlefield, with 14,200 taken elsewhere. One proconsul, namely Servilius, two quaestors, 29 military tribunes, a number of ex-consuls, praetors and aediles, and 80 senators, also perished with the army. Of the consuls, Paullus was killed and Varro fled from the field. Of the Carthaginians, some 8,000 'of his [Hannibal's] bravest men' were killed (Livy, *The History of Rome*, 22.52.6).

ROMAN MANPOWER

The Second Punic War revealed the latent power of Rome, that is, its capacity to produce soldiers. The majority of Rome's previous wars had been fought with two consular armies each of two legions and their usual complement of allied contingents, and Polybius (*The Histories*, 3.107.9) notes that the mobilization of eight legions for the Cannae campaign had never been done before. If Polybius is right in stating there were eight legions at Cannae, this means Rome had mobilized a total of ten legions – since there were already two in the city. By 211 BC there were 25 legions in the field, which, taking into consideration the allied contingents and the men serving at sea, represents something like 250,000 men. As Cineas, the trusted diplomat of King Pyrrhos, was said to have predicted, the many-headed monster could regenerate and struggle on.

This inexhaustible supply of manpower is an obvious reason as to why Rome finally defeated Hannibal. According to Livy, Rome lost more than 50,000 troops at Cannae – the army had suffered 80 per cent casualties. The casualty rate suffered by Britain and its colonial allies during the first day of the Somme in 1916 does not compare with this shocking figure (19,240 killed, 35,493 wounded, 2,152 posted as missing and 585 captured). Yet still Rome managed to survive and fight on.

Then as now, Cannae was a ruin. It was subsequently rebuilt in later Roman times and was still inhabited during the early medieval period. In AD 216 the site was employed as a magazine by the Roman Army to store grain and other supplies for the legions. Its attraction to Hannibal was that it lay firmly astride the strategically important grain-growing region of Apulia. Occupation of the site and domination of the surrounding region was bound to bring the Romans to battle. (Mark Healy)

Despite the massive defeat, Rome was 400km away, a distance that would take at least three weeks to cover with Hannibal's army marching at a forced rate of 20km a day, ample time for the Romans to organize the defence of the city. Moreover, Rome still had two legions sitting within the city itself, and a fleet stationed at Ostia, which raised a legion of marines after Cannae. It must also be remembered that the Roman Army was a citizen force; the population of Rome could be armed easily and by this means defend the walls of their city. Besides, if Hannibal had galloped away from southern Italy he would have left an area that was offering him vital support in his struggle with Rome. No part of Hannibal's long-term strategy involved a march on Rome, and even in 211 BC, when he stood at its gates, he was simply tempting the Romans to lift their siege of Capua.

No other state in antiquity could have survived such a shattering defeat. Rome also had a solid core of support amongst its closest dependencies, the Latin communities, despite a bout of war-weariness at Rome's endless calls on their manpower, and even those 12 that had refused to supply troops never opted to side with Hannibal. With northern and central Italy refusing to back Hannibal, his long-term strategy was not going to be a success. The evidence from negotiations between the defectors (mainly Samnites, Rome's traditional foes) and Hannibal shows that what they really wanted was autonomy and the chance to determine their own fate. Defection to Hannibal, who was after all an outsider, was changing one master for another, or so many feared.

After such an overwhelming victory the question arises as to why Hannibal did not then march on Rome. Instead he continued to try to bring about the dissolution of the

Roman confederation. Many explanations are possible, but even with hindsight it would be unwise to pass judgement on a complex decision about which we only have the most rudimentary knowledge. Before following Hannibal any further, mention should be made of the fact that though the Romans had suffered at home, the two Scipio brothers, Gnaeus and Publius, had landed in Spain and conducted a well-executed land and sea campaign. However, lacking the resources, they had been unable to achieve anything decisive.

THE WAR EXPANDS, 215–206 BC

When news of Hannibal's victory at Cannae reached Carthage, a wave of enthusiasm for the war swept through the city, ambitions rose and Hannibal's plans for broadening the canvas of the war were accepted. In essence Hannibal proposed a strategic encirclement of Italy, the execution of which would be the responsibility of the Carthaginian Senate, and an inner encirclement of Rome itself through the detachment of her allies, for which he would continue to be responsible.

After receiving more than 4,000 cavalry and infantry reinforcements and being relieved in southern Spain by a new army recently arrived from Carthage, Hasdrubal marched north to settle accounts with the Scipios. These two armies were of almost equal strength and when they met, in obvious imitation of his brother's tactics at Cannae, Hasdrubal thinned out the Spanish infantry, holding the centre, and concentrated the Libyans and cavalry on the wings. The Romans, however, broke through his centre, destroyed his army and regained the line of the Ebro. After two years of inconclusive fighting, the Scipios decided to divide their army between them; this separation of Roman force resulted in the brothers being handsomely defeated and counted amongst the dead. The opportunity for Hasdrubal to recover the whole of Spain came and went due to internal dissension among the Carthaginians. Time was allowed for Roman reinforcements to arrive in 210 BC, including a new commander-in-chief, the 25-year-old military genius who was later to be known as Scipio Africanus, the son and nephew of the Scipio brothers who had been killed two years earlier. The following year, after rallying his disheartened troops, Scipio struck at New Carthage rather than attacking the two Carthaginian armies lying near Gibraltar and Madrid, whose commanders were still not able to reconcile their differences and co-operate.

Statue from Herculaneum in the National Museum, Naples, showing a member of the Balbus family wearing the military dress of a proconsular or praetor. Though Augustan, the statue probably represents the dress of a military commander of the latter Republican period reasonably accurately. (German Archaeological Institute, Rome)

SCIPIO'S SIEGE OF NEW CARTHAGE, 209 BC
The Carthaginian foundation of the city lay in a lagoon with only one avenue of approach. Here we see the Romans attacking in a *testudo* ('tortoise') formation – a simultaneous assault on the north wall went unnoticed and the Romans were able to open the gates from within and seize the town. (© Adam Hook, Osprey Publishing)

It took Scipio seven days to reach New Carthage, and he began his assault on the city almost immediately, from both land and sea. As the day matured and the casualties mounted with no prospect of success, Scipio sounded the retreat before making his next move, which would prove to be decisive. Learning from some fishermen that at ebb tide it was possible to ford one of the lagoons and approach the city from the rear, Scipio sought surprise by deception. Renewing his assault on the section of the wall he had attacked the previous day, Scipio drew the defenders to what they regarded as the critical point while he led a 500-strong contingent across the lagoon and scaled the weakly defended northern wall. The city was soon secured, most of its citizens massacred and an immense amount of booty taken.

SARDINIA 215 BC

In 215 BC, the year after the battle of Cannae, a small Carthaginian expedition sailed for Sardinia but ran into a violent storm and was blown off course to the Balearic Islands, where the ships had to be hauled ashore for repair. All this caused considerable delay, and by the time the Carthaginians reached Sardinia, the Romans had been alerted and had reinforced the island with a second legion, quickly suppressing a premature revolt. When the Carthaginians landed, little effective support was available and, lacking adequate strength by themselves, they were soon defeated. Their commander was taken prisoner and the survivors were left with little alternative but to flee to their ships. Fate had not favoured the Carthaginians, but whether they would have prevailed had they not been delayed by the storm is far from certain.

Following the fall of New Carthage, Scipio turned his attention to the field armies and in 208 BC Hasdrubal, after suffering a defeat on the headwaters of the Guadalquivir, inexplicably decided to join Hannibal in Italy. As we will see later, it was a fateful move, both for him personally and for those he commanded. Though substantial reinforcements had arrived from Carthage, in 206 BC the Romans finally defeated the Carthaginians at Ilipa, some 16km north of modern Seville, to end the war in Spain.

SICILY, 215–210 BC

Hieronymus of Syracuse, who had inherited the throne and decided to side with the Carthaginians, was assassinated by members of the pro-Roman party and for a time it looked as though Carthaginian intentions had been thwarted. However, the pro-Roman faction behaved with such wanton cruelty that they in turn were overthrown. This caused the Romans to reinforce Sicily, as in Sardinia, with a second legion. Syracuse now became the Romans' primary objective, but with its formidable fortifications, which had been further strengthened by Archimedes' ingenious war machines that could hurl boulders and grapple ships, it was no easy undertaking. Indeed, the first land and sea assault was a costly failure. Meanwhile the Carthaginians had sent formidable reinforcements. The situation looked critical for the Romans, until two further legions were sent, thus enabling them both to lay siege to Syracuse and to confront the newly arrived Carthaginians.

In 212 BC, the Romans achieved a decisive victory. The Syracusans' enthusiastic indulgence during a religious festival had left them with unsteady legs and less than clear heads, and they were easily surprised. The Romans scaled the outer defences under cover of darkness to open one of the city's gates, and swarming in, they soon established themselves in an unassailable position ringing the inner defences. Deserted by their fleet and so deprived of any relief, the garrison surrendered. Having secured the city it was given over to plunder by the Romans, who destroyed three centuries of civilization and massacred the population, including Archimedes, one of the ancient world's greatest mathematicians and physicists. With the fall of Syracuse the campaign seemed to be coming to an end, but the arrival of further Carthaginian reinforcements prolonged the struggle for another three years.

THE WANING YEARS, 216–205 BC

After Cannae, Hannibal was faced with a dilemma from which he could find no escape. Following the secession of a number of Rome's former allies, he found himself having to protect them and, in so doing, losing the initiative he had previously enjoyed. If Hannibal were to win over more defectors, he would have to operate offensively, yet if he were to retain those cities he had already gained, he would have to act defensively. With an army that was not strong enough to undertake both commitments simultaneously, the clarity of Hannibal's operational aim was lost.

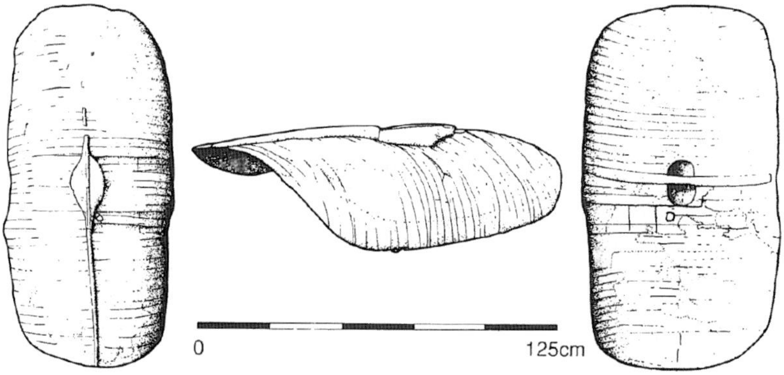

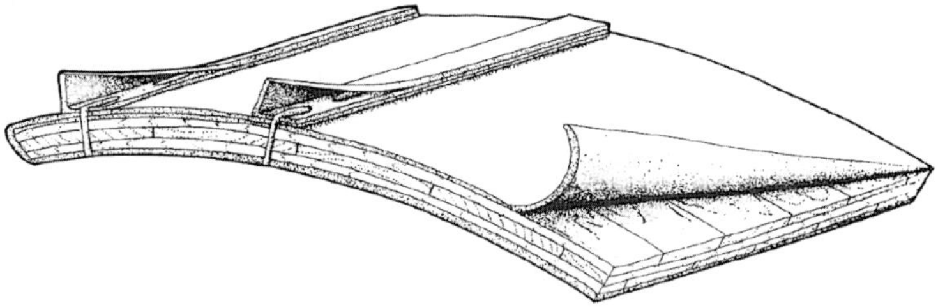

The *scutum* illustrated here is based upon the example found at Kasr el-Harit in Egypt. Though not Roman it is very similar to that shown carried by the legionaries on the alter of Domitius Ahenobarbus and the Aemilius Paullus monument. (Dr M. C. Bishop)

In contrast to Hannibal's restricted capability, the Romans had the means to hold the fortified cities, which then formed a defensive framework around which the field armies could operate. In this manner, wherever Hannibal decided to campaign offensively, the Romans would go on the defensive, but when he was not present, they would take the offensive against former allies who had deserted them. As such, Hannibal was forced into a restless pursuit of ever-shifting and elusive objectives.

Undaunted by his difficulties, however, Hannibal still managed to conduct a robust campaign and one that denied any prospect of early victory for the war-weary Roman population. Much Roman strength was already being diverted to reinforce Spain, Sicily, Sardinia and further campaigns in Illyria, however, by lowering the age of recruitment to 16 and enrolling slaves, the Romans were able to maintain 20 legions under arms in the various theatres of war, 16 of which were in Italy itself.

The most important city to defect after Cannae had been Capua, the capital of Campania, second only to Rome itself in size and prosperity. Retaining Capua was of prime importance to Hannibal if he were to have any hope of encouraging other cities to seek their independence from Rome. In 211 BC, Capua was being threatened by the Romans, who had constructed two lines of siege works round the city. Concerted attempts by Hannibal to break in, and by the garrison to break out, were repulsed, leaving Hannibal no alternative but to seek an indirect means of relieving Capua. He would march on Rome. Without any hope of being able to storm its formidable fortifications, his move was a bluff, intended to create such alarm that the armies besieging Capua would be summoned back to defend the threatened city.

Hannibal's sudden arrival before the walls of Rome caused consternation in the city. Having made this demonstration, Hannibal began his return march but, though he inflicted heavy casualties on the Romans pursuing him, he realized that he was incapable of relieving Capua. His gamble had failed, and while he still remained the undisputed master of the open battlefield, from now on Hannibal found himself in retreat. From the Romans' point of view events had not yet tilted decisively in their favour. Certainly in Italy the situation had improved, and in Sicily Syracuse had been captured, but in Spain the two Scipios had died with their legions after crossing the Ebro, and in Illyria Philip of Macedon was still on the offensive. Everything still hung in the balance.

In Capua all hope of relief had died; 27 of the senators wined and dined in generous excess before taking their own lives by poison. The next day the inhabitants opened one of the gates to the Romans, who rounded up the remaining senators, scourging and then beheading them, while the aristocrats died more slowly in various prisons and the rest of the population was sold into slavery.

Until 208 BC the fortunes of the campaign had ebbed and flowed, with neither Hannibal nor the Romans gaining the ascendancy, but in that year the important city of

THE ITALIAN PENINSULA, 3RD CENTURY BC

Tarentum (Taranto), on the heel of Italy, was captured by the Romans while Hasdrubal, who had marched from Spain, was wintering in Gaul with his 20,000-strong army. In the spring of 207 BC Hasdrubal crossed the Alps, following the same route as his brother had done, evidently without serious incident, and marched to the east coast, where he turned due south towards the Metaurus river, which flows through Umbria. Not knowing Hannibal's whereabouts, Hasdrubal had sent six horsemen to try to locate him, rather unwisely bearing a letter giving his intentions. After having ridden nearly the entire length of Italy, the horsemen were picked up by the Romans near Tarentum and the plan was revealed. Acting rapidly, the Romans closed in on the Metaurus, surrounded Hasdrubal and trapped him in the winding steep-sided river course. Seeing that all was lost, Hasdrubal rode into the thick of the fray, where he was killed together with some 10,000 of his men. A few days later Hasdrubal's severed head was thrown into one of

Hannibal's outposts and two African prisoners were released to recount the disaster. The Romans did not press their advantage and the following year saw little activity, but in 205 BC Publius Cornelius Scipio (later Africanus) stepped onto the scene and everything changed.

THE ROMANS CARRY THE WAR TO AFRICA, 205–201 BC

Hitherto it had been the Carthaginians who had held the strategic initiative with their attempted encirclement, but now it was the turn of the Romans, who would do no more than contain Hannibal in Italy while taking the offensive in Africa. Throughout 205 BC the preparations in Sicily for the invasion of Africa continued, and the next year the expedition sailed from Lilybaeum. Once ashore the Romans set about ravaging the fertile Bagradas valley, and after defeating a Carthaginian army, set siege to the important city of Utica on the coast. The military reverses brought about a realignment of political power in Carthage, where the big landowners and wealthy merchants who had always wished to avoid war with Rome in favour of their African territorial and commercial interests, ousted the Barcic faction and after 16 years in the wilderness came to power. Thirty members of the Council of Elders, superior even to the Senate, came to prostrate themselves before Scipio and after cravenly blaming everything on Hannibal, sought his pardon. Scipio acted with commendable moderation when he laid down his peace terms: all prisoners of war and deserters were to be handed over, all claims to Spain and Mediterranean islands were to be renounced, a substantial indemnity was to be paid, and only 20 warships could be retained, the remainder were to be surrendered. Probably realizing that the terms could have been much harsher, the Carthaginians accepted them and envoys were sent to Rome to seek ratification.

Meanwhile, Hannibal had been recalled to Carthage and with his arrival those wishing to prolong the fighting displayed a new truculence, first seizing a number of Roman ships that had been scattered in a storm, then intercepting and destroying others carrying envoys returning from Carthage. Despite the fact that a delegation had arrived from the Senate informing Scipio that his proposed peace terms had been accepted, the acts of treachery made Scipio determined to settle the long, drawn-out struggle between the Roman and Carthaginian peoples. Hannibal was to be brought to battle and his army destroyed before Scipio directed his attention to Carthage itself.

The two armies confronted one another at Zama, some 160km south-west of Carthage. Though the Romans had a superiority in cavalry, overall numbers were probably about equal, some 40,000 apiece. Although it would be difficult to overestimate the importance of Zama – with the Carthaginians fighting for their lives and homeland and the Romans for the supremacy of their empire – as the two commanders appear to have matched one another tactically the battle was little more than a grisly slogging match in which the Romans prevailed. The details need not concern us, but what is of interest about Zama is how it demonstrated the interplay between the operational and strategic levels of war. By ravaging the Bagradas valley, Scipio had drawn Hannibal away from his own secure coastal base into hostile areas inland where he had to fight on ground and conditions not of his own choosing. This manouevre would have been a difficult operational situation to have created in Italy but, by taking the strategic decision to transfer the war to Africa, it was achieved almost effortlessly.

Hannibal escaped from Zama and was able to exert a restraining influence on those who argued against accepting the Romans' terms of defeat, which were inevitably harsher than those originally proposed in 205 BC. The number of warships allowed was halved, the indemnity increased and Punic military rights were drastically curtailed, leaving Carthage as little more than a client state of Rome. The war that had brought devastation to the whole of the Mediterranean during the previous 17 years had come to an end, leaving Rome as an imperial power of unmatched military might.

Scipio Africanus returned to Rome, indisputably the most powerful figure in the city. As political in-fighting tore reasonable compromise apart, however, and the passage of time diminished Scipio's moderating influence, in 184 BC he finally withdrew from public life in disgust.

THE THIRD PUNIC WAR, 149–146 BC

Carthage had been built on a naturally strong defensive position and then extensively fortified. There were only two restricted land approaches, either along the 3,000m-wide isthmus to the north, protected by three lines of massive defence works towering one above the other, or along the narrow spit of sand to the south, which terminated at the foot of the city walls. The two isthmuses were separated by the unfordable Lake of Tunis and washed by the sea on their outer shores. The single 35km city wall enclosed the great harbour, the entrance of which lay just to the east of the southern sandbar, as well as the citadel constructed on the prominent Byrsa mound, not far from the harbour.

The Romans divided their forces between the two isthmuses, and when ready, attempted to take these two directly approachable defence works by storm. Not surprisingly, they met with a bloody repulse in the north. Undeterred, they flung themselves forward for a second attempt that was equally unsuccessful. On the sandbar to the south they fared somewhat better. By using massive battering-rams propelled by several hundred soldiers and sailors, a breach was made in the city wall, but the assault troops failed to exploit the opportunity, therefore allowing the Carthaginians to build fresh barriers during the night and man the surrounding rooftops.

Denarius struck by C. Servilius commemorating some military exploits by one of his ancestors. Here we can see that the 'Greek' cavalry shield with its *umbro* and spine has replaced the 'popanum' shield. (N. Sekunda)

It was a brief respite. Though the Romans were met with a hail of missiles and were driven back, when they resumed the attack the following day an unseemly withdrawal was prevented from turning into a rout only by the timely intervention of Scipio Aemilianus, the adopted grandson of Scipio Africanus, who was serving as a tribune with the legio IV. Roman impetuosity was then sharply curbed, and they settled down to the more prosaic business of blockading the city. The Carthaginians, however, did not rest on the defensive and made a determined sortie along the northern isthmus. Catching the Romans by surprise, they forced them to abandon their forward position in favour of one further back.

The following year, in 148 BC, demands were made for the appointment of a more vigorous commander, as, although the Romans had secured a number of small inland cities and others along the coast, there was an obvious lack of leadership. As a result, with the enthusiastic support of the Roman people and the army, Scipio Aemilianus was promoted to consul and given command in Africa. He at once set to work constructing a huge mole, which was was to extend from the sandbar across the harbour mouth and bottle up the Carthaginian fleet; it would also seal the Carthaginians off from any further supplies. At first the Carthaginians did not believe that the Romans could succeed, but as work progressed relentlessly, they took counter-measures and cut a new entrance from the inner harbour, giving access to the sea from the east. Fifty triremes then sailed out in a triumphal display of contempt; but it was an unwise gesture, as they lost the element of surprise and so the opportunity to destroy the Roman fleet, which was lying unmanned at anchor while the sailors toiled on the mole.

Undaunted, Scipio positioned his battering rams and other siege engines at the end of the now completed mole and made a partial breach in the Carthaginian defences, but during the night a Carthaginian raiding party swam out to the mole and set fire to the closely packed siege equipment. The Carthaginians then worked feverishly to repair the damage and raise additional towers along the wall. However, it was only a matter of

ROMAN INFANTRYMAN, BATTLE OF PYDNA, 168 BC
Some figures wear the familiar mail cuirass, but others wear the Italian muscle-cuirass, which can be recognized by its lack of shoulder guards. (© Angus McBride, Osprey Publishing)

time before the Romans had secured a foothold between the outer sea wall and that of the harbour, which enabled them to block the newly constructed harbour entrance. Cut off from both land and sea, the fate of Carthage was sealed. While the preparations for the final assault were under way, Scipo took the opportunity to mount a mopping-up operation into the interior and extinguish the last flickering embers of Carthaginian resistance beyond their capital's crumbling defences.

The final assault was mounted from the harbour area where the Romans had established themselves the previous autumn. After some desperate fighting they managed to breach the city wall and then penetrate into the sprawling dockyard buildings, which the Carthaginians set alight once their strength began to fail. A new defensive line was adopted, centred primarily on the citadel commanding the ridge of high ground extending west and east from the Byrsa. Every remaining house had been turned into a stronghold and was contested with the courage born of despair, and the Romans had to clear the whole area, house by house and street by street. For six days the battle raged; on the seventh, the Carthaginians offered to surrender, begging for their lives in return. After Scipio had accepted their request, some 50,000 terrified men, women and children, nearing the limits of exhaustion and starvation, filed out of the city, later to be sold into slavery, but 900 Roman deserters, who could expect only crucifixion if taken alive, fought on. At first they held out in the enclosure surrounding the temple crowning the Byrsa citadel. Then, as their numbers declined, they retreated to the temple itself and finally to its roof before committing suicide.

The city was then given over to plunder before the ruins were levelled to the ground. After six centuries, Carthage had been destroyed and the Phoenician race dispersed to suffer extinction, leaving no readily discernible religious, literary, political or social heritage. An eastern civilization had been planted in the western Mediterranean, but after a period of luxuriant growth, it had been violently uprooted and exterminated. Meanwhile Rome, in an unchallengeable position, was left free to subdue and pacify Europe.

EARLY REPUBLICAN STYLE OF FIGHTING

As discussed, Roman strength lay in the set-piece battle, the decisive clash of opposing armies that settled the issue one way or another. Polybius saw the Romans as rather old-fashioned in their straightforward and open approach to warfare, commenting that as a race they tended to rely instinctively on 'brute force' when waging war. Nothing illustrates his criticism better than Cannae, when Roman tactics subordinated the other arms very much to the heavy infantry.

The essential philosophy behind the manipular legion was that of winning a straightforward, mass engagement with the enemy. Only in the method of doing this did it differ from the Greek phalanx or Macedonian combination of the phalanx with shock. The same, quick decisive clash with the enemy was desired. In this role the manipular legion performed very well. Hannibal's obvious skill as a general inflicted a number of massive defeats on this Roman Army (e.g. Cannae 216), yet the same type of army, when better led and with higher morale, beat him in turn (e.g. Zama). As Polybius rightly states, 'the defeats they suffered had nothing to do with weapons or formations, but were brought about by Hannibal's cleverness and military genius' (*The Histories*, 18.28.7).

The inclusion of allied troops within the armies of this period did not change the essential tactical doctrines behind them. Many allied units were organized and equipped as legions and thus acted in a similar fashion, whilst the additional light-armed troops or cavalry were deployed to help achieve the same aim of breaking the enemy line.

Polybius does not offer his readers an account of the legion in battle, but there are a number of combat descriptions both in his own work and that of Livy. However, very few accounts describe tactics in detail; a contemporary Roman (or Greek) audience would take much for granted.

Despite this we can draw our own picture from the sources available to us. The legion would usually approach the enemy in its standard battle formation, the *triplex acies*, which was based, as we have seen, around the triple line of *hastati*, *principes* and *triarii*, with the *velites* forming a light screen in front. Each of the three lines consisted of ten maniples. The maniples were not drawn up side by side, instead gaps were left equal in width to their own frontage (*c.* 18m). The gaps in the line of the *hastati* were covered in the second line by the maniples of the more seasoned *principes*, and likewise the maniples of the veteran *triarii* covered the gaps in the line of the *principes*. Modern commentators conveniently call this battle formation the *quincunx*, from the five dots on a dice-cube.

Battle would be opened by the *velites*, who attempted to disorganize and unsettle enemy formations with a hail of javelins. Having done this they retired through the gaps in the maniples of the *hastati* and made their way to the rear. The maniples of the *hastati* now reformed to close the gaps, either by each maniple extending its frontage, thus giving individuals more room in which to handle their weapons, or, if the maniple was drawn up two centuries deep, the *centurio posterior* would move his *centuria* to the left and forward, thus running out and forming up alongside the *centuria* of the *centurio prior* in the line itself (Keppie, *The Making of the Roman Empire*, pp.38–39).

The *hastati* would discharge their *pila*, throwing first their light and then their heavyweight spears, some 15m – the effective range of a *pilum* – from the enemy. During the confusion caused by this hail of *pila*, which could be devastating, the *hastati* drew their swords and, says Polybius, 'charged the enemy yelling their war cry and clashing their weapons against their shields as is their custom' (*The Histories*, 15.12.8). He also says that the Romans formed up in a much looser formation than other heavy infantry, adding this was necessary in order to use the sword and for the soldier to defend himself all round with his shield. This implies the legionary was essentially an individual fighter, a swordsman. Yet Marcus Porcius Cato (the censor), who served during the Second Punic War as an *eques* and quaestor, always maintained that a soldier's bearing, confidence and the ferociousness of his war cry were more important than his actual skill with a blade.

Polybius, in an excursion dedicated to the comparison between Roman and Macedonian military equipment and tactical formations, says the following:

> According to the Roman methods of fighting each man makes his movements individually: not only does he defend his body with his long shield, constantly moving it to meet a threatened blow, but he uses his sword both for cutting and for thrusting.
>
> (Polybius, *The Histories*, 18.30.6)

What we are witnessing here is the intelligent use, by a swordsman, of the short sword. We know from the archaeological record that the *gladius* of the Principate ('Pompeii' type) was an amazingly light and well-balanced weapon that was capable of making blindingly fast attacks, and was suitable for both cuts and thrusts. However, Tacitus and Vegetius lay great stress on the *gladius* being employed by the legionary for thrusting rather than slashing. As Vegetius rightly says, 'a slash-cut, whatever its force, seldom kills' (*De Re Militari*, 1.12), and thus a thrust was certainly more likely to deliver the fatal wound. Having thrown the *pilum* and charged into contact, the standard drill for the legionary was to punch the enemy in the face with the shield-boss and then jab him in the belly with the razor-sharp point of the sword.

ROMAN SOLDIERS, 1ST CENTURY BC

The three figures here are (from left to right) a Roman tribune, a signifier and a legate or consul. The tribune is shown holding a spear of the Greek type, and the round shield is probably of the hoplite type. His armament is completely different to that of the legionary, being much more Greek than Roman. (© Richard Hook, Osprey Publishing)

In his near-contemporary account of the battle of Telamon (225 BC), Polybius tells us that 'Roman shields ... were far better designed for defence, and so were their swords for attack, since the Gallic sword can only be used for cutting and not for thrusting' (*The Histories*, 2.30.9). Soon after, when he covers the Gallic tumultus of 223 BC, it is disclosed that legionaries 'made no attempt to slash and used only the thrust, kept their swords straight and relied on their sharp points ... inflicting one wound after another

ROMAN CAVALRYMEN ON RECONNAISSANCE

Two cavalrymen on reconnaissance in Thessaly during the Second Macedonian War, gathering information from a *veles* (left). The horseman on the left, based on the Curtius relief, carries a shield of the 'popanum' variety. His comrade, based on the Servilius coins, carries a 'Greek' shield with a central spine. Both figures wear the cavalry cloak (*sagum*). (© Angus McBride, Osprey Publishing)

on the breast or the face' (2.33.6). In a much later passage (6.23.4) Polybius hints that they were trained to take the first whirling blow of the Celtic slashing-sword on the rim of the *scutum*, which was suitably bound with iron.

The use of the thrust also meant the legionary kept most of his torso well covered, and thus protected, by his *scutum*. The latter, having absorbed the attack of his antagonist, was now punched into the face of the opponent as the legionary stepped forward to jab with his *gladius*. Much like the riot shield of a modern policeman, the *scutum* was used both defensively and offensively to defect blows and hammer into the opponent's shield or body to create openings. As he stood with his left foot forward, a legionary could get much of his bodyweight behind this punch. Added to this was the considerable weight of the *scutum* itself.

Ideally, the *hastati* fought the main enemy line to a standstill, but if they were rebuffed, or lost momentum, the *principes* advanced into the combat zone and the process was repeated. Hand-to-hand fighting was physically strenuous and emotionally draining, and the skill of a Roman commander lay in committing his second and third lines at the right time. Obviously the survivors of the *hastati* and the *principes* reinforced the *triarii* if it came down to a final trial of strength.

Victory would eventually go to the side that endured the stress of staying so close to the enemy for the longest and was still able to urge enough of its men forward to renew the fighting. It was the inherent flexibility of the manipular system that made the legion a formidable battlefield opponent. In Polybius' measured analysis:

> The order of battle used by the Roman Army is very difficult to break through, since it allows every man to fight both individually and collectively; the effect is to offer a formation that can present a front in any direction, since the maniples that are nearest to the point where danger threatens wheel in order to meet it. The arms they carry both give protection and also instil great confidence into the men, because of the size of the shields and the strength of the swords, which can withstand repeated blows. All these factors make the Romans formidable antagonists in battle and very hard to overcome.
>
> (Polybius, *The Histories*, 15.15.7–10)

Hellenistic armies, by contrast, preferred to deepen their phalanx rather than form troops into a second line, and made little use of reserves, as the commander's role was usually to charge at the head of his cavalry in the manner of Alexander the Great. The deepening of the pike-armed phalanx gave the army stamina in the mêlée, but even the men in the rear ranks were affected by the stress and exhaustion of prolonged combat. The Roman system, on the other hand, allowed fresh men to be fed into the fighting line, renewing its impetus and leading a surge forward, which might well have been enough to break a wearying enemy.

In a consular army, the two Roman legions would form the centre with two allied *alae* deployed on their flanks – they were known as the '*ala* of the left' and the '*ala* of the right' (Polybius, *The Histories*, 6.26.9), a positioning reflecting the term *ala* (wing). In larger armies, however, legions and *alae* would probably alternate as they did at Cannae, where there were effectively four separate consular armies, each consisting of two legions and two *alae*, and each with its own commander. Although the *extraordinarii* had a special place in the line-of-march and in camp, they do not seem to have had a special role in battle and may have simply stood with the rest of the allies, that is, as part of their parent unit.

CAVALRY TACTICS

In its simplest form, the cavalry served to protect the flanks of the consular army. The citizen cavalry of the two legions are usually depicted as stationed on the right wing, the position of honour, whilst the Latin and Italian cavalry formed on the left. Still, given that there were often three times as many of the latter as the former, this may be an oversimplification. Even so, combat between cavalry invariably took place on the edges of the battlefield, flanking the general infantry contest.

Under normal circumstances, one side would apparently have been intimidated by the other and given way before colliding with them. This seems reasonable, for horses will not charge into solid objects, and a steady unit of enemy horsemen in close formation could well have been perceived as just an impenetrable object. Moreover, the riders would themselves have been all too aware of the potential catastrophe that could occur if the opposing forces crashed into each other. Under normal circumstances, the riders' nerve would fail. Steady cavalry nearly always relied upon morale rather than physical shock to cause the enemy to flinch, break and run.

Polybius' silence on the subject suggests that the allies were organized and equipped along Roman lines, which would certainly have been desirable as it would have enabled them to interact smoothly with the legions. Presumably their traditional arms and tactics were gradually replaced by Roman methods and weaponry.

Roman *velites* were essentially skirmishers. They operated in a very loose order, with a fluid formation, allowing each man great freedom to advance and retire at will.

In ideal circumstances, skirmishers were supposed to drive back their opposite numbers and then begin to 'soften up' the main body of the enemy, but such successes were exceptionally rare. *Velites* appear not to have had their own officers, instead they were commanded by the centurions stationed with the heavy infantry, yet they could be quite effective in battle. Livy describes them successfully skirmishing from a distance by throwing their javelins and then fighting at close quarters with their swords, using their shields to protect themselves. Polybius mentions how certain *velites* would wear a wolf's skin over their helmets so that they would be visible to their centurions from a distance; such individuals, being keen to impress, could well have led by example.

A high degree of courage would have been required in order to get close enough to hit the enemy, necessitating the need to enter the killing zone and exposing oneself as an individual to enemy fire. Thus the main importance of preliminary skirmishing was probably to boost morale or intimidate the enemy. Ancient writers are certainly right to regard this initial phase of battle as inconclusive and tactically insignificant, since it is quite likely that comparably few troops were killed or even wounded in it.

THE ARMY OF THE LATE REPUBLIC, 146–27 BC

INTRODUCTION: POLITICS AND THE ROMAN WAY OF WAR

Although originally a monarchy, Rome, as we have seen, had become a republic near the end of the 6th century BC. Such political revolutions were commonplace in the city-states of the ancient world, but after this Rome proved remarkably stable, free from the often violent internal disputes that constantly beset other communities. At first, the Romans gradually expanded their territory, and by the beginning of the 3rd century BC they controlled virtually all of the Italian peninsula. Conflict with Carthage, which began in 265 BC and continued sporadically until that city was utterly destroyed in 146 BC, resulted in the acquisition of overseas provinces. By this time, Rome dominated the entire Mediterranean world, having easily defeated the successor kingdoms which had emerged from the break-up of Alexander the Great's empire.

Roman expansion continued, and time and time again her legions were successful in foreign wars, never losing a conflict even if they sometimes suffered defeat in individual battles. Yet, the stability and unity of purpose which had so characterized Roman political life for centuries began to break down.

The Roman Republican system was intended to prevent any individual or group within the state from gaining overwhelming and permanent power. The Republic's senior executive officers or magistrates, the most senior of whom were the two consuls, held power (*imperium*) for a single year, after which they returned to civilian life. A mixture of custom and law prevented any individual being elected to the same office in successive years, or at a young age, and in fact it was rare for the consulship to be held more than twice by any man. Former magistrates, and the pick of the wealthiest citizens in the state formed the Senate, a permanent council which advised the magistrates and also supervised much of the business of government, for instance, despatching and receiving embassies. The Senate also chose the province (which at this period still meant sphere of responsibility and only gradually was acquiring fixed geographical associations) to be allocated to each magistrate, and could extend the *imperium* of a man within the same province for several years.

Previous page:
'The death of Caesar' by Nicolas Poussin. Caesar's death at the hands of those seeking to preserve the liberty of the Republic was finally avenged at the battle of Philippi in 42 BC. (Corbis)

Roman politics was fiercely competitive, as senators pursued a career that brought them both civil and military responsibilities, sometimes simultaneously. It was very rare for men standing for election to advocate any specific policies, and there was no equivalent to modern political parties within the Senate. Each aristocrat instead tried to represent himself as a capable man, ready to cope with whatever task the Republic required of him, be it leading an army or building an aqueduct. Men paraded their achievements and – as it was often the case that before election they personally had done little – the past achievements of their family. Vast sums of money were lavished on the electorate, especially in the form of games, gladiator shows, feasts and the building of great monuments. This gave great advantages to a small core of established and exceptionally wealthy families who as a result tended to dominate the senior magistracies. In the 1st century BC there were eight praetorships (senior magistracies of lower ranking than consulships), and even more of the less senior posts, but still only ever two consulships. This meant that the majority of the 600 senators would never achieve this office.

The higher magistracies and the consulship offered the opportunity for the greatest responsibilities and therefore allowed men to achieve the greatest glory, which enhanced

THE APPEARANCE OF THE ROMAN ARMY, *c*.104 BC
From left to right to figures are: a tribune, an *eques* and two infantrymen. The *eques* has a yellow plume on his helmet – Arrian mentions Roman cavalry wearing yellow plumes some 250 years later, but we have no idea when this became standard practice. (© Angus McBride, Osprey Publishing)

their family name for the future. The consuls commanded in the most important wars, and in Rome military glory always counted for more than any other achievement. The victor in a great war was also likely to profit from it financially, taking a large share of the booty and the profits from the mass enslavement of captured enemies. Each senator strove to serve the Republic in a greater capacity than all his contemporaries. The propaganda of the Roman elite is filled with superlatives, each man striving to achieve bigger and better deeds than anyone else, and special credit was attached to being the first person to perform an act or defeat a new enemy. Aristocratic competition worked to the Republic's advantage for many generations, for it provided a constant supply of magistrates eager to win glory on the state's behalf.

In the late 2nd century BC, however, the system began to break down. Rome had expanded rapidly, but the huge profits of conquest had not been distributed evenly, so a few families benefited enormously. The gap between the richest and poorest in the Senate widened, and the most wealthy were able to spend lavishly to promote their own and their family's electoral success. It became increasingly expensive to pursue a political career, a burden felt as much by members of very old but now modestly wealthy families as by those outside the political elite. Such men could only succeed by borrowing vast sums of money, hoping to repay these debts once they achieved the highest offices. The risk of failure, which would thus bring financial as well as political ruin, could make such men desperate.

During the 1st century BC, soldiers no longer provided their own equipment, instead they were issued with standard weapons, armour and clothing by the state. The differences between the various property classes in the legion vanished, as did *velites* and *equites*. All legionaries were now heavy infantry, armed alike with *scutum*, *pilum* and *gladius*. (Fields-Carré Collection)

At the same time men from the richest and most prestigious families saw opportunities to have even more distinguished careers than their ancestors by flouting convention and trying to build mass support. Both new men (*novi homines*; s. *novus homo*) and those from senatorial families were inclined to act as *populares*, an abusive term employed by critics to signify men who appealed to the poorer citizens for support by promising them entertainment, subsidised or free food, or grants of land. The *popularis* was an outsider, operating with methods unattractive to the well-established senators. It was a very risky style of politics, but one which potentially offered great opportunities. In 133 BC, Tiberius Sempronius Gracchus, a radical tribune (the ten tribunes of the plebs were magistrates without military responsibilities who were supposed to protect the interests of the people) from one of the most prestigious families, was lynched by a mob of senators when he tried to gain re-election to a second year of office. In 121 BC, his brother

Gaius, who pursued an even more radical agenda, was killed by his opponents in something that came close to open fighting in the very centre of Rome. Yet a small number of men began to have previously unimaginable electoral success, as many of the old precedents restricting careers were broken.

Social changes were also affecting the political map of Rome. Italy's economy and society had been profoundly changed by Roman expansion and the influx of huge numbers of slaves. The population of Rome itself had swollen to one million by the end of the 1st century BC, and a high proportion of the people were without steady employment. *Popularis* politicians who tried to address the problems of dispossessed farmers or the urban or rural poor were sure of winning support. All of these factors produced a dangerous instability. In 88 BC the consul Lucius Cornelius Sulla led his legions to seize power in Rome when Marius tried to seize the command allocated to him. Civil war followed, leading to Sulla eventually becoming dictator for more than a year. After this, stability never really returned to the Republic for more than very brief periods, as attempted coups, political violence and civil war followed each other with monotonous regularity. Sulla was a member of an old aristocratic family that had fallen on hard times, and had to use extreme methods to achieve the distinguished position within the Republic that he felt his birth warranted. There were several other men from similar backgrounds who acted in a similar way, and the most successful of these was Gaius Julius Caesar, probably the most famous Roman of all.

Before the advent of Caesar, however, between 104 and 100 BC, a successful general named Gaius Marius was elected to five successive consulships. In the same period the conversion of the Roman Army into a professional force fundamentally altered its relationship with the rest of society. Until this time the legions had been militia forces, all citizens who possessed a certain property qualification being obliged to serve when called upon by the Republic. The wealthiest, able to provide themselves with a horse and the necessary equipment, served as cavalry, the moderately well off as heavy infantry, the poorer as light infantry and the poorest rarely served at all. In a real sense the army represented a cross-section of Roman society under arms. For these men service in the army was not a career, but a duty to the Republic. As men of property – most were farmers – they easily returned to civilian life after each period of service. As the Empire expanded, however, wars tended to last longer and were fought further away, while there was a growing need for permanent garrisons to protect conquered territory. A decade of service in a garrison in one of the Spanish provinces could well mean ruination for the owner of a small farm. Service became increasingly unpopular and the eventual solution was to turn to men willing to make the army their profession.

A soldier's pay was low, the conditions of his service extremely harsh, and a military career tended only to be attractive to the poorest citizens, who in the past had not been

MOUNTED GENERAL IN WARTIME

A mounted general of senatorial rank is here accompanied on the right by two lictors each carrying *fasces* – a bundle of rods and an axe, symbolizing the magistrate's ability to inflict either corporal or capital punishment. On his left are two scribes. (© Angus McBride, Osprey Publishing)

obliged to serve. Such men proved excellent soldiers, but when the war ended and their legion was disbanded they had nothing to return to in civilian life. The Senate refused to acknowledge this change, maintaining that military service was a duty requiring no formal reward, and made no provision to provide for discharged soldiers. Individual commanders began to demand land for their veteran soldiers, wanting to settle them in colonies on conquered territory. Soldiers started to become more loyal to generals who offered such rewards than to the Republic which neglected them.

The rise of the professional army was probably the most important of the problems besetting the Republic with which the Senate failed to deal. For the Roman Army of the late Republic was truly a potent force, one that was winning respect across the known Western world for its fighting skills and personal tenacity. The fact that this military power was not properly controlled from the centre made the Roman state truly unstable.

THE MARIAN MACHINE

Gaius Marius is generally credited with taking the decisive steps that laid the basis for the professional standing army of the Principate. Rome was now the dominant power in the Mediterranean basin and the annual levying of what was in effect a part-time citizen militia was incompatible with the running and maintenance of a world empire. Moreover, decades of war overseas had turned out thousands of trained soldiers and many of them would have found themselves strangers to civilian life after their years of service abroad. The army had been their life and Marius called them back home. But besides these time-expired veterans, Marius also enrolled another more numerous kind of volunteer: the men with nothing.

Gaius Marius (157–86 BC). In many ways the spectacular career of Marius was to provide a model for the great warlords of the last decades of the Republic.

Lacking the means to provide themselves arms, these citizens were listed in the census simply as the *capite censi*, the 'head count'. However, Marius was not content to supplement his army for the African campaign by only drawing upon 'the bravest soldiers from the Latin towns' (Sallust, *Bellum Jugurthinum*, 84.2). Thus of all the reforms attributed to Marius, the opening of the ranks to the *capite censi* in 107 BC has obviously attracted the most attention, and the unanimous disapproval of ancient writers. And so Marius, a *novus homo* from a family that had never before held the consulship, stands accused of paving the way for the so-called lawless, greedy soldiers whose activities were thought to have contributed largely to the fall of the Republic a few generations later.

Yet we should not lose sight of the fact that Marius was not the first to enrol the *capite censi*. At times of extreme crisis in the past, the Senate had impressed them, along with convicts and slaves, for service as legionaries. In the aftermath of the crushing defeats at the Trebia, Lake Trasimene and Cannae, the Senate made the first of a number of alterations to the Servian constitution. In the dark days following Cannae, for instance, two legions were enlisted from slave-volunteers. Marius was merely carrying one stage further a process visible during the 2nd century BC, by which the prescribed property qualification for service in the army was eroded and became less meaningful. Now the only real prerequisites were Roman citizenship and a willingness to go soldiering.

Noticeably the ancient sources, unlike modern commentators, do not say that Marius swept away the qualification, or changed the law on eligibility. On the contrary, he merely appealed to the *capite censi* for volunteers, whom he could equip from state funds under the legislation drawn up by Gaius Gracchus in 123 BC, by which the state was responsible for equipping the soldier fighting in its defence.

Marius' common-sense reform should be seen as a logical development. What he did was to legalize a process that had been present for about a century and that the Senate had failed to implement, that is, open up the army to all citizens regardless of their property, arm them at state expense and recruit them not through the *dilectus* but on a volunteer basis.

With Marius the traditional link between property and defence of the state was broken forever. What is more, by the enfranchising laws of 90–89 BC the recruiting area for those who could serve in the legions was extended to all Italy south of the Po. So the *socii* disappeared, and the previous distinction between *legio* and *ala* ceased to have any purpose. The Roman Army was now composed of legions of citizen-soldiers recruited throughout peninsular Italy, and contingents of non-Italians serving either as volunteers or as mercenaries.

REFORMING THE LEGION

Marius is also credited with changes in tactical organization, namely he abolished the maniple and regularized the cohort as the standard tactical unit of the legion. The cohort as a formation of three maniples, as we have seen, was not an entirely novel innovation, as it appears to have been in use as a tactical, as opposed to an administrative, expedient from the time of the Second Punic War. Polybius, in an account of the battle of Ilipa (206 BC), pauses to explain the meaning of the term *cohors* to his Greek readership. Surprisingly, it receives no mention in his detailed account of army organization in either the 6th book or in his comparison of legion and phalanx in the 18th book, although, it should be stated, there is little on tactics in either of these narratives. On the other hand, some have detected the last reference to maniples manoeuvring as the sole tactical unit of the battleline in Sallust's account (*Bellum Jugurthinum*, 49.6) of the operations of Caecilius Metellus against Jugurtha (109–108 BC). Hence a belief that Marius swept them away either in 106 BC or during his preparations in 104 BC for the war against the Cimbri and Teutones.

It is recognized that the battle of Pydna (168 BC) was the triumph of the Roman maniple over the Macedonian phalanx, and this disposition was adequate till Rome came to meet an opponent who adopted a method of attack different from the slow methodical advance of the phalanx with its 'bristling rampart of outstretched pikes' (Plutarch, *Aemilius Paullus*, 19.1). The tactics of the Germanic and Celtic tribes, the latter armed with a long two-edged sword designed for slashing, was to stake everything upon a vigorous onslaught at the start of the battle, beating down the shields of the opposition and breaking into their formation. This was a terrifying thing, and at times could swiftly sweep away an opponent – especially a nervous one – but if it was halted the tribesmen would tend to lose their enthusiasm and retreat quickly.

To meet this brutal method of attack, where the perpetrators believed that fighting power increased in proportion to the size of the mass, the formation in three fixed battlelines of maniples was unsuitable. The units themselves were fairly small and shallow, and an attack strongly pressed home might easily overcome their resistance. In the war against the Celtic Insubres (225 BC) the *hastati* of the front line had attempted to circumvent this difficulty by substituting their *pila* for the thrusting-spears of the *triarii* stationed in the rear.

Yet the small size of the maniple was a major weakness against such a style of fighting, and Marius decided to strengthen his front line of defence by increasing the size of the individual units. With the cohort taking the place of the maniple as the standard tactical unit, the Marian legion was thus organized into ten cohorts of equal size, strength and purpose. Naturally, with the lowering of the property qualification and its eventual abolition, the legionaries were now equipped by the state at public expense. Consequently, variations in equipment originally linked to differing financial statuses now ceased to have any *raison d'être*.

The natural corollary of Marius' decision to enrol poor citizens in the army was that legions would not all automatically cease to exist when the men were discharged from duty. Soon enough the legion was to become a permanent organization into which new recruits could be added, keeping the same name and number throughout its existence. To mark this change in status, Marius gave each legion a permanent standard to represent it. As explained in Part 1, the Republican legion originally had five standards – eagle, wolf, minotaur, horse and boar. Elder Pliny places the adoption of the silver eagle (*aquila*) as the supreme standard of all legions precisely in 104 BC, at the start of preparations for the war against the Cimbri and Teutones. This selection of the eagle, a bird of prey associated with Jupiter, is thus firmly credited to Marius.

Certainly the best known of all Roman standards, the *aquila* not only worked to increase the loyalty and devotion of soldiers to the legion through fostering a corporate identity, but it was also reflective of the sweeping away of the old class divisions within the Roman Army. Moreover, legionaries who viewed the army as a career, not simply as an interruption to civilian life, came to identify very strongly with their legion, and these formations developed, in the fullness of time, tremendous corporate spirit. Admittedly an old provisional legion could be a first-class fighting unit, especially if seasoned by long service, but a new professional legion was on average better trained and disciplined than its predecessors, simply because it was more permanent. At the

THE SIZE OF THE MARIAN LEGION

Though we have assumed that the size of the Marian cohort was 480 men as it would be during the Principate, the size of the Marian legion has been a matter of controversy. It is likely that it averaged some 5,000 men all ranks, but the total complement could be higher (6,000) or, more likely, much lower (3,000). The ancient sources confuse the problem because, as Brunt (*Italian Manpower 225 BC–AD 14*, pp.687–93) points out, they normally multiply by 5,000 or so whenever they use the term *legio*. In other words, *legio* is equal to 5,000 regardless of actual size. Besides, sometimes disease, hardship and occasionally desertion thinned the ranks. Of course, sometimes it was the result of casualties. It is likely that casualties had reduced Caesar's legions in 49 BC to about 4,000 men each (Brunt, *Italian Manpower*, p.690), and the following year, when Caesar embarked seven legions at Brundisium (Brindisi) he had only 15,000 men fit for active duty. As Caesar himself says, 'many had been lost during all the campaigns in Gaul, the long march from Iberia had removed a great many, and the unhealthy autumn weather in Apulia and around Brundisium, after the wholesome regions of Gaul and Iberia, had seriously affected the health of the whole army' (*Bellum Civile*, 3.2.4).

time of Marius, the legions were probably still reconstructed every year, but by Caesar's day they certainly began to retain their identity. Service was, in the first instance, for six years, though the total period of liability to serve in the legions was 16 years. Of course individuals could, and did, volunteer to serve longer.

The adoption of the cohort as the standard tactical unit probably also marked the elimination of the light infantry *velites*. The youngest and poorest citizens eligible for military service under the old Servian system, they were now assimilated into the regular structure of the centuries, which were all made the same size, and armed in like fashion to the other legionaries.

The last specific mention of *velites* as such occurs in Sallust's account (*Bellum Jugurthinum*, 46.7) of Metellus' African campaigns. The Roman Army now provided the same function through the use of non-Italian auxiliaries, which were either mercenaries hired for the occasion or local levies taken from amongst Rome's provinces or client states. Rulers of native peoples who inhabited the fringes of the empire were obliged through their treaties with Rome to supply a certain number of troops to serve in the Roman Army, usually in or near their homelands. In other instances, native princes and chieftains beyond the empire chose to serve as mercenaries, and brought with them their warrior bands, in order to advance their own personal or their peoples' causes. All together, these auxiliaries included light-armed infantry such as Numidian javelineers, Cretan archers and Balearic slingers.

THE ARMY DURING THE JUGURTHINE WAR, 110–105 BC
Here we see a cavalry officer (left), legionary (centre) and centurion (right) of the late 2nd century BC. Notice the geometric patterns on the legionary's shield – such patterns, probably based on Gallic prototypes, are shown on a number of archeological monuments of the period. (© Angus McBride, Osprey Publishing)

Along with the phasing out of the *velites*, the citizen cavalry was gradually withdrawn from the legion. The inferiority of the mounted arm had been demonstrated by the war with Hannibal, and so it became customary to hire or levy the more efficient services of foreign horsemen. Hence following Hannibal's defeat, Numidian mercenaries were being employed, especially in Iberia, as Roman auxiliaries.

By Caesar's day the legion had no citizen cavalry whatsoever, and during his Gallic campaigns he made exclusive use of horsemen raised in Gaul, Iberia and Germania. Indeed, the absence of Roman horsemen is sufficiently shown by the fact that, when Caesar goes to meet the Germanic war leader Ariovistus for a parley, he ordered some legionaries of legio X to mount up on the horses of his Gallic cavalry so as to form a Roman escort. Caesar's cavalry arm was rarely more than 4,000 strong and was mainly raised from Gallia Transalpina, from his allies the Aedui and minor tribes associated with them. The high-quality Germanic horsemen from the far side of the Rhine were only a few hundred strong, but in most encounters with Gallic horse they seemed to have a psychological edge over them.

WEAPONS AND ARMOUR

All legionaries were now equipped with a bronze Montefortino helmet, a mail shirt (*lorica hamata*), the *scutum*, two *pila*, one heavy the other light, and *gladius Hispaniensis*, plus a dagger (*pugio*). Greaves disappeared, except on centurions. Here we should note that Varro calls Roman mail 'Gallic' (*De Lingua Latina*, 5.116), believing that the Romans acquired their knowledge of mail-making from the Gauls, who, it seems, were also its original fabricators.

Regarding the *pilum*, Plutarch (*Marius*, 25.1–2) attributes Marius with a modification that made it more certain that the spear would bend on impact, namely he replaced one of the two iron rivets, which held the iron shank of the *pilum* to its wooden shaft, with

LEGIONARY EQUIPMENT

The legionary, like all professional foot soldiers before his day and after, was grossly overloaded – alarmingly so according to some accounts. It has been estimated that the legionary was burdened with equipment weighing as much as 35kg if not more. It appears, therefore, that another of Marius' apparent reforms was to reduce the size of the baggage train (*impedimenta*). The legionaries now had to shoulder much of their gear: bed-roll and cloak, three or more days' rations of grain, a bronze cooking pot (*trulleus*) and mess tin (*patera*), a metal canteen or leather flask, a sickle for cutting grain and foraging, a wicker basket for earth-moving, either a pick-axe (*dolabra*) or an iron-shod wooden spade (*pala*), a length of rope and a stake (*pilum muralis*) for fortifying the overnight marching camp. This gear was slung from a T-shaped pole (*furca*), and Plutarch writes (*Marius*, 13.1) that the soldiers were nicknamed *muli Mariani* (Marius' mules), a wry description that would remain in popular currency. Each *contubernium* on the march was also allowed one four-legged mule to carry the heavier items such as its leather tent and millstones.

a wooden rivet. With this modification the wooden rivet would snap upon impact, resulting in the shank bending. Archeological evidence from one of the five Roman camps east of the Iberian stronghold of Numantia, near modern-day Burgos, indicates that it was the heavy *pilum* that was modified in this way. Similar examples were recovered from the site of the siege at Alesia, showing both types of *pila* were still in use in Caesar's day. Whereas a long tang and two rivets were used for the heavier type, the lighter version was simply socketed onto its wooden shaft.

Experimentation with the pilum did not end there, however. Later it was decided to move away from Marius' adaptation by choosing to leave the iron shank untempered instead. This innovation (often wrongly accredited to Caesar) meant that the head of the *pilum* retained its murderous penetrating capacity while the rest would buckle upon impact.

Straight sword and dagger from Almedinilla, Córdoba, 4th or 3rd century BC. These weapons remind us that Iberian straight swords and daggers were the forebears of the *gladius* and *pugio*. Note the 'atrophied antennae' pommel, a characteristic feature of Iberian straight-bladed weapons. (Fields-Carré Collection)

AUXILIARIES

As for auxiliaries, locally raised horsemen fought in their traditional manner with their own weapons, thereby saving the Roman Army the time and expense of training and equipping them. Moreover, native horsemen usually provided their own horses and found their own remounts, though Caesar says (*Bellum Gallicum*, 7.65.6)

AUXILIARY SLINGERS

Slingers normally served as a complement to archers, the sling not only out-ranged the bow but a slinger was also capable of carrying a larger supply of ammunition than an archer. Slingshots were not only small stones or pebbles, but also made of lead, acorn- or almond-shaped, and weighing some 20–30g. These leaden bullets, the most effective of slingshots, could be cast bearing inscriptions, such as symbols – a thunderbolt emblem on a bullet from Alesia for instance – or a short phrase, usually only a few letters. The sling, as deadly as it was simple, was made of non-elastic material such as rush, flax, hemp or wool. It comprised a small cradle or pouch to house the bullet, and two braided cords, one of which was secured to the throwing hand and the other held, simultaneously, between the thumb and forefinger of the same hand. It was then cast, after a single twirl around the head, the bullet being fired at the moment that the second cord was released, its range being related to the angle of discharge, the length of the whirling cords and the amount of kinetic energy imparted by the thrower. Fast-moving slingshot could not be seen in flight and did not need to penetrate armour to be horrifically effective. A blow from a slingshot on a helmet, for instance, could be enough to give the wearer concussion.

The adoption of mail by the Romans stems from their having borrowed the idea from the Celts, amongst whom it had been in use at least since the 3rd century BC, albeit reserved for use by aristocrats such as the Vachères warrior. Note shoulder-doubling for extra protection against downward sword strokes. (Fields-Carré Collection)

he had to remount his Germanic horse-warriors on mounts requisitioned from the military tribunes and other equestrian officers serving with him. Presumably during the winter months they returned to their homes and were thus removed from the ration list.

Of course, the negative side of such an arrangement was that the Roman commander had to rely on the good faith of local princes and chieftains.

Yet it was worth the risk as cavalry provided the highest-quality troops in native society. In Gaul, for instance, they were drawn chiefly from the nobles – the *equites* mentioned by Caesar – and their retinues and clients. Because of their recruitment from the wealthier and more prestigious warriors, equipment was of good quality and consisted of a shield, javelins, short spear and long slashing-sword, and often helmet and iron mail armour. They were always well mounted, paying high prices for good horses, of which they were very fond and which they would often decorate with bronze or silver ornaments attached to the harness. Added to this was the four-horned saddle, later adopted by the Romans, a key technical innovation that provided a thoroughly secure seat. Tactics were normally aggressively simple: a shower of javelins were thrown, and followed up by a charge using spears and swords. Naturally, discipline was normally poor, so that they were difficult to rally from pursuit or rout.

Germanic horse-warriors, despite their physically inferior native mounts, were highly motivated and skilled. They mainly practised forward movements and turns or wheels that did not expose their unshielded side. They believed that horsemen who employed the Celtic saddle were effeminate and would normally charge them on sight no matter the odds. In cavalry battles they often dismounted and fought on foot, unhorsing the opposition by stabbing their horses in the belly. Their weapons were mainly javelins and short spears, with the occasional sword. Body armour too was in short supply and helmets rarer still. They could also fight in conjunction with foot-warriors, operating in pairs. If necessary, the foot-warriors could help themselves along by clutching the manes or tails of the horses. They were lightly armed and chosen for their speed, and presumably their function was not only to protect any unhorsed comrades but also to hamstring the enemy horses and dispatch their riders.

The foremost horse-warriors were Numidians – especially those from the arid steppe areas of the Sahara where the nomadic life still prevailed. Numidian horsemen were formidable and well respected by the Romans, but disunion made them difficult allies politically. Such was their mastery of their desert horses that Roman sources made much of Numidian 'bareback horsemen', who rode 'without bridles'. Though obviously he was one with his mount, it seems more likely that the Numidian rode on a saddlecloth and guided his mount with a bozal. This was a bridle of leather or rope to which a lead-rein was attached without using a metal bit in the horse's mouth.

COMMAND AND CONTROL

The tradition of the Republic was that a senator should be prepared to serve the state in whatever capacity it demanded. Thus in the late Republic the principal military command still lay in theory with the two consuls, who were supposed, as of old, to have the first four legions of each year as their consular armies. However, since the time of Sulla it became the norm for the consuls to remain in Rome during their year of office, and the command of the legions fell to men of proconsular rank wielding proconsular power (*imperium pro consule*) in that part of the empire where their campaigns were to

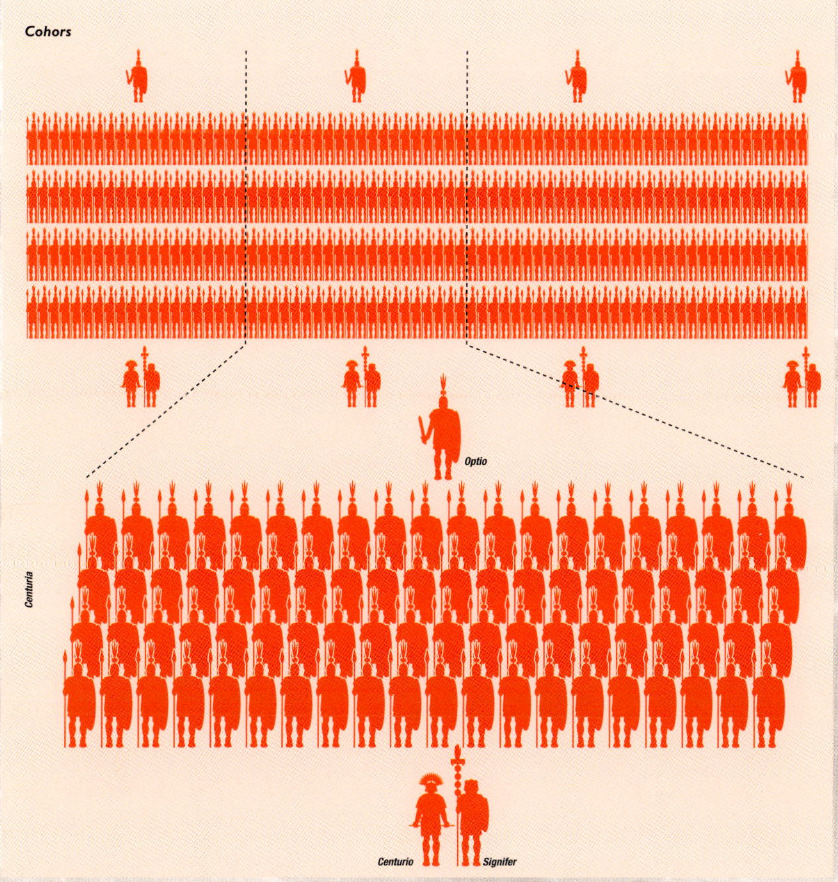

The new tactical unit, the cohors, consisted of six *centuriae* each of 80 legionaries armed alike with *pilum* and *gladius*. Each *centuria* was commanded by a *centurio* supported by an *optio*, a signifer, a *cornicen* and a *tesserarius*. Within each cohors the order of seniority amongst the six *centuriones* was *pilus prior, pilus posterior, princeps prior, princeps posterior, hastatus prior* and *hastatus posterior*, with the overall command of the cohors being the duty of the *pilus prior*, who presumably left his *optio* in charge of his *centuria*.

be conducted. As an outward indication that their armies were not consular ones, the custom arose of omitting numbers I to IV in the enumeration of their legions, these numerals being reserved for the consuls should they have to raise an army during their year of office. Thus Caesar, on taking up his command in Gaul in 58 BC, calls his first unit legio VII, while Pompey does not make use of the consular numbers till he himself is consul in 55 BC. The commander of an army received no formal training as such and would, in fact, be expected to learn the art of generalship himself, from books or the harder lesson of battle itself. The qualities of a good general, according to Cicero, were 'military knowledge, courage, authority and good luck' (*De imperio Cnaeo Pompeii*, 28).

Although during the late Republic there was no permanent legionary commander, and this situation would remain so until the establishment of the Principate under Augustus, there were still, as in the days of the manipular legion, six military tribunes, *tribuni militum*, in each legion. Likewise, tribunes were still being elected by the citizens in the *comitia centuriata*, and both Caesar and the younger Cato were elected tribunes in this fashion. On the other hand, additional tribunes could be chosen by a general himself. Here demands of nepotism were met by taking family, friends and the sons of political associates onto his staff, who were thus able to acquire some military service and experience that would stand them in good stead for their future excursion into politics.

With the increase in size of the armies under the command of one man from a nominal two or four legions – the traditional consular or double-consular army – to a strength of anything from six to 12 legions, the question of the command of individual legions became of supreme importance. Thus we note that there is no instance of a military tribune commanding a legion in action during Caesar's campaigns in Gaul. As they were invariably short-term politicos, who had an eye cast in the direction of Rome, tribunes could be rather an embarrassment at times. In 58 BC, when Caesar was preparing to march against Ariovistus, these young blades became so terrified that they tried to excuse themselves from duty and some even wept openly.

In their place Caesar started to appoint a senior officer, usually a legate (*legatus*, pl. *legati*), both for the command of individual legions and as a commander of an expeditionary force detached from the main army. The quaestor was an elected magistrate, a senator at an early stage of his *cursus honorum* (lit. 'course of honours', the sequence of public offices) who was supposed to administer the finances of the province and act as the governor's deputy. Unlike military tribunes, these legates were not elected but chosen by Caesar from amongst his *amicitiae*. Usually of senatorial rank, some of these men might be former proconsular governors or army commanders, providing the leadership, experience and stability that the legion needed to operate effectively. The frequency of foreign wars and the not-uncommon outbreak of civil conflict in the late Republican period allowed many legate officers to see almost continual military service.

As legates they provided the professional military skill and experience for proconsular governors like Cicero who were themselves either without such experience or without any great military competence.

In the late Republic, centurions were normally promoted on merit from the ranks to the lowest grade of centurion, from which they worked their way up, the most senior grade being that of *primus pilus* ('first spear', formerly known as the *centurio primi pili*), the chief centurion of the legion who nominally commanded the first century of the first cohort. On retirement, many of them were granted equestrian status, and their sons could therefore take up the military profession as tribunes.

The centurions in each cohort bore the following titles: *pilus prior* and *pilus posterior*, *princeps prior* and *princeps posterior*, and *hastatus prior* and *hastatus posterior*. Within each cohort, the order of seniority amongst the centurions reflected their former positions in the old three-fold battlelines of the manipular legion (see diagram on p.33). The senior centurions of the legion were those of the first cohort with the *primus pilus* at their head, and the junior those of tenth cohort. Promotion thus consisted of a movement towards a lower numbered cohort.

Each *centurio* was assisted by a second-in-command, an *optio*, with *centuriones* choosing their own *optiones*, a standard-bearer (*signifer*), a musician (*cornicen*) and a guard commander (*tesserarius*). The *optio*, who would take command if the *centurio* fell, traditionally stood at the rear of the *centuria*, while the *tesserarius* supervised the posting of the sentries at night and was responsible for distributing the following day's watchword, which he received each night inscribed on a wooden tablet (*tessera*). Each *centuria* carried a standard (*signum*) basically consisting of an assemblage of discs (*phalerae*) mounted on a pole surmounted by a spear point or effigy hand, below which could be an inscribed tablet indicating the number of the *cohors* the *centuria* belonged to (e.g. COH(ors) V). As no more than six *phalerae* seem to be placed on any one *signum* in

THE *AQUILIFER* IN BATTLE

The famous incident involving the anonymous but heroic *aquilifer* of legio X Equestris is the classic example that immediately springs to mind. Caesar had just landed off the coast of Britain and his troops were somewhat hesitant to jump down from the relative safety of their ships and wade ashore against stiff opposition. It was at this point that the *aquilifer* of Caesar's favourite formation yelled: 'Jump down, comrades, unless you want to surrender our *aquila* to the enemy; I, at any rate, mean to do my duty to my country and my general' (Caesar, *Bellum Gallicum*, 4.25.3). His comrades, inspired by his bravery, quickly followed him over the side.

The frieze from the headquarters of the legionary fortress at Mainz in Germany dates to more than a century after the Gallic Wars, but gives a good idea of the classic fighting stance of the legionary – crouching slight to gain the maximum protection from his shield, with his left leg advanced and sword thrust underarm. (AKG Berlin/Erich Lessing)

the many illustrations of them on coins and sculptures, it has been suggested that the number of discs denotes the number of the century in its cohort.

The new eagle standard (*aquila*) was carried into battle by a senior standard-bearer, the *aquilifer*, second only to a centurion in rank. It was under the personal care of the *primus pilus*. While its safe custody was equivalent to the continuance of the legion as a fighting unit, however depleted in numbers, its loss brought the greatest ignominy on any survivors and could result in the disbandment of the legion in disgrace, a practice that was to long continue.

The *aquilifer* played an important if comparatively minor leadership role in battle too. He was, after all, the man who served as a rallying point during the chaos of battle, and could urge hesitant troops forward during a particularly dangerous moment.

Closely associated with the standards was the *cornicen*, a junior officer who blew the *cornu*, a bronze tube bent into almost a full circle with a transverse bar to strengthen it. Three successive calls controlled the departure of the army from camp: at first call, the tents were struck and equipment packed; at the second, tents and surplus baggage were loaded on to the mules; at the third, the army moved off in the regulation fashion. On the battlefield itself different calls, accompanied by visual signals such as the raising of the standards, would sound the alarm or order a recall. When the troops charged into contact and raised their war cry (*clamor*), the *cornicines* blew their instruments so as to encourage their comrades and discourage the enemy.

THE ROMANS GO OUT TO CONQUER: GAUL

The Roman Army that campaigned in Gaul in the 1st century BC was to all intents and purposes a professional one, with many soldiers in the legions regarding their military service as a career. The soldiers were equipped, trained and paid by the state, often serving for many years at a stretch. The Gallic armies were completely different. Gallic warfare was based on the values of a warrior society; while the elite warriors may have been able to spend time raiding neighbouring tribes and may have possessed high quality arms and armour, tribes were unable to maintain armies for long because of the lack of any organized supply system and the need for many of those fighting to return to their fields. The Roman conquest of Gaul was a clash between two cultures employing very different methods of waging war.

Gallic and Roman fighting styles were the complete antithesis of each other. The Gallic fighting style allowed the warrior to display himself on the battlefield, either through fighting naked or by wearing elaborately decorated armour, and he showed his valour by fighting as an individual. The warrior's long sword required him to have a fair amount of space around him on the battlefield in order to operate properly. The Celtic sword was essentially a slashing weapon and in the hands of a tall Gallic warrior with a long reach, could be a deadly blade, particularly against shorter opposition with short swords. But the Gallic warriors fought as individuals; though training and especially experience must have provided them with some understanding of tactics, and commands could have been communicated on the battlefield through musical instruments, they did not possess the same degree of training to fight as a unit that Roman soldiers did. When forced to retreat, they could not always maintain ranks and withdraw in good order, something that required considerable training and absolute trust in one's fellow soldiers. This made them vulnerable to outflanking manoeuvres and to cavalry attacks on retreating warriors. Lack of space to swing their swords could also cause havoc in the Gallic ranks. When forced together, Gallic warriors could not use their swords properly, and this made them vulnerable to an enemy who could operate at very close quarters with deadly efficiency.

The Roman legionary's equipment did not make him reliant on his neighbour's shield for protection in combat as in a Greek phalanx formation, as he fought as an individual, but he was dependent on the strength of his unit. If his comrades in his century, cohort or legion gave way, he would eventually become exposed to attack on the flank or rear.

The might of the Roman Army lay in the strength of its formations, and that was based on unit morale, discipline and training. These can clearly be seen when Caesar's legions came under sudden attack by the Nervii in the second season of campaigning. The legionaries did not even need their officers to give them orders: they automatically dropped their entrenching tools, picked up their weapons, and formed a battleline. Their training ensured that even though they were not with their own units and the men they normally fought with, they were resourceful enough to create an effective line of battle. Roman soldiers were not automatons in a 'military machine': they were trained to think and use their initiative as well as follow orders. The training and discipline instilled in the soldiers meant that Roman units could move over battlefields in formation and even retreat while maintaining a defensive formation, an invaluable technique in warfare for minimizing casualties. Usually, in pitched battle Roman discipline triumphed over Gallic flair.

58 BC – THE FIRST CAMPAIGN

In the first year of his governorship, Caesar fought and won two major pitched battles and set himself up to conquer Gaul. The speed and decisiveness with which he operated must have impressed his political rivals in Rome, and terrified the Gauls. Caesar had freed them from the menace of the migrating Helvetii and the German king Ariovistus, but now he threatened their independence himself.

Caesar was still in Rome when news arrived in mid-March that the Helvetii were on the move, heading west towards Geneva and southern Gaul, dangerously close to the Roman province. He immediately headed for Provence, ordering the only legion stationed there to make for Geneva and to destroy the bridge over the Rhône. He levied auxiliary troops in Provence and raised two new legions in northern Italy. Playing for time, he agreed to consider a request that the Helvetii be allowed to pass, but then refused once his troops had built defences that forced the Helvetii away from Roman territory and into central France. He then dashed back to Italy to collect the two new legions and three veteran legions in garrison at Aquileia, marched them through the Alps in early summer and caught up with the Helvetii as they were crossing the Saône. Three-quarters had crossed, but Caesar attacked those remaining. Some escaped into the woods, but his legions slaughtered the rest. The casualty figures are not recorded.

Crossing the Saône in a single day on pontoons, Caesar caught up with the main body of Helvetii and trailed them at a discreet distance, refusing to be drawn into combat except on his terms. The Helvetii were keen to avoid battle and tried to negotiate, but Caesar's demands were too severe, perhaps intentionally since he was probably eager to fight when the tactical situation became favourable. It did a few days later and a force under Labienus

JULIUS CAESAR, 100–44 BC

In this period Rome produced a remarkable series of great soldiers; following Marius and Sulla came the unconventional Sertorius, and then the great Pompey himself. Talented men indeed, but they all lacked that touch of genius had by Caesar.

At the core of Caesar's success was his quickness of action at both the strategic and tactical levels, the legendary *Caesariana celeritas*. For not only did Caesar always move his forces with amazing rapidity, but he also acted quickly to gain the advantage in any opportunity that presented itself. On Caesar's system of warfare Suetonius says that he 'joined battle, not only after planning his movements beforehand but also on the spur of the moment, often at the end of a march, and sometimes in miserable weather, when he would be least expected to make a move' (*Divus Julius*, 60.1). Appian too pinpoints the kernel, the central theme, of Caesar's concept of warfare, remarking that 'he always exploited the dismay caused by his speed of execution and the fear engendered by his daring, rather than the strength created by his preparations' (*Bellum Civilia*, 2.34). His crossing of the Rubicon with just one legion was audacious in the extreme, and Caesar's general philosophy of war was uniformly simple and to the point.

It is said that fortune favours the bold, and the Romans certainly considered luck as an indispensable attribute of leadership. On the banks of the Sabis (Sambre) the Nervii had outflanked Caesar's right wing, most of the centurions had been killed or injured and the ranks became too packed together to operate effectively. The situation was critical. Caesar dismounted and snatched a *scutum* from a man in the rear, then made his way to the forefront of the battle, yelling orders for the ranks to open up and the men to form a square so they could defend themselves from attack on all sides. His own energetic reaction and presence on foot helped to stiffen resistance until aid arrived in the form of the die-hard legio X Equestris. Caesar's over-confidence had led to a near disaster, but his personal bravery and the loyalty of his more seasoned legions – the knowledge, too, that defeat meant massacre – turned it into a significant victory.

Caesar, in speeches to his army, deliberately addressed his men as 'comrades' (*commilitones*) rather than 'soldiers' (*milites*). His flattering concern for his soldiers was one of the reasons for their extreme loyalty to him, so much so that, at the outbreak of the civil war, each and every centurion offered to equip a cavalryman from his savings and all the common soldiers volunteered to serve under him without pay or rations. Caesar understood the chemistry of morale better than most. Though he allowed no deserter or mutineer to escape severe punishment, he turned a blind eye to much of his soldiers' everyday misconduct. 'My soldiers fight just as well when they are stinking of perfume,' he was said to have once boasted.

took the high ground above the Helvetian camp in preparation for an attack, but a veteran scout panicked and wrongly reported to Caesar that the flashes of arms he had seen on the hill were definitely Gallic, not Roman, so the attack had to be aborted.

Caesar continued to tail the Helvetii, but was finally forced towards Bibracte to collect supplies from his Aeduan allies, his own supply train being stuck on the Saône. Perhaps hoping to cut the Romans off from their supplies, the Helvetii decided to give battle and attacked the Roman rearguard. Caesar deployed on a slope under cover of a cavalry screen.

The Roman forces consisted of six legions numbering *c.*24,000–30,000 men, as well as unknown numbers of auxiliary infantry and cavalry. Two of the legions were newly recruited and many of the auxiliaries were Gauls – their fighting capabilities must have been suspect. There are no figures for the size of the Helvetian army; however, we know that their allies, the Boii and Tulingi, numbered *c.* 15,000, and it is unlikely that the total Gallic army was more than *c.* 50,000 men.

Caesar deployed his two new legions and the auxiliary infantry on the high ground as a reserve and to guard the Roman encampment; the four veteran legions deployed as a *triplex acies* on ground sloping down towards the Helvetii. (Four cohorts were in the front line, with two further lines of three cohorts each as a reserve force.) The Helvetii formed up in very close order. They gathered their baggage, wagons and families beyond the left wing of their battleline, along with their allies, the Boii and Tulingi.

The Helvetii's first attack was easily repulsed by the Romans, who had the advantage of the slope and superior weaponry in the form of their *pila*, which stuck into the enemy's shields, weighing them down and pinning them together. The Helvetii were forced back, but this attack may have been a feint. As the Roman cohorts followed the retreating Helvetii, the Boii and Tulingi outflanked the Roman right. At this point the Helvetii renewed the fight and the Romans were surrounded. Close-quarter infantry combat ensued. The brilliant tactical flexibility of the legion enabled Caesar to order the rear line of cohorts to turn round and the legions fought the battle on two fronts. The Roman reserves on the hill were not even engaged. The Helvetii fled; the Boii and Tulingi were forced back against the wagons and slaughtered, along with the women and children.

In the aftermath of the battle, Caesar rested for three days to see to his wounded before continuing his pursuit of the Helvetii, who promptly surrendered. Concerned that Germanic tribes might move into the lands vacated by the Helvetii, Caesar ordered the survivors home. Caesar claims that of the 368,000 who set out on the migration, only 110,000 returned.

Surviving leaden sling-bullets are typically about 35mm long and about 20mm wide, and weigh approximately 28g. These acorn-shaped examples probably belong to the time of the Greek siege of Motya in the 4th century BC. Whereas slingshots are common finds, slings themselves are exceptionally rare. (Fields-Carré Collection)

After dealing with the Helvetii, Caesar turned on the German tribes who occupied land on the left bank of the Rhine under their king, Ariovistus. Caesar needed a good reason for attacking a king who was a 'Friend and Ally of the Roman People', and claimed that the Germans were raiding allied Aeduan territory and other Gallic tribes had asked for help. Both sides aimed to occupy the strategically important town of Besançon, but Caesar got there first. Eventually, the Romans forced Ariovistus to deploy by marching in battle formation right at the German encampment.

The Germans parked their wagons behind their battleline, Caesar says to prevent the warriors escaping, but it may equally have been to prevent an outflanking manoeuvre by the Romans. The engagement began with the Germans charging so quickly that the Romans had no time to throw their *pila*, and an intense period of hand-to-hand combat ensued. The German left was routed by the Roman right under the personal command of Caesar, but the Roman left was coming under pressure. The officer in command of the cavalry, Publius Crassus, saw this and had the initiative to redeploy the third line of each legion to attack the German right. Again it was the flexibility of legionary tactics that turned the battle and the Germans fled, pursued the full 24km to the Rhine. The German losses are reported at 80,000 and the battle was clearly an outright victory for the Romans. In just one year Caesar was able to report to his rivals in Rome that he had defeated two of Rome's traditional and most feared enemies, the Gauls and the Germans. He wintered his legions near Vesontio and returned to northern Italy to attend to the civil aspects of his governorship.

57 BC – CONQUEST OF THE EAST

By early 57 BC, if he had not already resolved to do so the previous year, Caesar had decided to conquer the whole of Gaul. Caesar raised two more legions, bringing the total to eight (32,000–40,000 men, plus auxiliaries), and at the start of the campaigning season, headed for northern Gaul. His intention was to defeat the powerful Belgic tribes and cut them off from German support to the east. The Belgae caught up with him near Bibrax and tried to capture the *oppidum* (the main settlement in any Roman administrative area) from the occupying Remi who were being assisted by lightly armed missile troops Caesar had sent to help. Unable to capture the town, the Belgae instead ravaged the land and then turned towards Caesar's camp by the River Aisne. Neither side wished for battle at this point, although Caesar had prepared by linking artillery redoubts to the camp by means of trenches to prevent a Belgic outflanking manoeuvre should battle ensue. Skirmishes followed, but still no battle. Eventually each side's supply requirements effected a result of sorts: Caesar attempted to precipitate a general engagement by sending

GALLIC LOYALTIES

By 57 BC, some Gallic tribes were persuaded to form alliances with Rome because of the protection and influence such a relationship would bring within Gaul, and they may have felt, probably correctly, that as conquest was inevitable, it was better to be on the winning side. The Aedui in central Gaul were encouraged to remain Caesar's staunchest ally by his willingness to let them expand their influence over defeated Gallic tribes. The Remi in northern Gaul preferred to fight with Rome rather than against her, providing Caesar with intelligence during the campaign. However, the majority of Belgic tribes feared Rome's growing power in the region and prepared to resist, soliciting help from the Germans. Caesar claims the Belgic tribes could muster an army of 200,000 warriors.

his cavalry and light infantry against the Belgae because he was concerned about being cut off from his supplies. But the Belgae, too, were running short of supplies and because they had no logistical support, simply disbanded their army, to re-form if, or when, Caesar threatened them directly. They may also have recognized that Caesar's prepared battlefield made the terrain too unfavourable for a successful Belgic engagement.

The speed at which Roman armies could move proved an important factor in the success of this year's campaigns. Caesar pounced on the *oppidum* of the Suessiones at Noviodunum (on the River Aisne), hoping to capture it before the warriors returned after the Belgic army had disbanded. Though the warriors were able to sneak in at night, they quickly surrendered when they saw the siege preparations: clearly they had never experienced anything like Roman siege warfare before. The psychological effects of this surrender were widespread, with the Bellovaci and Ambiones surrendering to the Romans without resistance. The next tribe though, the Nervii, decided to resist, formed an alliance with the neighbouring Atrebates and Viromandui and planned to ambush Caesar's army as it was marching or at its most vulnerable when encamping. Making use of the terrain, the land patched with dense woodland and divided by high hedgerows, the Nervii set an ambush in woods on the far side of the River Sambre. The Romans began fortifying camp on the near side of the river, and their cavalry and light infantry crossed the water to scout and keep the Nervii away while the legionaries completed the encampment. They were easily repulsed by the Nervii, who then charged very fast at the entrenching Roman soldiers. Caesar had failed to deploy a screen of infantry to protect those entrenching, standard procedure when encamping in the presence of the enemy, and his legions were caught dispersed and unprepared. The two rookie legions forming the rearguard had not even arrived at the campsite.

Cohortal tactic

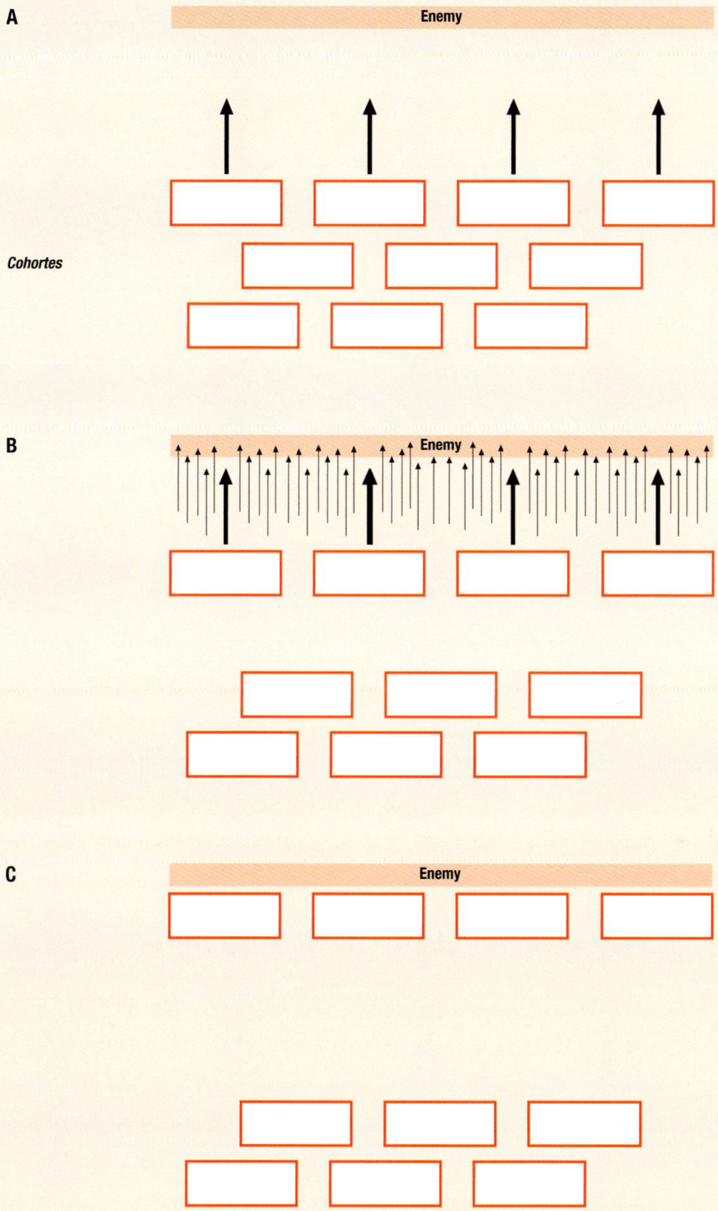

Much of the success of the Roman Army on the battlefield lay in the soldier's knowledge of close-formation fighting: legionaries were trained to fight as a team, to trust each other and to remain steady under pressure. It was this difference that gave the legion its decisive tactical edge.

Roman soldiers building camp, their arms neatly stacked within reach. Caesar defied military theory by building camps near woods and consequently, his troops were attacked whilst entrenching. When the Nervii attacked his army in 57 BC, he was lucky that they were able to form a battleline and retaliate. (Trajan's Column, AKG)

Caesar employed eight legions, two of which were still marching, and an unknown number of auxiliary infantry and cavalry. The Nervii had at least 60,000 warriors of the Nervii, Atrebates and Viromandui. Faced with a sudden attack, the Roman legionaries did exactly the right thing. Both they and their officers had a year's more experience than when they had panicked in the face of Ariovistus the previous year, and their training and discipline kicked in. They grabbed arms and automatically created a line of battle. The IX and X legions held the left wing, the VIII and XI the centre, and the VII and XII the right wing. The Nervii created a very strong left wing; the Viromandui held the centre and the Atrebates the right wing.

The two cavalry forces were already engaged, with the Gallic cavalry mauling the Romans. Despite the battleline being cut up by the hedgerows, the Romans held the line fast and stopped the Belgic onslaught. The Roman centre was successful and the left wing repulsed the Atrebates, pursuing them across the Sambre. This success left the half-built Roman camp and the right wing of the battleline exposed and the Gauls captured the camp.

Meanwhile, the Roman right wing was outflanked by the Nervii, several of the officers had been killed and the ranks had become too packed together to operate effectively: the situation was critical. Taking up position on foot with the front rank soldiers, Caesar ordered the ranks opened up and the two legions to form a square so they could defend themselves from attack on all sides. His own presence helped to stiffen resistance until help arrived in the form of the legio X, which had been sent back to assist after capturing the enemy encampment, and the two rookie legions of the rearguard which had finally arrived. The combined force of five legions turned the tide of battle and obliterated the Nervii, who refused to surrender or withdraw.

Caesar's over-confidence had led to a dangerous situation, but his presence and the experience of his army turned it into a significant victory. This successful engagement broke the power of the Belgae to such an extent that even German tribes beyond the Rhine sent envoys to Caesar offering submission. In operations towards the end of the year, one legion was sent to pacify the tribes on the Atlantic seaboard and with the remainder of his army, Caesar reduced the Aduatuci, who as allies of the Nervii were legitimate targets. Because they broke the terms of their surrender, all the Aduatuci were sold into slavery. The profit from selling 53,000 Aduatuci into slavery was, by rights, Caesar's alone.

Towards winter, Caesar sent one of his senior officers, Galba, to open up the road over the Great St Bernard pass into Italy, allegedly for trade purposes. But he had been given an inadequate force of one under-strength legion and when Galba billeted his troops in the village of Octodurus he came under heavy attack from the local tribes who were concerned, probably rightly, that the Romans were more interested in conquest than trade routes. Galba's legion, the XII, was depleted after its mauling in battle with the Nervii and the poorly defended position they held was untenable. Galba was forced to abandon the campaign and break out, though according to reports they managed to kill some 10,000 Gauls on the way. Despite this setback, at the end of this second year, Caesar reported that Gaul was at peace and the Senate in Rome voted him an unprecedented 15-day public thanksgiving, which greatly increased his political and military reputation. He returned again to northern Italy to spend the winter; his legions were quartered in northern Gaul, the tribes there being forced to provide for the soldiers.

Portrait bust of Caius Julius Caesar, (*c.*102–44) the Roman politician and general who conquered Gaul in the mid-1st century BC. (Ancient Art and Architecture)

56 BC – NAVAL WARFARE AND THE CONQUEST OF THE WEST

Gallic resentment at the compulsion to feed the Roman legions over the winter showed itself when the Venetic tribes in north-western Gaul detained Roman officers sent out to procure grain and other supplies. Roman prestige demanded a heavy response. Since the Veneti were essentially a maritime force, ships were requisitioned from Gallic allies, warships were ordered constructed on the Loire, and oarsmen recruited in Provence with a view to beginning the naval campaign as early as the weather permitted. The Veneti knew that the capture of Roman officers would bring the invading army down on them and also prepared. They had the advantage of knowledge of both the land and the sea: warfare on the Atlantic with its storms and strong tides would be rather different from the kind of naval warfare Rome was used to in the Mediterranean. The Veneti fortified their hill forts, many of which were situated on isolated spits of land more accessible by sea than land, and gathered allies from Aremorica (modern Brittany), the Channel coast and even the British tribes with whom they traded.

Caesar divided his forces and sent them to campaign in different parts of northern and western Gaul, proof that his claims that Gaul was at peace or had been conquered were something of an exaggeration. Throughout his governorship, Caesar was worried about incursions by German tribes and always kept a strong force in the Ardennes with cavalry to provide mobility against the Germans. This force also helped to hold down the Belgic tribes. Other forces were sent to Aquitania under Crassus, and Normandy under Sabinus. Caesar himself led a force of nearly four legions to meet with his newly gathered fleet, probably near the mouth of the Loire.

The Venetic campaign was a tough one. Sieges and assaults took care of the hill forts, but the wealth and resources of the Veneti were mobile and when one hill fort was about to be taken they loaded up their ships with people and possessions and simply sailed off to another. The newly built Roman fleet, designed for Mediterranean conditions and warfare, lacked the sturdiness needed to face Atlantic conditions and was stuck in harbour. The Romans, despite their professional army, sophisticated siege equipment and brand new fleet, were facing an impasse and Caesar was forced to pause until his fleet could join him. Eventually the sea was calm enough to allow the Roman fleet to sail, and it encountered the Venetic navy off the coast of Brittany. In an engagement lasting from late morning till sunset, most of the Venetic ships were destroyed, the Romans relying on the *corvus* and boarding tactics.

Having lost their naval power, the Veneti could no longer retreat; they had nothing to protect them against the Romans or against other Gallic and British tribes and were forced to surrender. To serve as an example, Caesar executed the elders and sold the remainder of the population into slavery.

NORMANDY AND AQUITANIA

Sabinus easily defeated a coalition of Venelli, Curiosolites and Lexovii when they charged the encampment he had located at the top of a long rise. They were so exhausted by the time they reached the camp that when the Romans sortied they routed them easily. All the tribes involved surrendered, placing the regions of modern Normandy under Roman control.

With just over one legion and a cavalry attachment, Publius Crassus had a tougher task against the tribes of Aquitania, so he raised additional infantry and cavalry from Provence and marched south of the Garonne and towards the Pyrenees, repulsing an attack by the Sontiates on the marching column. There was tougher opposition from the Vocates and Tarusates, who had Spanish allies that had fought alongside the rebel Roman general Sertorius in the 70s BC. They aimed to cut Crassus off from his supply lines, a strategy that forced the Romans to seek pitched battle. But, having learned from the successful guerrilla tactics Sertorius had employed against Roman armies in Spain, the Gallic and Spanish tribes refused battle, instead blocking roads and supplies, and

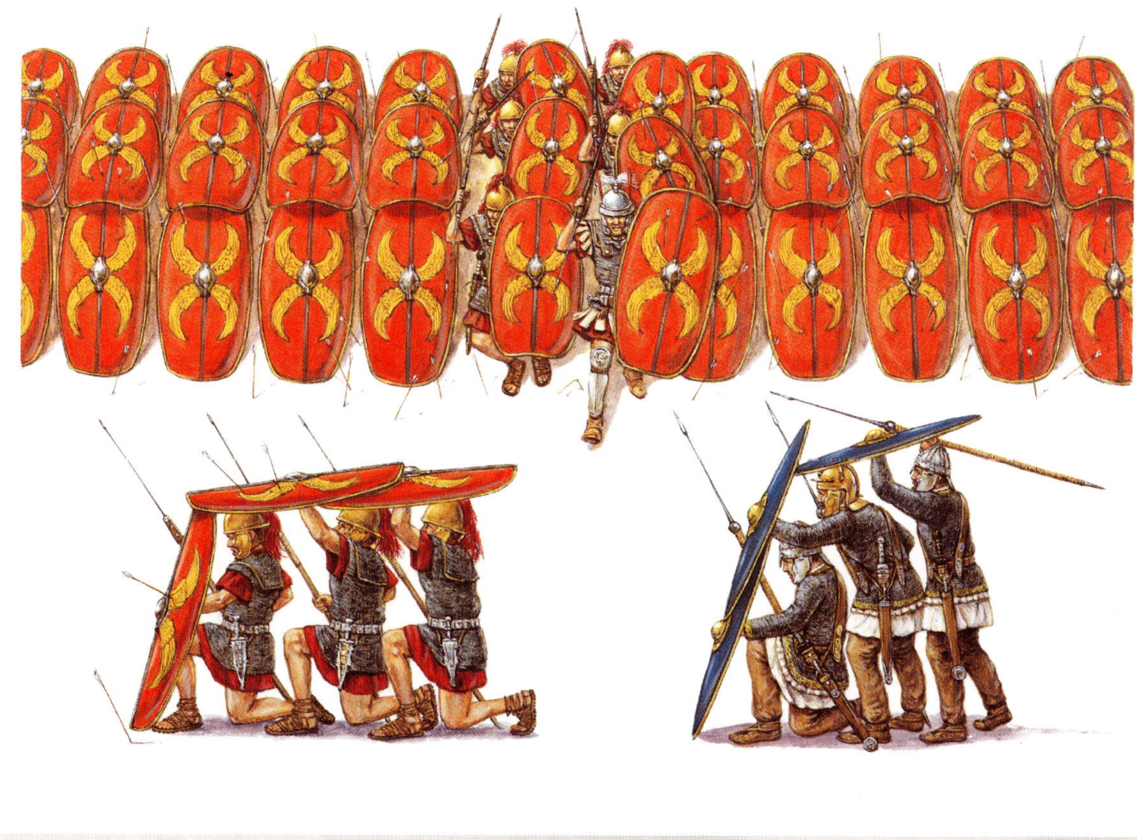

THE *TESTUDO* FORMATION

The *testudo* ('tortoise') formation is famous for its use in siege warfare, but it was also widely employed in field battles, because it offered excellent protection against missiles. Here we see part of the *testudo* formed by Mark Antony against horse archers during his retreat from Parthia in 36 BC. (© Adam Hook, Osprey Publishing)

attacking Crassus' marching column. If he wanted a result from the campaign, Crassus had to force an encounter, so his army attacked the enemy encampment. The camp was only properly fortified at the front, and once he learned of this, Crassus ordered reinforcements to circle round and attack the rear of the camp. The army of about 50,000 Gauls was taken by surprise and, completely surrounded, attempted to break out and flee, pursued by Crassus' cavalry force. Crassus reported to Caesar that only about 12,000 escaped the slaughter, and most of the tribes in the surrounding area surrendered. This was a significant victory and Crassus had succeeded in forcing the surrender of a huge area of south-western Gaul.

Towards the end of summer, Caesar turned on the Morini and Menapii on the Channel coast. They had supported the Veneti and that was reason enough for an attack, but Caesar was probably already considering his campaigns for the following year, which would require a settled situation in northern Gaul. However, the poor weather and enemy tactics of withdrawing into forested and marshy land meant that Caesar was only able to ravage farmland rather than engage the enemy, and he withdrew for the winter. The legions went into winter quarters in the land between the Loire and Saône that belonged to recently conquered tribes, their punishment for having resisted.

55 BC – PUBLICITY STUNTS

Caesar's two campaigns of 55 BC were dictated more by events in Rome than by military requirements in Gaul. His two closest political allies, the same men who were his greatest rivals, Pompey and Crassus, were consuls in Rome. The chief magistrates of the Roman state, their positions enabled them to seize all the publicity and buy the people's affections and votes with gifts, grain and public banquets. Aware of the need to remain in the public eye, Caesar decided to enhance his reputation by being the first Roman to lead an army across the Rhine into Germany and over the 'ocean' to the mysterious island of Britain.

Two German tribes, the Usipi and Tencteri, had crossed the Rhine in search of land after being ousted from their own by stronger Suebi, but following the policy he had established in his first year of office, Caesar refused to allow them to settle in Gaul. With a small force of 800 cavalry these German tribes then routed a Roman cavalry force (actually made up of Gauls) some 5,000 strong, killing 74. In retaliation, Caesar attacked their camp, caught them by surprise and massacred them, men, women and children, driving them into the nearby Rhine. Though there was probably nothing like the 430,000 casualties Caesar claims, it is likely that tens of thousands were killed, with no Roman losses. Roman warfare was often brutal, but this was excessively so, and Caesar's enemies in Rome threatened to prosecute him for war crimes once his governorship and its accompanying immunity from prosecution came to an end.

Caesar then decided to cross the Rhine to intimidate the Germans further, if they were not terrified enough by his massacre of the Usipi and Tencteri. Because this was a publicity stunt to gain prestige amongst both the Germans and his fellow Romans, Caesar decided to build a bridge and march across the Rhine rather than row across. In ten days, his troops had built a timber bridge on wooden piles driven into the riverbed and Caesar marched into Germany, burned some empty villages, marched back before the powerful Suebic Army could muster, and destroyed the bridge. The first Roman invasion of Germany lasted 18 days.

The expedition to Britain was as brief as that to Germany. Caesar crossed the Channel late in the campaigning season, his justification for the campaign being the military assistance the British tribes kept giving the Gauls, but that was a mere excuse. The expedition to Britain was hardly an invasion; Caesar took only two legions with him, VII and X, and the cavalry force never got across the Channel, seriously limiting Roman operations. It is not known where in Kent Caesar landed, but the land-fall was protected by cliffs and the Britons were waiting, so he moved seven kilometres up the coast to a flat, more open beach. The British had sent on their cavalry and chariots to oppose the landings and the deep-hulled Roman transports had to disembark the legionaries in deep water. Up to their waists in water and fully loaded with kit, the legionaries struggled ashore to be met by the terrifying barbarians, cavalry and chariots. Despite artillery support, the legionaries were reluctant to leave the safety of their ships. They were inspired to do so by the example set by the famous *aquilifer* of the legio X. Jumping into the sea, this unnamed soldier forced his fellow legionaries to follow him by taking the standard into battle. To lose a standard was the ultimate disgrace and the soldiers of the legion began disembarking. Once the scout ships began ferrying more legionaries to shore, the infantry was able to form up and force a landing.

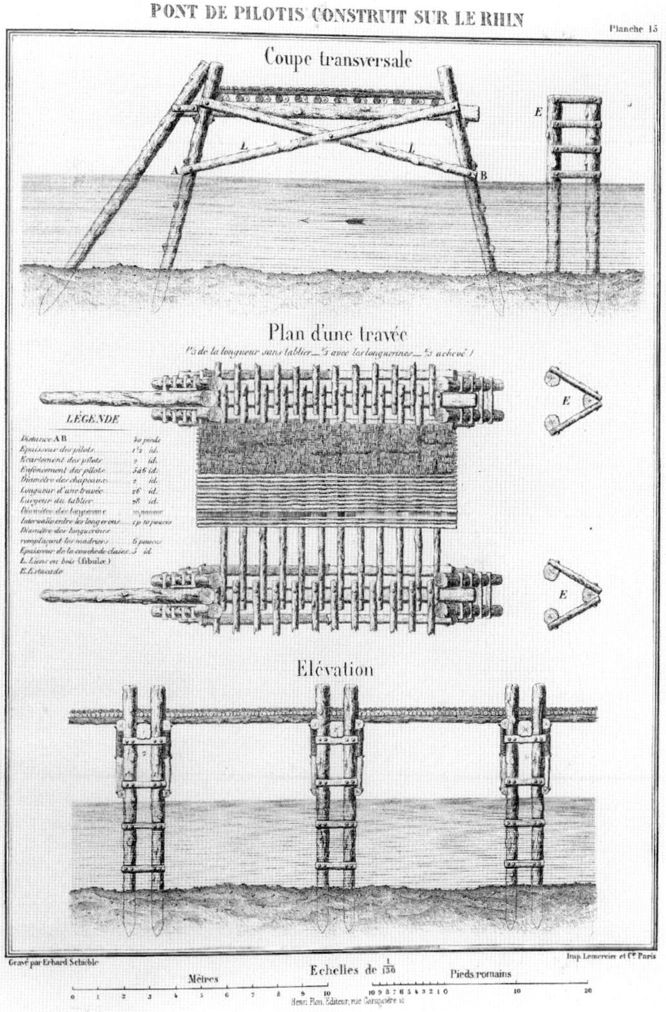

The engineering skills of the Roman Army are best illustrated by the bridge Caesar's soldiers built in ten days across the Rhine. The bridge was built entirely of wood and required hundreds of timbers to be driven into the river bed from barges built specially for the purpose. Once they were in place, a timber roadway was constructed on top, allowing the Roman Army to march across the river into Germany. (Glasgow University Library)

The British fled, but the failure of the cavalry to make the crossing meant the Romans were unable to finish the battle decisively.

In the following days the Roman expeditionary force suffered nothing but setbacks. Again, the cavalry failed to make the crossing, high tides caused serious damage to a number of the ships and transports, and the small Roman force was in no position to winter in Britain, as it was inadequately supplied. To cap all this, a detachment of the legio VII was ambushed while harvesting grain and although a rescue party had driven the British off, this only inspired them to gather a large force to attack the seemingly vulnerable Romans. A short pitched-battle ensued in front of the Roman encampment, but Caesar gives no details except that the Britons were easily repulsed and once again the lack of cavalry prevented any pursuit. Caesar demanded hostages from the defeated British tribes, but could not wait for them to be handed over. With the rapidly approaching equinox and the likelihood of storms, Caesar withdrew, having never got beyond the coast of Kent. The expedition to Britain could have been a disaster. Caesar had risked everything by leading an under-strength and poorly supplied force to Britain. But the crossing of the Channel caught the imagination of the Roman public more sharply even than the bridging of the Rhine. Caesar became a hero and a public thanksgiving of 20 days was decreed in Rome, trumping any popularity Pompey and Crassus had been able to achieve in the capital.

Although this engraving depicts a romanticized view of Caesar's landing in Kent, it is possible that legionaries had to fight whilst still wading ashore, having disembarked in deep water. (Ancient Art and Architecture)

Transports suitable for operations in the Channel were designed and built over the winter and a force of five legions and 2,000 cavalry made an unopposed landing in Kent in 54 BC. Caesar left three legions and a further 2,000 cavalry to hold down northern Gaul, and the fact that he took various untrustworthy Gallic chieftains to Britain with him indicates that Gaul was by no means pacified. Nonetheless, the Roman Army disembarked and Caesar immediately took four of the legions and most of the cavalry to find the British who had gathered some 19km off. The Britons utilized hit-and-run tactics for most of the campaign and gained some success in hampering Caesar's advance. But the weather caused problems and again the ships were damaged by a storm. Caesar was compelled to return to the beachhead, fortify it securely and arrange for repairs to the ships before heading back out to find the British. The Britons used the delay to gather a larger army under the leadership of Cassivellaunus, king of the powerful Catuvellauni tribe.

The mobility of the British infantry, cavalry and especially the chariots caused the Romans problems and forced them to remain in close formation on the march, lest they become isolated and picked off by the Britons. But when Cassivellaunus attacked a foraging party and was comprehensively repulsed, serious British resistance was

Images of fighting were common in ancient Rome including, as in this case, on sarcophagi. This late 2nd-century AD sarcophagus from Rome has a stylized depiction of battle between Romans and barbarians that portrays the confusion and urgency of pitched battle. (Museo Nazionale Romano)

crushed. The Romans crossed the Thames, aiming for the Catuvellaunian capital, a hill fort surrounded by trees, perhaps Wheathampstead in Hertfordshire. At this point, various tribes began surrendering to Caesar, offering hostages and grain. Caesar's willingness to accept these overtures encouraged others to capitulate, and once the hill fort was easily taken by storm, Cassivellaunus also requested terms. Eager to withdraw from Britain before the equinoctial storms, Caesar agreed, demanding hostages and an annual tribute paid to Rome. The second expedition to Britain was far more successful than the first, and could truly be described as an invasion. Tribute had been exacted from the tribes and they could be considered subject to Rome. Caesar had no need to return to the island, and events in Gaul prohibited that anyway.

The winter of 54/53 BC was one of considerable disturbance in Gaul, showing how superficial much of the Roman conquest had been. Poor harvests throughout the province forced Caesar to divide his legions up when they went into winter quarters in north-eastern Gaul and probably increased discontent amongst the tribes, who were forced to supply scarce grain to the occupying legions. The scattering of the legions provided an opportunity for the Gauls, and within two weeks the winter camps were coming under coordinated attack.

The furthest east of the winter camps, Cotta's was the most exposed Roman base and therefore the one most vulnerable to attack. One inexperienced legion and five cohorts were attacked by the Eburones under their dynamic leader Ambiorix, who claimed that all northern Gaul was in revolt and German mercenaries had crossed the Rhine to join in. He promised safe conduct to the Romans if they left their camp. Foolishly, Sabinus took him at his word and, despite the protestations of his fellow officers he led his force out of the safety of camp in a formation inappropriate to the tactical situation, straight into an ambush the Gauls had laid in a steep-sided valley. The inexperienced troops panicked, unable to maintain proper formation in terrain that denied them any opportunity to manoeuvre. The Romans were wiped out, Sabinus ignominiously being killed when trying to parley with Ambiorix, whom he still felt he could trust. A few escaped with their lives, others made it back to the encampment where they committed suicide during the night to avoid capture.

Quintus Cicero, the brother of Rome's most famous orator, had one legion encamped in the territory of the Nervii. Encouraged by the massacre of Sabinus' force, the Aduatuci, Nervii and their dependent tribes attacked Cicero's camp, trying to sell him the same story about general revolt and a German invasion. Unlike Sabinus, Cicero refused point blank to discuss terms, strengthened the camp's defences and tried frantically to contact Caesar. Under guidance from Roman prisoners, the Nervii built a circumvallation of rampart and ditch and moved siege towers up to the Roman fortifications. There followed a desperate couple of weeks in which the legion successfully held off attacks that continued both day and night. Cicero's troops refused to leave the ramparts even when the barracks were fired and their possessions were burning, but injuries were taking their toll. By the time Caesar relieved the siege, the legion had suffered 90 per cent casualties.

When Cicero did finally get a message to Caesar, he acted immediately, redeploying his legions and hurrying by forced marches to Nervian territory, covering up to 32km a day. Though he had only two legions and a small cavalry force, Caesar destroyed a Nervian army 60,000 strong, which abandoned its siege of Cicero's camp to head off the relieving army. Cicero's dogged resistance and the outstanding bravery of his officers won high praise from Caesar.

NEW CAMPAIGNS AND THE GREAT REVOLT

Following the disastrous winter of 54 BC, the season's campaigns concentrated on re-establishing Roman military superiority in north-eastern Gaul. Caesar recruited two more legions and borrowed one from Pompey, bringing the total to ten (40,000–50,000 legionaries). The size of the army allowed operations to be conducted, often simultaneously, against numerous tribes who had either been involved in the winter's uprisings or whom Caesar did not trust. At the end of the campaign most of the legions were quartered together on the Senones; the remaining four were quartered in pairs on the Treveri and Lingones, to prevent a repeat of the previous winter's attacks.

Before the campaigning season had properly begun, Caesar launched a surprise attack, concentrating on destroying property and capturing prisoners and cattle. The Nervii were swiftly forced to surrender and the legions returned to winter quarters.

In early spring Caesar marched suddenly on the Senones, taking them before they were able to withdraw into their fortified town or *oppidum*. With their people and supplies vulnerable, they had no alternative but to surrender. Caesar marched into the Rhine delta with seven legions. Menapian tactics were to withdraw into the marshes, but the Romans built causeways to allow them access to the area, then destroyed all their property, capturing cattle and taking prisoners as they advanced. With their wealth destroyed, the Menapii were forced to surrender.

The Treveri were still unsettled after the winter and were awaiting promised German reinforcements before attacking Labienus, who was encamped with 25 cohorts of legionaries and a large cavalry force. Keen to defeat the Treveri before help arrived, Labienus tricked them into attacking on terrain that was very unfavourable to them. Labienus pretended to be withdrawing and the Treveri charged up a very steep riverbank to fall on the Romans. The Romans formed up their battleline and the Treveri, disordered

Permanent bases were protected by two or more V-shaped ditches, each more or less five Roman feet (1.48m) wide and three Roman feet (89cm) deep. Here we see the double ditches defending the west side of Rough Castle, Falkirk. Note the causeway that crosses them from the *porta principalis sinistra* (the gate at the left-hand end of the transverse street of a Roman fort or camp, as viewed from the front of the headquarters or general's tent). (Fields-Carré Collection)

and out of breath from their uphill charge, were routed within minutes of the battle commencing; Labienus' powerful cavalry force mopped up those fleeing. Help would never be forthcoming from the Germans now, so the whole tribe of Treveri surrendered.

For a second time Caesar bridged the Rhine and marched into Germany to punish the tribes for sending help to the Gauls and discourage them from doing so again. But supply problems limited the scope of operations and Caesar seems to have been unwilling to risk battle against the powerful Suebi so he withdrew.

In the Ardennes two columns of three legions each raided much of modern Belgium, destroying property and taking prisoners. The burning of crops threatened the Gauls with starvation and many tribes, including the Eburones, surrendered.

In the space of a year, northern Gaul was totally reduced through vicious punitive raids aimed at destroying the property and wealth of the tribes. In the winter of 53/52 BC the general revolt that had been threatening erupted, perhaps because the tribes realized that coordinated resistance could prove effective against the Romans, and possibly because a tribal council Caesar held the previous year indicated that Gaul was now being treated as a province of Rome. Taking advantage of Caesar's return to northern Gaul and the political turmoil and uncertainties in Rome caused by the death of the popular politician Publius Clodius, the Gauls began to plan their campaign. Amongst the tribes leading the call for revolt was the Carnutes, whose territory included consecrated land supposed to be the centre of Gaul, and where the druids met annually to settle disputes between Gauls. This sacred space was now being threatened by Roman advances and was of interest to all Gauls, encouraging them to put aside their previous differences. The massacre of Romans settled in the town of Cenabum (Orleans) signalled the beginning of the revolt and enabled a charismatic young Arvernian, Vercingetorix, to build a coalition of Gallic tribes around his own leadership. Caesar, who had been in Italy, reacted swiftly to try to prevent the whole of Gaul getting caught up in the revolt and rushed to Provence with a small force. Having arranged the defence of Roman territory, Caesar marched through the Massif Central and used Agedincum as his base to threaten Arvernian territory and force Vercingetorix to abandon an attack on Gorgobina, capital of the Boii who were still allied to Caesar.

The Roman troops detoured in order to capture several *oppida*, partly to spread terror, but perhaps more importantly, to capture supplies of grain and fodder. As it was still winter there was no forage available and the Roman Army was finding it difficult to supply itself. The Gauls realized this and Vercingetorix's strategy was to avoid general engagements with the Romans, instead attacking foraging parties and supply trains. The Gauls cut off the Romans from all sources of food by withdrawing the population and supplies to the strongest *oppida* and adopting a scorched-earth policy, abandoning all other *oppida*. Vercingetorix did not want to defend the *oppidum* of Avaricum (Bourges) despite its strong defences, but was persuaded to do so by the Bituriges. Caesar immediately invested it.

The *oppidum* was virtually surrounded by a river and marshes, but Caesar entrenched where there was a gap in the natural defences and constructed a siege terrace of earth and timber 100m wide and 24m high. Despite the cold, rain, sorties and attempts by the Gauls to undermine and fire the terrace, it was completed in only 25 days. Camped with a large force outside the *oppidum*, Vercingetorix had unsuccessfully tried to attack Roman foraging parties and wanted to abandon the defence of Avaricum before it was captured. He was unable to persuade those whose home it was to do so, however: they were confident in the strength of their defences. Under cover of a heavy rainstorm when the Gallic sentries were less vigilant, Caesar ordered siege towers into position and his troops to assault the walls. The Gauls valiantly but vainly defended the breach and the Roman artillery took its toll, clearing an entrance

A Montefortino-style helmet. Although this example dates from the 2nd century BC, with its cheek-guards and ample dome, it is fairly typical of the kind of helmets issued to soldiers in the late Republic. (Ancient Art and Architecture)

ARTILLERY

Catapults were an important weapon in the armoury of the Roman Army and were the ancient equivalent of canons and machine guns. Torsion artillery had been invented by the Greeks in the 4th century BC and developed during the subsequent Hellenistic period. By the late 1st century BC the machines available were both sophisticated and highly effective in warfare. There were two basic types of catapults, the *ballista*, which hurled stones, and the *scorpion*, which fired quarrels similar to the later crossbow. The catapults were powered by coils of rope or sinew, which could be tightened up using a ratchet, and when the stored energy was released, the missile could be projected with terrific speed and noise. Specialist architects and engineers were attached to Roman armies who would build and maintain these machines, but in the field they would have been operated by the soldiers.

for the legionaries who then took possession of the circuit of walls without risking street fighting by descending into the town proper. Once possession was secured the soldiers turned from disciplined attack to rape and pillage. No prisoners were taken and Caesar claims 40,000 died.

Despite the setback at Avaricum, Vercingetorix had the authority to maintain the Gallic coalition and it was strengthened by the revolt of the Aedui. Some Aedui remained loyal and Caesar continued to command and use Aeduan cavalry, but it caused another blow to his already precarious supply lines, although the capture of supplies at Avaricum must have helped. Now the campaigning season had begun and fodder was becoming available in the open, Caesar ordered Labienus with four legions and cavalry to crush the Parisii and Senones, while he marched the remaining six legions down the Allier to Gergovia. Unlike Avaricum, which Vercingetorix had not wished to defend, this was one of the *oppida* he did intend to hold, probably because it was very strongly fortified, but perhaps also because it was the hill fort of his own tribe, the Arverni.

The hilly terrain dominated the Gergovia campaign. On arrival the Romans as usual entrenched camp, then captured a high hill opposite the *oppidum*, which dominated the principal water supply. Caesar had a smaller camp constructed there and linked his two camps with a wide ditch. This allowed him to move his forces around without interference from enemy sorties or cavalry. The next step was to capture another hill much closer to the hill fort and which actually adjoined the *oppidum*. The Gauls were not patrolling it properly and the legionaries were able to take it without much difficulty, crossing a 2m-wall built to prevent such an action. In his *Commentaries*, Julius Caesar claims he was only intending to take this hill and then halt the action. Either the soldiers failed to hear the recall he claimed to have sounded, and disobeyed orders, or he had actually intended to launch an attack against the *oppidum* itself if this first phase proved successful. Whatever the truth, the Romans did proceed to make a direct attack on Gergovia's defences, the enthusiasm of the centurions for being the first onto the walls driving them on against the defenders who hugely outnumbered them. The Romans were driven back; 700 men were killed including 46 centurions. Caesar blamed his men for the defeat and may have been less than clear in reporting his intentions in his *Commentaries* to distance himself from blame for a serious setback.

Caesar's forced withdrawal from Gergovia must have greatly increased Vercingetorix's reputation and encouraged more tribes to join the revolt. He continued to attack the Roman supply lines while calling in reinforcements. The Romans, too, obtained reinforcements, from the Germans who proved effective in routing the Gallic cavalry attacks on the Roman marching columns. The next *oppidum* Vercingetorix decided to defend was Alesia in the territory of the Mandubii and after the victory at Gergovia he must have been confident of success.

About 48km north-west of modern Dijon, Alesia was a large hill fort on a lozenge-shaped plateau protected by steep slopes and rivers on two sides. There was a plain at one end and at the other, the eastern end, the Gallic army was encamped. It was clear

ROMAN SIEGE WORKS

The Roman siege works at Alesia were extraordinary in their size and complexity. After digging a deep ditch on the plain to prevent cavalry attacks on the working parties, the Romans built a rampart with palisade and towers at regular intervals, and a double ditch, one filled with water diverted from the rivers where possible; seven camps and 23 redoubts were added at strategic points. This line covered a circuit of 18km. Caesar was not happy even with this formidable system of defences, and lines of booby traps were extended for several yards in front of the trenches. These comprised rows of sharpened stakes, then covered pits with sharpened stakes planted in them, and finally rows of wooden stakes with barbed iron spikes stuck into them. Once this circuit was completed Caesar had another identical line built outside, 22.5km in circumference, to protect the besiegers from the relieving army. The whole system took about a month to construct. Archaeological investigations have indicated that the fortifications were not as complete as Caesar suggests. There may have been gaps in the lines, particularly where the terrain provided natural protection, but the systems held up to concerted attacks by both Gallic armies even when they were prepared with bridging materials to cross the outer defences and ditches.

CAESAR'S SIEGE OF AVARICUM, 52 BC
This scene depicts the construction of a massive siege embankment, designed to level out the steeply shelving terrain outside Avaricum. Caesar's intention was to enable a massed infantry assault on the Gallic ramparts, but similar structures were used on other occasions to bring battering rams up to the walls of enemy towns. Two siege towers were erected, in order to command the battlements and provide the workers with covering fire, and the workers were protected by lines of shelters as they moved backwards and forwards along the embankment. (© Adam Hook, Osprey Publishing)

that an assault was out of the question, particularly after Gergovia, so the Romans would have to blockade. This was Vercingetorix's intention, for he allowed himself to be hemmed in at Alesia and ordered a relieving army to be gathered with all possible speed. The intention was to catch the Roman Army in a pincer movement with simultaneous attacks by the besieged under Vercingetorix and a relieving army, which Caesar claims (perhaps dubiously) was nearly a quarter of a million strong.

Ultimately the Romans did not have to starve out the defenders at Alesia, and no attempts were made to take the *oppidum* by assault. Violent coordinated attacks by both

CAESAR'S SIEGE OF ALESIA, 52 BC

This scene depicts an assault on Caesar's inner line of siege works. The assault was supported by Gallic slingers and archers. Caesar records that the Romans drove back the Gauls 'with slings throwing 1lb stones, as well as with stakes which had been distributed within the siege-works, and sling bullets', and adds that 'many missiles were discharged from the artillery' (Caesar, *Bellum Gallicum*, 7.81). Many who survived the barrage trod on the spikes or stumbled into the lily pits in Caesar's obstacle zone, and the assault finally failed. (© Adam Hook, Osprey Publishing)

Gallic forces on the Roman siege works had no effect and although the lines came under enormous pressure in one attack, reinforcements arrived in time and the Gauls were repulsed. It became clear that the extraordinary defences the Roman Army had constructed were not going to break and the failure of the revolt and starvation for those shut in Alesia were inevitable. The relieving army disbanded and Vercingetorix surrendered. Caesar distributed most of the prisoners amongst his men in lieu of booty. Vercingetorix was kept alive, to be displayed six years later in Caesar's triumphal procession in Rome, after which he was ritually strangled.

51–50 BC – MOPPING UP

The legions were distributed throughout Gaul over the winter to keep down the defeated tribes, and to protect the Remi who alone had been unswerving in their support for Rome. Caesar's last full year of campaigning in Gaul involved mid-winter terror raids against the Bituriges and Carnutes and, once spring had begun, Roman forces were sent that crushed all remaining thought of rebellion amongst the Belgic tribes, the Bellovaci, Eburones, Treveri and Carnutes. The only remaining serious resistance was in south-western Gaul. Here two men, Drappes, a Senonian who was nonetheless able to exert influence amongst other tribes, and Lucterius, a local Cadurcan, took over the *oppidum* of Uxellodunum which was extremely well fortified.

With only two legions, the general Caninius invested the *oppidum*, building three camps at strategic points and starting a circumvallation. Drappes and Lucterius clearly knew what to expect because they sortied to collect supplies, but were intercepted by Caninius, and Drappes was captured. Roman reinforcements arrived during the siege, and Caesar personally attended to the final crushing of the revolt.

Section of Caesar's siegeworks at Alesia, reconstructed at Beaune. Here we see the double ditches, behind which stands the earthwork crowned with a timber palisade. Forked branches are embedded in the earthwork, while towers overlook the defences. The original ran for 11 Roman miles, with a corresponding circumvallation of 14 Roman miles. (Ancient Art and Architecture)

Despite the disaster that befell Drappes' foraging party, Uxellodunum was very well supplied and the forces bottled up there were nothing like as numerous as those at Alesia the previous year. Potentially, they could have held out for some time, but Caesar was keen to take the town swiftly to serve as an example and so attacked the water supply. Like many Gallic *oppida*, Uxellodunum was dependent on an external water supply and artillery was set up to cut the defenders off from the rivers, leaving only a spring from which water could be obtained. The Romans then built a huge ramp and tower to dominate the spring and fire on those collecting water, and secretly dug tunnels towards it. Parts of the tunnels were discovered by archaeologists in the 19th century. The Gauls sortied in an attempt to destroy the siege ramp, rolling flaming casks down onto the woodwork, but their diversionary attack was repulsed and the Roman soldiers were able to extinguish the incendiary devices before serious damage was done. Finally, the Roman tunnels reached the spring and the Gauls, ignorant of what had caused their ever-reliable spring to run dry, interpreted it as a divine signal and surrendered. Instead of massacring the defenders, Caesar cut off their hands and set them free, to serve as an example of the punishment meted out to those who resisted Rome.

So Gaul was conquered, or at least the tribes had all surrendered to Roman power. The legions were brigaded throughout Gaul over the winter and virtually no campaigning took place the following year because the province was largely at peace, and Caesar had already turned his attention back to Rome. Civil war was becoming inevitable and Caesar would be one of the key players.

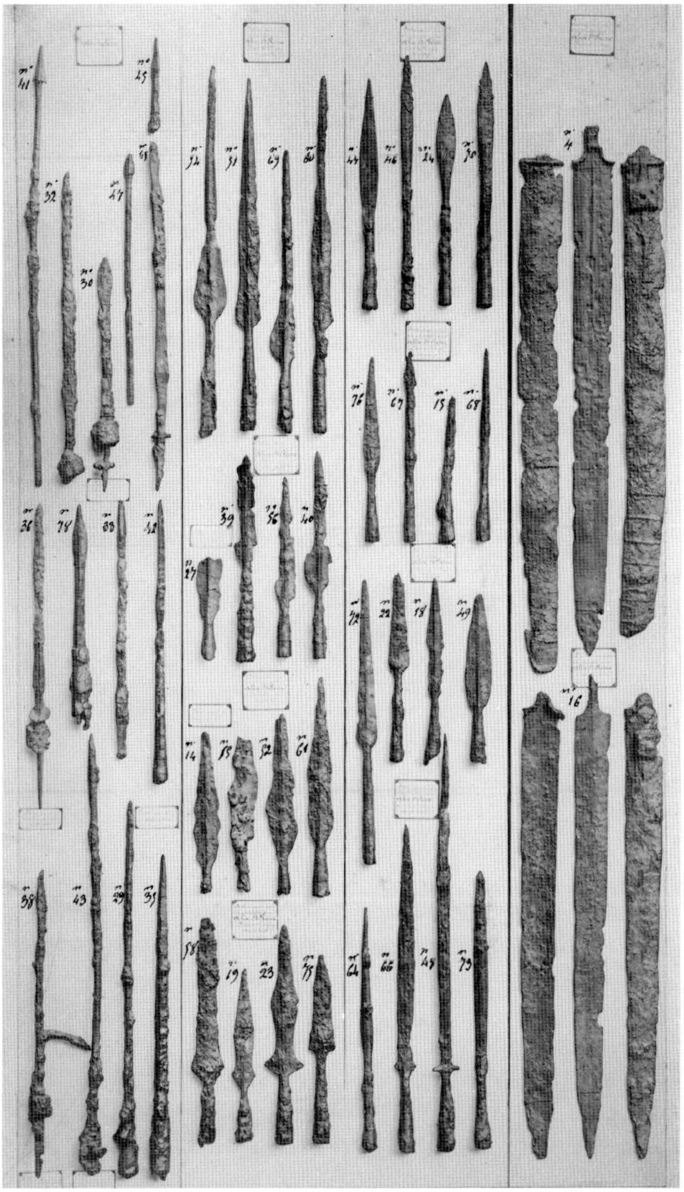

Finds of weapons from the Roman siege at Alesia. The site was explored by Napoleon III in the 19th century and many of these iron spearheads, *pilum* shafts and catapult bolts were found at Monte Rea where the fiercest fighting took place.

LATE REPUBLICAN WARFARE

The Romans attached a great deal of importance to training, and it is this that largely explains the formidable success of their army. The basic aim of this training was to give the legions superiority over the 'barbarian' in battle, hence the legionary, as we have seen, was taught to attack with his *gladius* by thrusting and not by slashing.

As with the old manipular legion, the Marian legion moved ahead in three battlelines at a walking pace, each cohort advancing alongside its neighbours under the direction of its centurions. During this steady advance the soldiers had to make sure they never lost sight of their standards and listened out for orders. The six centurions of each cohort were distinguished from the common soldiers by helmets with transverse crests, brushes across the helmet from ear to ear, so the soldiers could follow 'not only their standard, but also the centurion' (Vegetius, *De Re Militari*, 2.13). The soldiers were ranged behind him by *contubernia* (ten eight-man sub-units).

It may have been necessary at some point for the advance to stop and the cohorts to align themselves before the final approach. Any gaps could be filled in at this time too. And then, at the signal, the soldiers began their attack, probably a short jog of perhaps 40 or 50m; running in armour, *scutum* and *pila* in hand while in a formation must have been out of the question. As they approached the enemy, they would cast their *pila*, perhaps at a distance of 15m or so, and then draw their *gladii* and prepare to close. This means the soldiers probably came to a near halt, perhaps involuntarily, to be sure of their neighbours.

THRUSTING VS SLASHING

As Vegetius emphasizes (*De Re Militari*, 1.12), a thrust with the sword has penetrating power, whereas the slash, which often is difficult to aim and control, may strike a bone or the opponent's shield and thus will do comparatively little damage. The thrust is delivered with the strength of the entire body, while the slash is executed solely by the elevation of the right arm and carries the weight of the weapon. On the other hand, a slashing blow can be performed more quickly than a thrusting one, and with the latter technique there is always the danger of getting the blade stuck. Nevertheless, to raise the arm to make a slashing blow exposes the entire right side of the body. The swordplay itself had a typical scenario that pitted the training and discipline of legionary against the courage and individualism of a 'barbarian'.

According to Caesar, the raising of a war cry was usually associated with the volley of *pila* and final charge into contact. At or about the moment of impact, the narrow gaps between the cohorts were filled naturally by men from the rear ranks, and so the two opposing lines stayed face to face, so long as one did not break and allow itself to be struck in a suddenly exposed flank. The centurions at the front urged their men forwards and pressed them to come to actual blows, crossing swords themselves when they needed to lead by example. At any place where the line thinned as soldiers pulled out from exhaustion or injury, a second-line cohort would be sent to brace them. It is impossible for us to imagine the nasty realities of hand-to-hand fighting, to actually comprehend what it was like to be in the thick of it with comrades falling around you and your own end likely at any moment.

At the battle of Aquae Sextiae (Aix-en-Provence) in 102 BC, Marius is said by Plutarch to have 'sent officers all along the line ordering the soldiers to stand firm and keep their ground, to hurl their javelins when the enemy came into range, and then to draw their swords and force them backwards with their shields' (*Marius*, 20.5). Whether he instructed them this way or not, the advice reflects the usual Roman practice of disordering the enemy with *pila*, knocking them with *scuta* and closing with the *gladius*. It differed only in that the legionaries were to stand fast and receive the enemy charge instead of them advancing. Obviously Marius thought it prudent to await the enemy's inevitable onslaught from his superior position and then advance down the slope once the enemy had been disordered. Nonetheless, his instruction to discharge 'javelins' and then join battle with sword and shield is such as we might expect to be given to an army that had adopted the *pilum* and *gladius Hispaniensis*. Likewise, if this is so, the offensive use of the *scutum* tells us that the tactical doctrine commonly associated with the Roman Army of the Principate was now firmly in place and had been since Polybius' day.

Having drawn his *gladius*, the Republican legionary then hunkered down in the manner described in Part 1, with the left foot forward, holding the *scutum* horizontally in front with the left hand and using it to cover the upper legs, the torso, and lower face, and thrusting out with it as a punching weapon. Essentially two methods of combat could be employed by the legionary, namely pro-active or re-active fighting. The first necessitated striking the first blow, perhaps through overwhelming his opponent with the *scutum*: here its sheer size was a premium. The second method involved taking the opponent's sword strike on the *scutum*. This would entail moving the shield a relatively short distance to meet the incoming blow: here the metal binding around its rim was a premium. The advantage here was that the parry and punch could be combined, the legionary moving in closer all the while to deliver the deadly jab. In both cases, however, we should be aware of the fact that the final position of the legionary would have been a few inches from his opponent.

In terms of late Republican auxiliaries, they would open battle by attempting to disorganize and unsettle enemy formations with an extended hail of javelins, arrows and slingshot. In doing so they also prevented the legionaries from being harassed by similar enemy light-armed troops. This done, they retired through the gaps in the main battleline and made their way to the rear, thereby allowing the legionaries to move forward into the combat zone. In the late Republican period of Roman history, however, such troops were relatively few in number and were predominantly armed with long-range projectile weapons, for example the bow or the sling. Yet the role of the archer, for instance, could be many-sided. On one occasion in Africa Caesar mingled them with slingers to provide a protective screen against cavalry attacking his flanks, on another, he placed detachments of them 'at specific parts of the line, and especially on the wings' (Anonymous, *Bellum Africum*, 60.3). In another instance he posted them with slingers in the course of a cavalry attack (*Bellum Africum*, 78.3), and again, in Gaul, while on the move he used them either at the head of the column or as its flank guard (Caesar, *Bellum Gallicum,* 2.19.3). In fact the typical arrangement when marching through enemy territory was to place the auxiliaries and cavalry at the head and rear of the column, and the legions in the central part, protecting the baggage train.

As we would expect, the normal battle arrangement was to place the legionaries in the centre, screened by the auxiliaries, and the cavalry on the wings. Though the Roman by custom and practice was a foot soldier, cavalry was essential to the success of the army, not only for flank attacks and encirclement but, once the battle had turned, for speedy pursuit of a broken enemy. As Napoleon succinctly puts it, 'charges of cavalry are equally useful at the beginning, the middle and the end of a battle' (*Military Maxims*, 50).

DIVIDE AND RULE: THE CIVIL WAR

THE ROMAN CIVIL WAR of the mid 1st century BC reminds us that the Roman military was as much about internal politics as it was about protecting the state from external aggressors. Caesar's military victories had brought him great power and prestige, but also significant numbers of political enemies, who feared his ascendancy. In 60 BC, together with other Roman power players, Marcus Licinius Crassus and Gnaeus Pompeius Magnus (Pompey), Caesar had formed the First Triumvirate, a trio of Rome's most influential men. The triumvirate ended with the death of Crassus in 53 BC at the battle of Carrhae. Caesar's relations with Pompey deteriorated, and in 50 BC Pompey guided the Senate to a decision that ordered Caesar to disband his army and return to Rome, his term as proconsul having come to an end. Caesar recognized that compliance would emasculate him in Rome's political future.

On the night of 10 January 49 BC, Caesar, with a single legion, crossed the Rubicon (the river frontier of Italy) and marched into Italy where Pompey had only to stamp his foot upon the ground and armed legions would form. Surprisingly, Pompey abandoned Italy and fled to Epeiros (17 March). Though Caesar was welcomed in Italy, he encountered neutrality in Rome, where he was appointed dictator for 11 days, just enough time for him to set up constitutional machinery for the consular elections of 48 BC. He then dashed off to Iberia, defeating the Pompeians in an almost bloodless campaign, which culminated at Ilerda (Lérida). Meanwhile, Caesar's legate, Curio, was defeated and killed in Africa.

In January 48 BC, Caesar crossed over to Epeiros, only to narrowly avoid total defeat at Dyrrhachium in July. Favoured by fortune, he turned the tables on Pompey and decisively defeated him at Pharsalus on 9 August (see p.129 for a more detailed study of this battle). Pompey fled to Egypt, where he was murdered on arrival by the followers of the boy-king Ptolemy XIII on 30 September. Caesar arrived soon after and swept into Alexandria, but had to survive an unexpected siege, during which he succumbed to the charms and wiles of Ptolemy's sister, Cleopatra. While Caesar dallied on the Nile, Pharnaces II of Bosporos defeated his legate, Domitius Calvinus in Pontus.

One of the *denarii* from the remarkable coin series issued by Mark Antony to honour his legions prior to Actium. On one side ANT(onius) AVG(ur) IIIVIR R(ei) P(ublicae) C(onstituendae) with a warship, and on the reverse LEG(ionis) XII ANTIQVAE with an aquila flanked by two signa. (Ancient Art and Architecture)

THE ITALIAN PENINSULA AND CAESAR'S ADVANCE, 49 BC

In August 47 BC Caesar routed Pharnaces at Zela (Zilleh, Turkey), near to where Pharnaces' father Mithradates had earlier trounced a Roman army. Such being the sharpness and rapidity of Caesar's victory, this was the occasion of the famous 'veni, vidi, vici' dispatch to the Senate (Plutarch, *Caesar*, 50.2). Caesar now settled the east and returned to Italy, where he had to quell a mutiny amongst his veterans and settle social unrest fanned during his absence by the likes of the bankrupted Marcus Caelius Rufus, Cicero's friend, and the debauched patrician Publius Cornelius Dolabella, Cicero's son-in-law.

Early in the new year (46 BC), Caesar opened his operations against the Pompeians, headed by Marcus Porcius Cato Minor and Quintus Caecilius Metellus Pius Scipio, who were firmly entrenched in Africa. After a hard slog, he found victory at Thapsus (Ras Dimasse, Tunisia), and in the aftermath many of the Pompeian leaders met their deaths, most notably Cato and Metellus Scipio. Caesar returned to Rome and celebrated four triumphs (Gaul, Egypt, Pharnaces and Iuba).

The year 45 BC, the penultimate for Caesar, brought another campaign in Iberia, where the remnants of Pompey's support had rallied round his two sons, Pompeius Magnus Minor and Pompeius Magnus Pius. A close-run battle was fought at Munda on

17 March, with Caesar emerging as the victor. Gnaeus was hunted down and executed, but Sextus remained at large. Meanwhile Caesar had returned to Rome and celebrated his fifth triumph, that over 'Iberia', and as a result of his final victory, Caesar paid 150 million *denarii* into the state treasury. He then began preparations for a military operation in the east against the Parthians, Crassus' recent undoing. As the poet Ovid says, with this campaign Caesar was planning to 'add the last part of the orbis' (*Ars amatoria*, 1.177).

On 15 February 44 BC, Caesar was appointed dictator for life (*dictator perpetuus*) by the Senate. Having reached the summit of power, on the Ides of March Caesar fell to the daggers of conspirators anxious to preserve the liberty of the Republic – he perished at the foot of the statue of his old foe Pompey. Rome's civil wars were not over, however.

THE COLLAPSE OF CAESAR'S COUNTERATTACK AT DYRRHACHIUM

On the morning of 9 July 48 BC, Pompey finally succeeded in breaking through the siege lines with which Caesar had pinned him to the coast south of Dyrrhachium. Caesar scraped together all the reserves he could muster – 33 cohorts – and led them in two columns against the old camp. The attack was a disaster. Here Caesar, in his red cloak, faces an attack from one of his panicking men with the butt end of a standard; he pays by having his arm cut off by Caesar's German bodyguard. (© Adam Hook, Osprey Publishing)

A new triumvirate emerged, this time formed by Gaius Octavius Thurinus (Octavian, later Augustus), Mark Antony and Marcus Aemilius Lepidus. Caesar was Octavian's great-uncle, and Octavian inherited the impetus for greatness. Octavian and Mark Antony fought together to defeat the forces of Caesar's assassins Marcus Junius Brutus and Gaius Cassius Longinus, who were eventually crushed in the battle of Philippi in Macedonia in 42 BC (see below). Yet such victories did not hold the triumvirate together in the long run. When the Second Triumvirate eventually spun apart, it was Octavian who took supremacy, forcing Lepidus into exile and driving Antony, following his defeat at the battle of Actium, to commit suicide. With these triumphs, and his establishment of the Principate in 27 BC, the age of the imperial Rome had begun.

On the field of battle each *centuria* usually fought in four ranks, with 1m frontage for each file and 2m of depth for each rank. This gave ample room for the use of *pilum* and *gladius*. The number of ranks could be doubled if extra solidity was required. In fact a convenient march formation was an eight-man-wide column (i.e. one *contubernium* wide), and this only needed a right wheel, march to the flank, halt, front and double files to become a fighting formation.

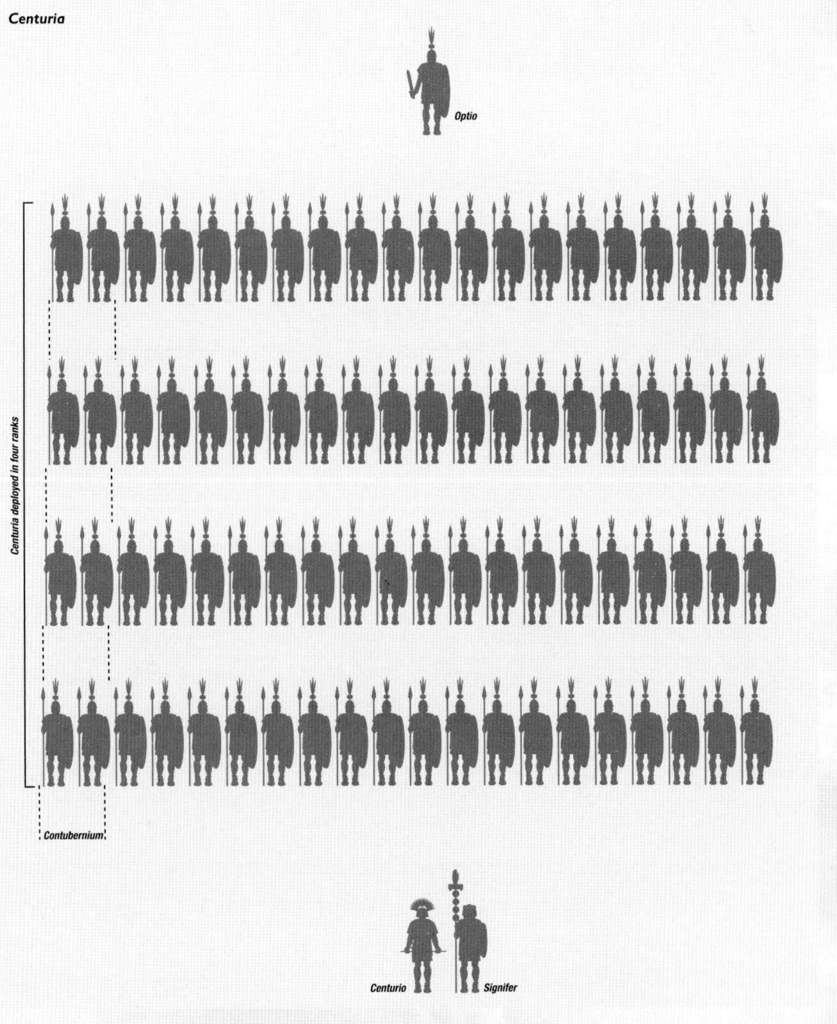

BATTLE: ROMAN AGAINST ROMAN – PHARSALUS, THAPSUS AND PHILIPPI

PHARSALUS, 48 BC

Taking a step back, our study of the Republican Roman Army is interesting set in the context of three critical civil war battles – Pharsalus, Thapsus and Philippi. Caesar himself never mentions Pharsalus, the most famous engagement of the Second Civil War. In fact, in his whole narrative of events immediately preceding and following the battle, and the battle itself, he mentions no place at all except Larissa (Lárissa). Such topographical information as is given in his account and in other sources is of little help in identifying the exact location of the battlefield.

While Appian, Plutarch and Suetonius refer to 'the battle of Pharsalus', Frontinus, Eutropius, Orosius and the author of the *Bellum Alexandrinum*, believed by many to be the soldier-scholar Hirtius, give the additional detail that it was fought somewhere near 'Old Pharsalus', a stronghold on a hill in the territory of Pharsalus proper. Pharsalus is generally agreed to be the modern Fársala about 5km south of the River Enipeios. The site of Old Pharsalus is disputed. One possibility is that the battle was fought on the north bank of the river, at the western end of the plain, which is almost entirely closed on the remaining sides by hills. Pompey was camped on a hill at the western end of the plain, Caesar in the plain further east. Old Pharsalus was across the river, not far from the site of Caesar's camp.

Caesar's battle report, on the other hand, does allow us to see the armies down to the level of the individual cohorts. On paper, Pompey had the equivalent of 11 legions made up of 110 cohorts, 45,000 legionaries plus 2,000 time-expired veterans (*evocati*) at Caesar's estimation. However, this ignores the fact that Pompey had left up to 22 cohorts on detached garrison duty, so that the two sides were more evenly matched than Caesar suggests. Caesar himself was able to field eight legions in 80 under-strength cohorts, totalling 22,000 legionaries by his own reckoning (*Bellum Civile*, 3.88.5, 89.1).

Pompey's legions may have been stronger, but they were certainly less experienced than Caesar's. On the left were the two legions Caesar had handed over 'in obedience to the decree of the Senate at the beginning of the civil strife' (*Bellum Civile*, 3.88.1), now

THE FRONT LINE AT PHARSALUS, 9 AUGUST 48 BC
Note how the legionary on the right delivering a fatal blow is showing good technique with both sword and shield. The *scutum* was designed to be effective in an offensive as well as defensive role, with the wielder gripping the handle in his fist and using it to punch forward, hoping to drive his opponent off-balance by striking them with the thickest part of the iron ridge running its length. (© Adam Hook, Osprey Publishing)

numbered I and III, in the centre were his legions from Syria, on the right legio Gemella from Cilicia and some cohorts that had found their way from Iberia. Lucius Domitius Ahenobarbus commanded on the left, Metellus Scipio in the centre, and Lucius Afranius on the right. The *evocati*, who had volunteered their services, were dispersed throughout the battleline. Having little confidence in the majority of his legionaries, Caesar ordered the cohorts to deploy ten deep and await the enemy charge at the halt, hoping to keep his raw recruits in a dense formation and prevent them from running away (Frontinus, *Strategemata*, 2.3.22). Pompey was relying upon his numerically superior cavalry, about 7,000 strong and supported by archers and slingers, to outflank the enemy right and roll up Caesar's line.

Like Pompey's army, Caesar's was deployed in the customary *triplex acies*, but it was vital that its front should cover much the same frontage as their opponents, so his cohorts were probably formed four or even six ranks deep. Realizing the threat to his right flank, Caesar took one cohort from the third line of six of his legions and formed them into a fourth line, angled back and concealed behind his cavalry. As usual, in his order of battle, Caesar posted legio X Equestris on the right, and legio VIIII on the left, and, as it had suffered heavy casualties in the Dyrrhachium engagements, he brigaded it with legio VIII. He posted the remaining five legions in between them. Mark Antony was in command on the left, Domitius Calvinus in the centre, and Publius Cornelius Sulla, the nephew of the dictator Sulla, on the right. Caesar himself would spend most of the battle with legio X Equestris, his favourite unit, on the crucial right wing. For the battle Caesar's men were given the watchword 'Venus, Bringer of Victory' in reference to his divine ancestor, while Pompey's men put their trust in 'Hercules, Unconquered'.

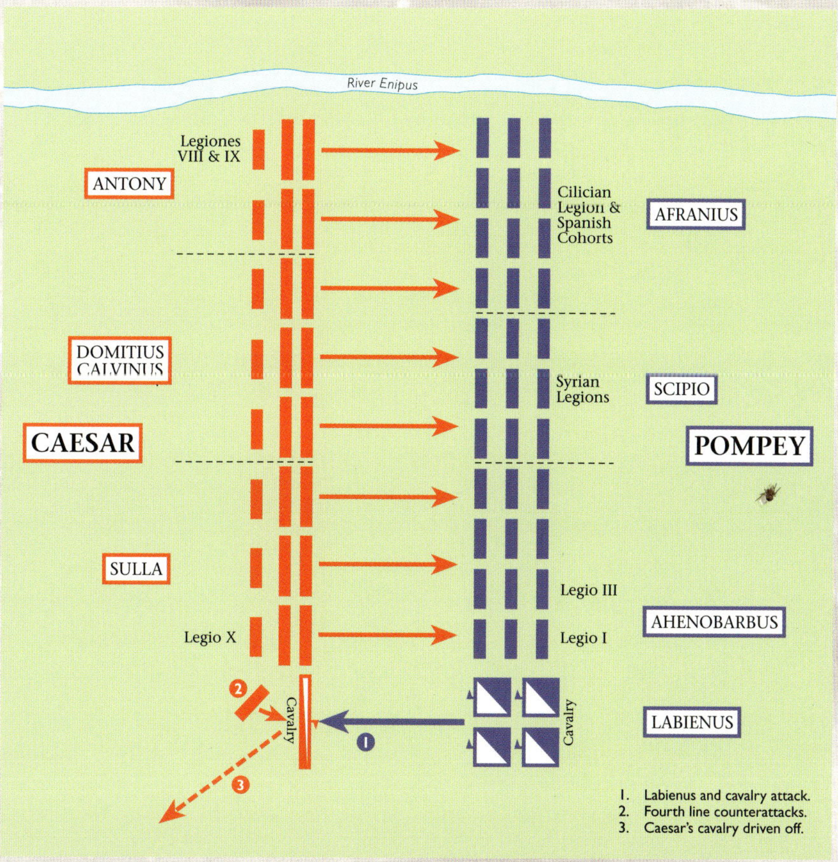

THE BATTLE OF PHARSALUS, 48 BC, PHASE ONE

THE BATTLE OF DYRRACHIUM, 48 BC

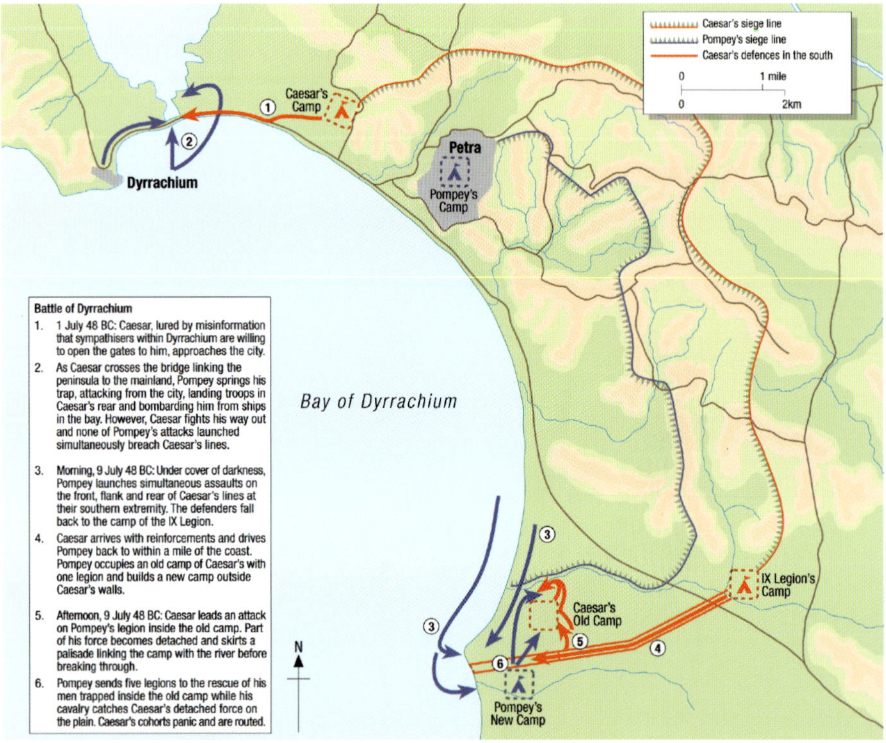

CAESAR'S FIVE CAMPAIGNS IN THE MEDITERRANEAN

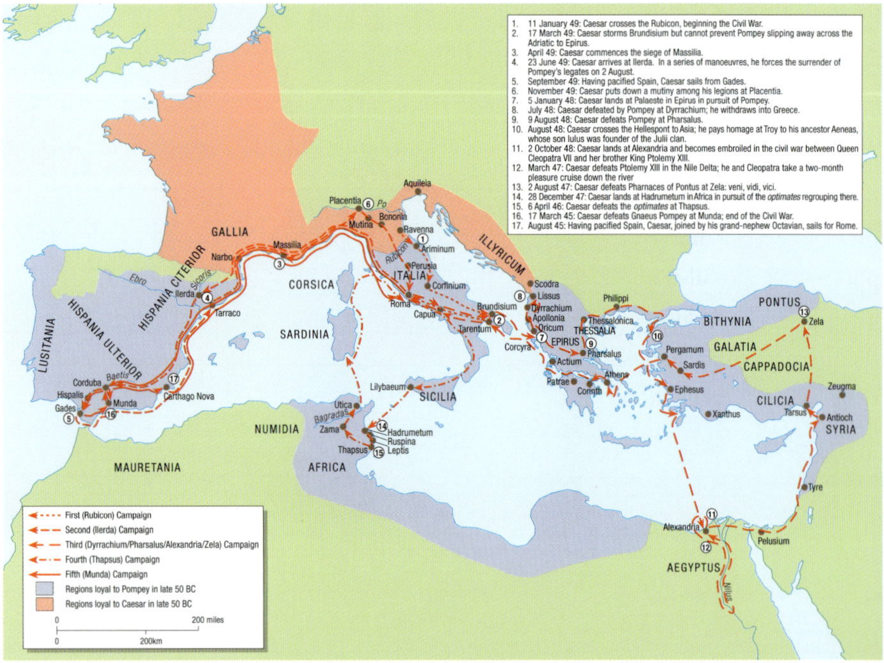

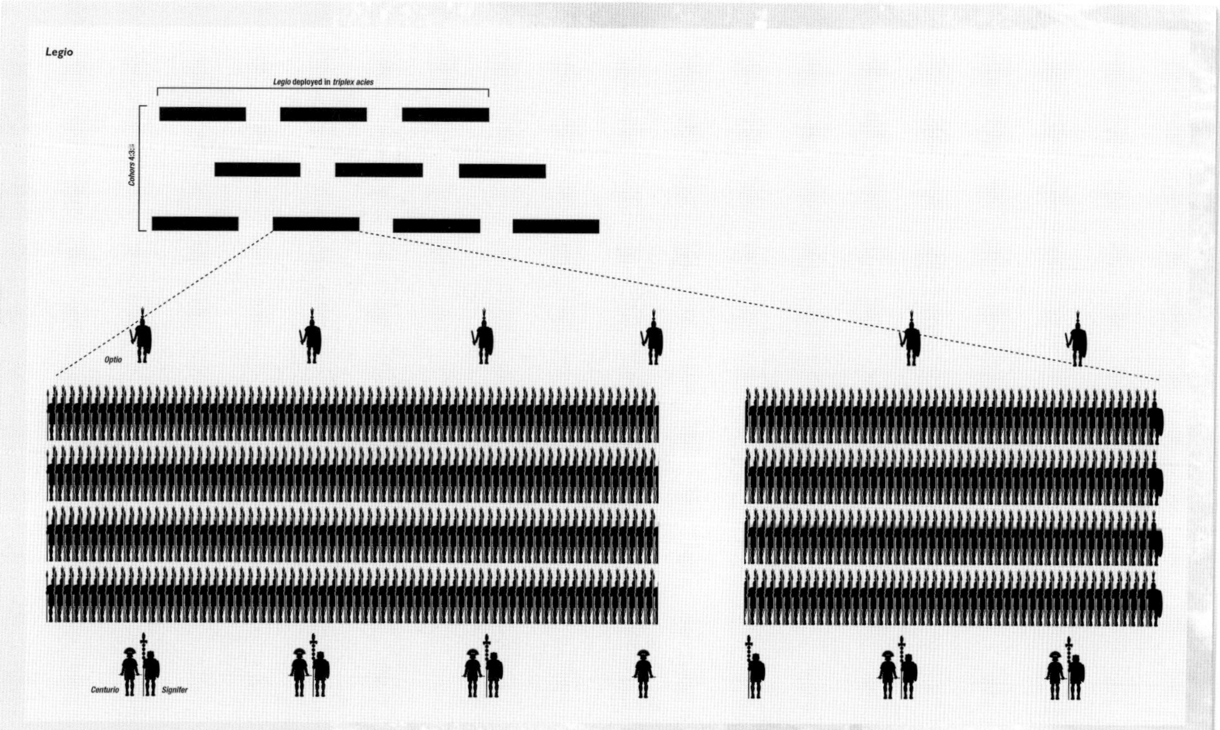

In effect, the old three-fold battle array of the manipular legion was cut into ten slices from front to back, with the *cohors* being a large but manageable unit that deployed with 480 men as nominal strength. When deployed for battle, the ten *cohortes* of a legio still formed up in the traditional *triplex acies*. The uniformly armed and sized *cohortes* could be deployed anywhere, unlike the *manipuli* they had replaced, which had been restricted to fixed positions.

Labienus, Caesar's former second-in-command, led Pompey's massed cavalry against the Caesarian right wing and soon put the enemy horsemen, who only numbered 1,000 or thereabouts, to flight. However, in the process these inexperienced horsemen lost their order and merged into one great mass – many of the men supplied by eastern potentates were ill-trained and both Appian and Plutarch describe them as young and inexperienced. Suddenly Caesar's fourth line, the back-up legionaries, burst from behind the main battleline and charged this milling throng of cavalry, stampeding them to the rear in wide-eyed flight. In the *sauve qui peut* that followed, Pompey's auxiliaries were left in the lurch and massacred or dispersed by Caesar's legionaries. Pompey's main attack had failed.

Meanwhile, the main infantry lines clashed, Caesar's superbly disciplined men stopping to re-form when they realized that the Pompeian cohorts were not advancing to meet them, as was the norm, and that they had begun their charge too early. Centurions, having re-dressed the ranks, ordered the advance to resume. When the

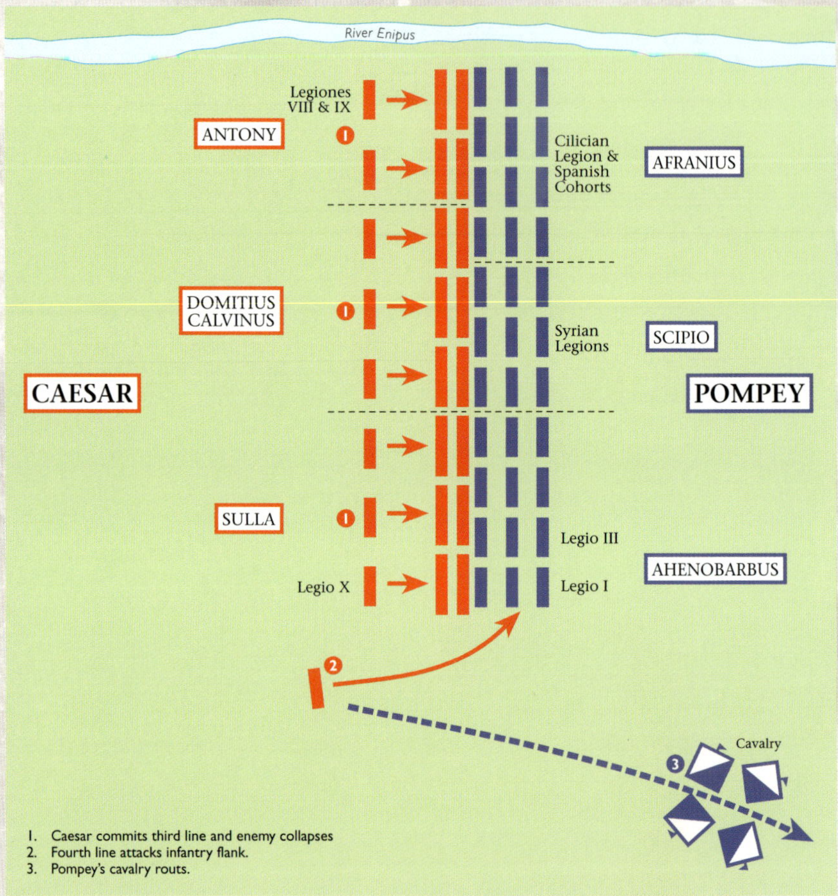

THE BATTLE OF PHARSALUS, 48 BC, PHASE TWO

Caesarians were within 20m of the enemy they discharged their *pila*, then charged into contact with drawn swords. A fierce struggle followed, and the second-line cohorts were drawn in. In other words, the Pompeians stood their ground and vindicated their general's battlefield tactics.

As the fourth-line cohorts swung round to threaten the now exposed left flank of the Pompeian legions and Caesar committed his third-line cohorts to add impetus to the main assault, Pompey's army collapsed. Casting aside his general's cloak, or so it was said, Pompey rode hard for the coast. His camp, in which victory banquets had been prepared and tents decked with laurel, was taken. That night Caesar dined in Pompey's tent, and 'the whole army feasted at the enemy's expense' (Appian, *Bellum Civilia*, 2.81). When it came down to it, experience won over numbers. The Pompeians had lost the psychological advantage they would have got from making the first charge. As it was,

Caesar's veterans spotted the trap. They stopped short of the Pompeian lines to regain their breath and re-form their lines.

Caesar claimed that he lost only 200 men and, because of their typically aggressive style of leadership, 30 centurions. Of Pompey's army, 15,000 had died on the battlefield while 24,000 now found themselves prisoners of war. Nine eagles were captured. Most Pompeian leaders were pardoned, amongst them Junius Brutus, whose mother, Servilia, had been the great love of Caesar's life, and it was even claimed that Brutus was their love child. True or not, Brutus' legal father had been one of the many victims of the First Civil War, but the high-principled stoical Brutus, by favouring the murderer of his mother's husband over her old flame, had chosen the cause of legitimacy.

PHARSALUS, 9 AUGUST 48 BC

Caesar's reserves rout Pompey's cavalry and turn the tide of history at Pharsalus. Pompey's trump card at Pharsalus was his overwhelming superiority in cavalry. To undermine this, Caesar withdrew six cohorts of infantry from his legions and stationed them behind his cavalry at an oblique angle to his front line. Caesar attacked with this reserve once Pompey's cavalry had attacked, and shifted the battle in his favour. (© Adam Hook, Osprey Publishing)

THAPSUS, 46 BC, THE REPUBLICAN SUNSET

Thapsus was a port town that sat on a cape overlooking the azure waters of the Mediterranean Sea, and it was here, on 6 April, that Caesar with 20,000 legionaries, 2,000 archers and slingers and 1,200 cavalry fought a Pompeian army of 28,000 legionaries and 12,000 Gallic, Iberian and Numidian cavalry. In support were 64 Numidian elephants, split equally between the two wings, and large numbers of Numidian auxiliaries.

Caesar had his main force of legions, which were deployed in the customary *triplex acies*, screened by auxiliaries, legiones X Equestris and VIIII forming the right of the line of battle and legiones XIII and XIIII its left. Five cohorts of legio V Alaudae, whose legionaries had been given a crash course in elephant fighting, were posted, along with auxiliaries, as a fourth line obliquely – as at Pharsalus – in the rear of each wing. Caesar had no intention of employing his own elephants in battle – he is said to have considered the lumbering, tusked bull elephant a menace to both sides. The cavalry, intermingled with the newly trained light-armed legionaries, were deployed on the extreme right and left.

The battle began with an unauthorized charge by Caesar's troops. Most of the elephants were killed, but those on the Pompeian left turned and stampeded through the troops lined up behind them. Caesar's redoubtable legio X Equestris exploited the resulting confusion, and as the Pompeian left swiftly unravelled, the rest of Metellus Scipio's main battleline dissolved. Labienus, the irrepressible commander, escaped the carnage and reached Iberia where he joined up with Pompey's sons, Gnaeus and Sextus. Surrounded and cut down from his horse, he would die outside Munda fighting to his last breath. Likewise Afranius, Iuba and Petreius escaped, but the first was eventually captured and delivered to Caesar, who put him to death for his perfidy, and the other two, who expected no mercy from the dictator, fought an after-dinner duel in which one killed the other and then killed himself.

Likewise, Caesar's chief antagonists, Cato and Metellus Scipio, chose suicide rather than capture. Metellus Scipio ended his life in a manner worthy of his patrician ancestors, jumping overboard when his fleeing ship was run down. Cato, ever the man of stoic principle, first read, three times over, Plato's *Phaedo*, in which Socrates comforts his companions by offering them proofs of immortality of the soul before serenely drinking the hemlock, and then took his sword and succeeded at the second attempt. Thus through death Cato escaped the death of the Republic, which to Cato was what Caesar symbolized, and his 'martyrdom' in the cause of Republicanism was to be a real embarrassment to Caesar. Ironically, the architect of the triumph himself was laid low by an epileptic fit early in the battle (Plutarch, *Caesar*, 53.5–6). Even so, with this victory he had defeated the Pompeians so effectively that Republican opposition in Africa ceased.

Modern-day view of the site of the battle of Philippi, looking west from the acropolis. It was on this plain, hemmed in by mountains to the north and marshes to the south, that the legions of the triumvirs and the Liberators clashed. The latter were camped just below, and traces of their extensive fieldworks can still be seen. (Fields-Carré Collection)

PHILIPPI, 42 BC, THE FINAL BOUT

Brutus and Cassius, the chief assassins of Caesar who called themselves the 'Liberators', were in control of all the Roman provinces east of the Adriatic, including the vital ones of Macedonia and Syria. They commanded 19 legions, numerous cavalry and a substantial fleet. Meanwhile the triumvirs mustered an army of 22 legions, including all the re-formed Caesarian formations. Over the summer of 42 BC they were ferried across the Adriatic to Dalmatia and, with Lepidus left behind in Italy as caretaker, Mark Antony and Octavian advanced eastwards along the Via Egnatia towards Philippi.

BALKANS THEATRE OF OPERATIONS, JANUARY–APRIL 48 BC

The Liberators had taken up a strong position just west of the town astride the Via Egnatia. A ditch, rampart and palisade connected their two camps, cutting the road and equipped with a central gateway that allowed troops from either camp to be deployed in the plain beyond. This plain was flanked by Mount Pangaeus inland to the north and by marshes southwards towards the sea. Here, firmly entrenched and well supplied, Brutus and Cassius awaited the anticipated approach of the two triumvirs.

The first engagement was forced by a hazardous frontal assault by Antony, whose battle-hardened legions broke through the front of Cassius and pillaged his camp. Cassius despaired too soon. Believing that all was lost he fell upon his sword and died. But the legions of Brutus, without awaiting orders, had swept over the Caesarian lines and captured the camp of Octavian, who was not there but hiding in a nearby bog. Both sides drew back, damaged and resentful.

It was nearly three weeks later when the impatience of his men compelled the 'last Republican' to try the fortune of battle again. It appears Antony was attempting to execute a dangerous infiltration between Cassius' camp, now occupied by Brutus, and the marshes, but after a tenacious and bloody contest Brutus' men were swept away. The poet Horace joined in the 'headlong rout, his poor shield ingloriously left behind' (*Odes*, 2.7.9–10). Escaping from the field Brutus persuaded his slave Strato to run him through with a sword. This time the decision was final and irrevocable, the dying embers of the Republic were quenched in Roman blood; its last defenders, like itself, perished not by the sword of the enemy, but by their own. After the victory, Brutus' body was brought to Antony's camp. He took off his general's cloak and cast it over the corpse and ordered an honourable funeral for his erstwhile comrade.

* * *

Engagements such as Pharsalus, Thapsus and Philippi illustrated that discipline and fortitude were just as important in Rome's internecine wars as in those directed at foreign enemies. With Mark Antony's nautical downfall at Actium in 31 BC, Rome began a new era under the unassailable power of Augustus. As we shall see, the Roman Army now faced new frontiers of warfare, as Rome began a period of imperial expansion unrivalled in its previous history.

THE EARLIER ROMAN EMPIRE,

27 BC–c.AD 200

INTRODUCTION: WINNING AND RUNNING AN EMPIRE

OCTAVIAN'S VICTORY OVER ANTONY at Actium concluded two decades of almost constant internal conflict, but it did not entail even a pause in Roman military activity. Although the new civilian controller of Rome, the *princeps* Augustus, proudly proclaimed that he had on three occasions shut the gates of the Temple of Janus, the action which traditionally commemorated the cessation of all hostilities, he also oversaw and organized the most substantial expansion of Roman territory: these conquests far outstripped those of his adopted father Julius Caesar and were presented to the Roman people with great pride in the statues and temples which adorned the newly constructed Forum of Augustus. These contrasting propaganda displays reflect the conflicting demands on Roman leaders. One the one hand there was the desire for peace and stability on the part of the civilian inhabitants, especially the propertied classes and those in the more central provinces. On the other, there were the expectations of military success, fuelled in part by historical tradition, in part demanded by the existence of a powerful military machine which could not remain inactive indefinitely.

ROMAN FRONTIERS

Roman imperial frontiers can be divided into three main sectors, the Rhine, Danube and Euphrates, with Britain as the fourth area of significance. It is no accident that in the first three instances a river accorded the frontier sector its basic structure. Although the defensive value of rivers has been debated, that they constituted some sort of barrier is demonstrated by the greater ease with which enemies breached European frontiers, at least, either in the depths of winter when the rivers were frozen or at the height of summer when they might become fordable. They could certainly be crossed, but often at identifiable points which could be watched by Roman guards, with the fleets to supplement this protection. Where rivers did not exist to demarcate different territories, the Romans tended to create visible alternatives, though these were not necessarily a continuous structure: in the face of the north African desert the Romans constructed various linear earthworks, whose purpose seems to have been to channel the natural movement of the inhabitants of marginal lands along observable routes, but not to prevent it altogether. At the same time Roman frontiers are rightly no longer seen as simple barriers, best represented by what appears to be the solid obstacle of Hadrian's Wall, but zones of communication and integration, with the Romans always keen to push their influence out beyond their defensive installations while their neighbours regularly crossed over.

Previous page:
'The Taking of Jerusalem' by Titus is said to be inspired by the 'Fall of the Temple of Jerusalem' by the Jewish historian and soldier Josephus, who was present at the siege of Masada. (Bridgeman Art)

LEGIONARY OF LEGIO II AUGUSTA, BRITAIN AD 43
Legio II Augusta was under the command of Vespasian during the invasion of Britain. It fought in 30 engagements and captured 20 hill forts. Here we see a legionary re-equipped for the expedition, but many would have been equipped similarly to their late Republican predecessors with bronze helmets, mail armour and curve-sided *scuta*. His curved rectangular *scutum* was probably more widespread now but not the standard pattern. (© Angus McBride, Osprey Publishing)

Augustus began an imperial momentum that ran strong from the next 200 years. When the Roman Empire reached its peak extent under the Emperor Trajan (r. 98–117), the Empire stretched from the Scottish borders and Spain in the west, through to Mesopotamia and Armenia in the east, and coastal North Africa, with the entire Mediterranean world under the Roman standard. While one consequence of the

THE ROMAN EMPIRE, AD 14

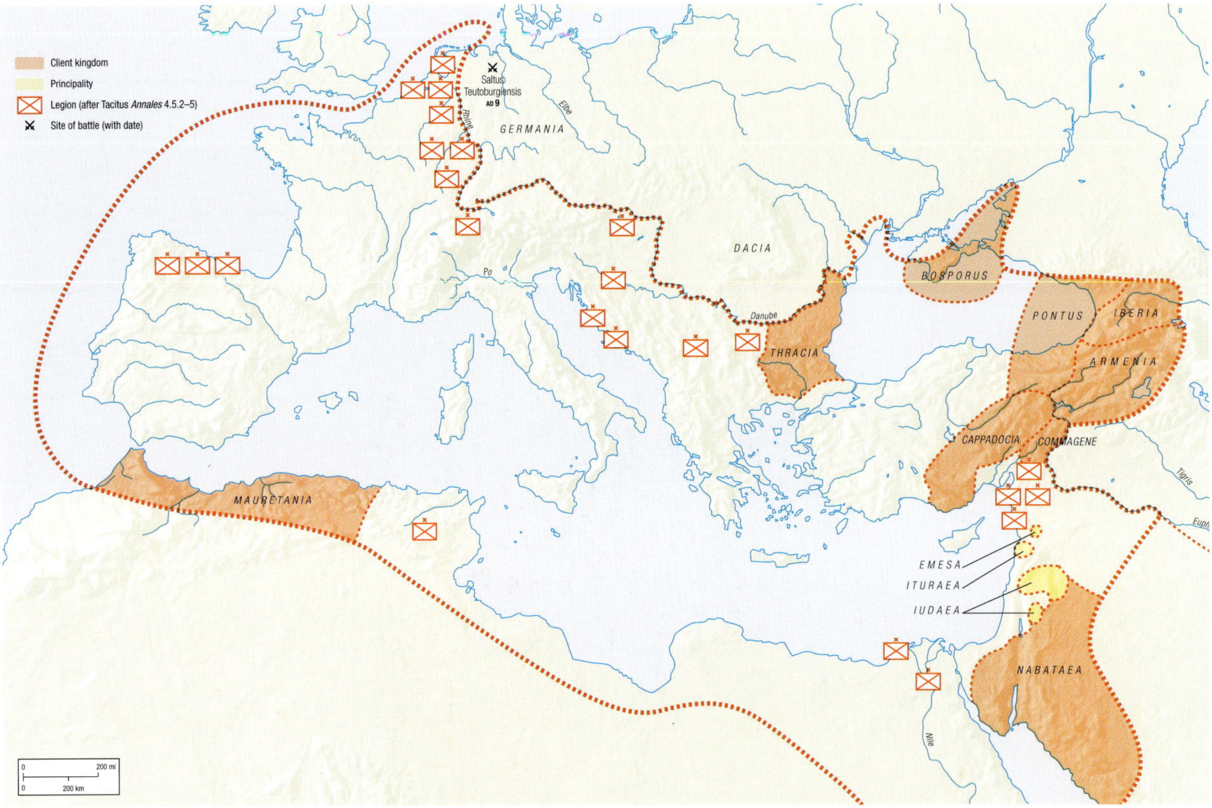

expansion was increased wealth for many Roman citizens, emperors also had to consider a variety of external threats, while remaining alert to the dangers of provincial revolt and the presence on the fringes of settled society of bandits, who would be encouraged by any loss of official authority or reduction in vigilance to extend their depredations.

It is argued that generals and Emperors were more interested in the rewards of external conquest than in routine defence of the Empire's inhabitants, and that from the military perspective provinces more often required subjugation than protection. Exchanges across frontiers, the significance of military glory, and the preservation of law and order are all valid considerations, but the ideology of *pax Romana* was also important: emperors were believed to have a duty towards the civilian members of the Empire, or at least their performance of this role was an issue which might be picked up in speeches of praise or defamatory tracts. In many years internal policing and repression tasks probably absorbed as much military manpower as action on or beyond the frontiers, but their recurrent and small-scale nature made them less newsworthy; along the frontiers we are better informed about grand campaigns than the run-of-the-mill patrolling and surveillance which will have occupied much of the garrisons' time.

THE DEVELOPMENT OF THE IMPERIAL ROMAN ARMY

Following his victory at Actium in 31 BC and his conquest of Egypt in 30 BC, Octavian found perhaps 60 legions under his control. He immediately began a massive settlement programme for time-served veterans, and over the period of seven years whittled down the number of legions to 28, retaining especially the units raised by Julius Caesar and, as a symbol of unity, the most renowned of Antony's legions. Where before legions had been raised for specific wars and disbanded after six years,

BATTLE OF TEUTOBURG FOREST, GERMANY, AUTUMN AD 9
Marcus Caelius (centre), a leading centurion of legio XVIII, leads a small band of veterans and *calones* (army slaves) against Arminius' Cherusci during the three-day battle in which three legions (XVII, XVIII, XIX) and nine auxiliary regiments were destroyed. (© Angus McBride, Osprey Publishing)

these 28 legions were permanent formations composed of long-service professionals. (The number of legions dropped to 25 after the Varian disaster of AD 9.) As Augustus, he was the first leader to lay down clear terms of service, rates of pay and pensions for the successful completion of service. The chaos of the late Republican period was not to be repeated. The legions were no longer a citizen militia; no one but Augustus had the right to raise new legions and they depended upon him for their pay and owed their loyalty to him alone.

Legions consisted of ten cohorts, with six centuries of 80 men in each cohort, apart from the first cohort (*cohors prima*), which from AD 70 or thereabouts was double strength, that is five centuries of 160 men. Commanded by a centurion and his second in command (*optio*), a standard-size century was divided into ten eight-man sub-units (*contubernia*), each *contubernium* sharing a tent on campaign and pair of rooms in a barrack block, eating, sleeping and fighting together. Much like small units in today's regular armies, this state of affairs tended to foster a tight bond between 'messmates' (*contubernales*). Male bonding would explain why many soldiers preferred to serve their entire military career in the ranks despite the opportunities for secondment to specialized tasks and for promotion. Nonetheless, a soldier who performed a special function was excused fatigues (daily duties and patrols), which made him an *immunis*, although he did not receive any extra pay (*Digesta*, 50.6.7).

Finally there was a small force of 120 horsemen (*equites legionis*) recruited from amongst the legionaries themselves. These *equites* acted as messengers, escorts and scouts, and were allocated to specific centuries rather than belonging to a formation of their own. Thus the inscription (RIB 481) on a tombstone from Deva (Chester) describes an eques of legio II Adiutrix pia fidelis as belonging to the centuria of Petronius Fidus. Citizen cavalry had probably disappeared after Marius' reforms, and certainly was not in evidence in Caesar's legions. However, apart from a distinct reference to 120 cavalry of the legion in Josephus (*Bellum Judaicum*, 3.68), they seem not to have been revived as part of the Augustan reforms.

When territory was added to the Empire, a garrison had to be put together to serve in its defence. New legions were sometimes raised, but normally these green units were not themselves intended for service in the new province. So when an invasion and permanent occupation of Britain became a serious possibility under Caligula, two new legions, XV Primigenia and XXII Primigenia, were formed in advance. Their intended role was as replacements for experienced legions earmarked to join the invasion force: XV Primigenia to release legio XX from Novaesium (Neuss), and XXII Primigenia to release XIIII Gemina from Mogontiacum (Mainz). The invasion force that eventually sailed for Britain in the summer of AD 43 consisted of XX and XIIII Gemina, along with II Augusta, which had been at Argentoratum (Strasbourg), this camp was now left vacant, and VIIII

Hispana from Siscia (Sisak) in Pannonia (Tacitus, *Annales*, 14.32.6).

Nevertheless, transfers of legions to different parts of the Empire could leave long stretches of frontier virtually undefended, and wholesale transfers became unpopular as legions acquired local links. An extreme case must be that of II Augusta. Part of the invasion army of AD 43, this legion was to be stationed in the province for the whole time Britain was part of the empire. As discussed below, many recruits were the illegitimate sons of serving soldiers or veterans, that is to say, *origo castris*. Therefore, the custom developed of not sending an entire legion to deal with emergencies, but detachments drawn from the various legions of a province.

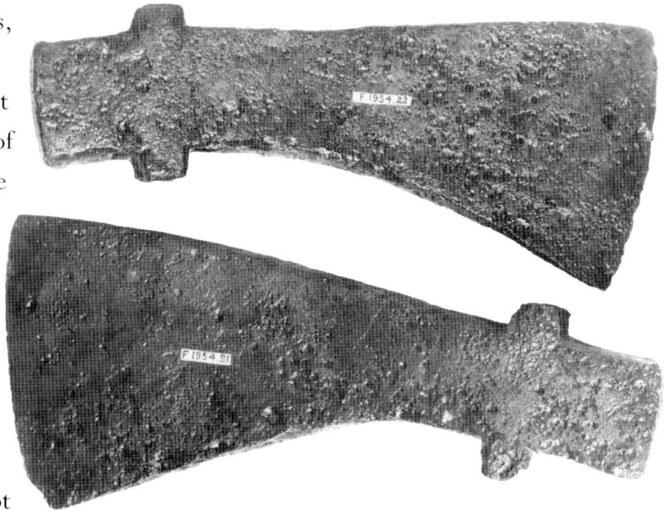

Roman military axes from Loudoun Hill, Scotland, 1st–2nd centuries. The legions excelled in construction and in peacetime would often work on civil projects. (Hunterian Museum, University of Glasgow)

Detachments from legions operating independently or with other detachments were known as *vexillationes*, named from the square flag, *vexillum*, which identified them. Until the creation of field armies in the late empire, these *vexillationes* were the method of providing temporary reinforcements to armies for major campaigns. Thus Domitius Corbulo received a *vexillatio* from X Fretensis, then stationed at the Euphrates crossing at Zeugma, during his operations in Armenia. Later he was to take three *vexillationes* of 1,000 men (i.e. two cohorts) from each of his three Syrian legions (III Gallica, VI Ferrata and X Fretensis) to send to the aid of Caesennius Paetus, whose army was retreating post-haste out of Armenia (Tacitus, *Annales*, 15.8–17).

* * *

The origins of the soldiers who defended the Empire evolved over the first three centuries, though they were always predominantly from rural backgrounds. Under Augustus, Italy, especially the colonies of the Po valley, was the prime recruiting ground for the legions, to be joined by the colonies and other veteran settlements of southern Gaul and Spain; in the Greek-speaking east where colonies were fewer, legionary recruitment amongst the provincials began under Augustus, with citizenship being the reward for enlistment. By the end of the 1st century AD the proportion of recruits from Italy was already in decline. There is evidence for imperial interest in supporting the population in several areas, but veteran settlements in the Danube provinces now emerged as an important resource to supplement other provincial suppliers of manpower.

One important factor that encouraged recruitment from veteran families was the prohibition, until the reign of Septimius Severus, on marriage for serving soldiers.

This meant that the children of the soldiers' inevitable liaisons were illegitimate and hence excluded from Roman citizenship, which, however, they could secure by joining the legions. The same incentive operated for the auxiliaries; originally these were raised amongst particular ethnic groups, whose name would be preserved in the unit title, for example Batavian, Sarmatian or Thracian, but such connections would be diluted when

LEGIONARY PRESS-GANG IN OSTIA, PORT OF ROME, AD 6–9
Suffering a manpower crisis, Augustus resorted to levying recruits in Rome and the surrounding area. Few men came forward voluntarily and the Emperor began seizing property, removing citizenship and resorting ultimately to executions. (© Angus McBride, Osprey Publishing)

the unit was deployed away from its point of origin and recruits would tend to be found wherever a unit was stationed.

If citizenship was one important incentive to enlist, the terms and conditions of life were another. Legionary pay was reasonable, 9 *aurei* (225 *denarii*) in the 1st century AD and 12 *aurei* in the 2nd century AD, a good wage for an unskilled workman, especially considering that it was regular. In addition, troops received occasional bounties or donatives, at accessions between Claudius (r. 41–54) and Vespasian (r. 69–79) and again consistently from Marcus Aurelius (r. 161–69), sometimes for service on particular campaigns when booty was also a powerful lure, and occasionally by bequest at an Emperor's death. On the other hand there were compulsory deductions for food, including fodder for cavalry mounts, clothing, and boots, so that any residue to be deposited for safe-keeping at the shrine of the legionary standards was likely to be small unless an individual had struck lucky with booty. On discharge veterans received 3,000

EMPEROR CONSTANTIUS IN HIS GILDED CHARIOT
He is flanked on the left by a *cataphract* of the *Scythae* regiment and, on his right, an infantry guardsman of the Cornuti. (© Angus McBride, Osprey Publishing)

denarii in the 1st century, which had increased to 5,000 by the early 3rd century, with a sizable allotment as an alternative where land was available. Auxiliaries undoubtedly received less favourable terms than legionaries, but there is insufficient evidence to chart how these changed over the centuries.

Regular payment, especially in coins minted with the Emperor's head and bearing a suitable slogan on the reverse, was one important mechanism for ensuring military allegiance. New recruits swore an oath of loyalty to the Emperor and Rome; this was renewed annually, and attention to the Emperor and his ancestors was sustained by regular commemorations of significant dynastic days and by the presence of imperial images next to the standards which focused the military cohesion of units. Most Emperors also had some experience of command and so could genuinely refer to soldiers as 'fellow-campaigners', thereby creating an important bond of shared memory.

Such positive measures were reinforced by the harsh punishments that indiscipline would incur, at least from strict commanders, with the result that mutiny was rare: discontent undoubtedly existed, but it usually required a particular catalyst to erupt into serious trouble, such as the death of Augustus or the arrival of a very lax commander. Most serious threats came not from the rank and file but from ambitious generals. Augustus had acted to limit potential competition from other generals, ensuring that the aristocratic Crassus was denied credit for personally killing an enemy commander in battle, denying triumphs to anyone outside the imperial family, and, after the celebration by his supporter Balbus in 19 BC, Augustus terminated the long Republican tradition of competitive displays; Balbus was also the last 'outsider' allowed to construct and name a major public building in central Rome. Thereafter many important campaigns were led in person by the Emperor or a close relative. Careful attention was devoted to the selection of the governors of frontier provinces with substantial armies under their command, they were personally chosen by the Emperor from amongst former consuls. In most reigns, generals were monitored quite carefully, even at a distance, and inappropriate actions might be countermanded or the culprit removed in disgrace.

BACKBONE OF THE IMPERIAL ROMAN ARMY: THE ROMAN LEGIONARY

TRADITIONALLY ALL ROMAN MALE CITIZENS between the ages of 17 and 46 were liable for military service. Most recruits to the legions were aged between 17 and 23, with the peak age of enlistment being 20, but recruits as young as 13 and 14, and as old as 36 are known. Many legionaries, if not the majority, were conscripts, and not necessarily educated to any great standard. The *dilectus* or levy was necessitated by the huge scale of the civil wars and the Augustan conquests. Volunteers were preferred but emperors were resigned to the necessity of conscription. A legionary recruit was supposed to be a Roman citizen, but the civil wars had resulted in the wide dispersion of the legions and the need for rival commanders to recruit on the spot.

The real requirement for entry into the legions, whether as a conscript or volunteer, was free birth, not Roman citizenship; citizenship could be granted at enlistment or at some point during service.

In AD 23, the Emperor Tiberius (r. 14–37) bemoaned the lack of suitable Italian recruits coming forward to serve in the legions and announced his intention to tour the provinces in order to discharge the large number of eligible veterans, and to replenish

SOLDIER HEIGHT

The ideal height of the legionary was 6 Roman feet (1.77m) and men of at least 5 Roman feet and 10 inches (1.72m) were preferred in the first cohort (Vegetius, *De Re Militari*, 1.5). However, the reality was different. Nero's legio I Italica was notable for two reasons: its composition of Italian recruits and the fact that all the men were at least 6 Roman feet in height (Suetonius, *Nero*, 19). That this is worthy of note suggests that men of smaller stature were regularly accepted into the other legions. The skeletal remains of a soldier who died in Pompeii in AD 79 suggest he was about 1.7m tall, but a soldier from the fort at Velsen in Holland was 1.9m tall. He may have been a local recruit from the Frisii. Evidence from the 4th century AD shows that men of 1.65m were admitted into the elite units of the army, suggesting that this was actually the upper limit of height in the rural population from which recruits were drawn (Theodosian Code, 7.13.3).

the legions by conscription. That so many soldiers were eligible for discharge suggests they had been recruited in large-scale levies more than 20 years before. Similarly, in AD 65 the urgent need to replenish manpower in the Illyrian legions after discharges attracted the attention of the Emperor Nero (r. 54–68), suggesting that the veterans had been conscripted en masse 25 years before (service had been extended; Tacitus, *Annals*, 13.40). If long-established units were maintained by voluntary recruitment this should have meant a minimal number of annual discharges. In times of relative peace a legion of 5,000 men probably suffered a decremental mortality rate of about 40 per cent over a 25-year service period (indicative of the endemic diseases in the Roman world), and a further 15 per cent through soldiers invalided out of service. Consequently the legion would require 280 recruits annually to maintain optimum strength. This level of recruitment can hardly have troubled the Emperors. They had problems because every 20 or 25 years they had to replenish much of a legion's strength at a single stroke.

Reconstruction of a 'cut-down'-style *scutum* in use by Augustus' time. The face was decorated with the unit's insignia – either in applied panels or painted. However, it is not clear whether the entire legion shared a common shield device, or whether each cohort was distinguished in some way, perhaps by colour. (Fields-Carré Collection)

We see no better explanation for the extent of Roman conquest than the Romans' military training, camp discipline and practice in warfare. Legionary recruits trained daily for four gruelling months. Training began with practising the military steps, 'for nothing should be maintained more on the march or in battle, than that all soldiers keep ranks as they move' (Vegetius, *De Re Militari*, 1.9). Recruits were required to march 29km in five hours at the regular step, and 35km in five hours at the faster step, loaded with a pack about 20.5kg in weight. This burden was merely for acclimatization; the weight of his arms and armour alone could be far greater. Strict maintenance of the ranks was enforced during drill, the centurions and training officers using their staffs to beat any laggards.

Once the recruits could march in time and follow the commands relayed by the trumpets and standards, manoeuvres were practised endlessly. They practised different formations: the hollow square, wedge, circle and the *testudo* ('the tortoise' – a mobile formation entirely protected by a roof and walls of shields). They were trained in overcoming obstacles, in charging and breaking off combat, in changing lines and relieving engaged units. The recruit was also taught to spring out of the line – this might prove useful in combat (Plutarch, *Antony*, 45).

Weapons training was conducted with swords, javelins and shields made of wood and wicker, but twice the weight of the real thing. These weapons were used against 1.8m practice posts. The instructors emphasized covering the body effectively with the shield while using the sword point instead of the edge, for this caused deeper wounds and was more efficient than slashing. Weapons training might occur twice a day. If possible, recruits were also taught to swim so that a campaigning army's advance would not be impeded by rivers. They were also given cursory instruction in archery, the sling and riding, so that they had knowledge of all arms.

Drill was maintained when the recruit became a regular, and he was expected to complete three route marches every month. At the end of these marches soldiers

LEGIONARY FIGHTING TECHNIQUES

(Top left) A typical heavy-armed legionary of the first half of the 1st century AD throwing his heavy *pilum* prior to charging with his sword. (Top right) A dedicated light-armed legionary. His flat oval shield is more manoeuvrable than the regular *scutum*, and his light javelins allow him to fight in advance of the battleline or deliver missile support over the heads of his comrades. In battles characterized by missile duels, such legionaries would have dominated the fighting. (Bottom left) Here is a regular legionary advancing without armour. Caesar, Tacitus and Dio all refer to heavy infantry relieved of their body armour to increase their speed and manoeuvrability in battle. (Bottom right) An Augustan legionary in a crouch stance, an option for a legionary wishing to get under the guard of an opponent armed with a slashing sword. (© Angus McBride, Osprey Publishing)

constructed a fortified camp with ditches and earthen ramparts. This, with its orderly internal structure, was fundamental to Roman military practice.

The training that imperial Roman soldiers underwent in advance of campaigns, and the daily weapons drill they performed when marching towards the war-zone, was crucial. This was especially true in peacetime because units were often under-strength, sometimes half their optimum size. Many soldiers were detached on various duties across the province, providing garrisons and acting as police (*stationarii*), or employed in various building projects, tax collecting or performing bureaucratic tasks for the provincial administration. Endemic disease also resulted in a steady rate of attrition. Only when a legion was required to fight in a major war might the majority of its manpower ever be assembled together, and its sub-units perform the manoeuvres they might carry out in battle (Josephus, *Bellum Judaicum*, 3.81ff).

The Roman legion is often described as a military machine, but the legion was only as good as the sum of its men and this was dependent on their morale. Legionaries were as apt to panic and as susceptible to defeat as any other demoralized soldiers throughout history. Legionaries therefore depended on the charismatic and fair leadership of their officers. Caesar, Antony, Germanicus, Caecina and Vespasian are obvious examples of generals willing to lead by example and share the soldiers' hardships. The centurions frequently cited by Caesar and Josephus were courageous and steady, able to assert their authority in crisis situations and avert the onset of panic amongst the rank and file. But not all officers had the necessary confidence, courage or charisma to lead their men effectively. Many were brutal and corrupt. When fair leadership was lacking, performance in battle was poor and legionaries were readily disposed towards mutiny and rebellion.

What made the legionary truly effective in battle was his feeling of belonging to his century and in particular to his *contubernium*. Such identification with the unit and loyalty

LEGION IDENTITY

Legionaries came to be identified by the numerals or titles of their legion (see Tacitus, *Histories*, 2.43). Identity was enhanced by the veneration of specific emblems, perhaps alluding to founders (the Bull for Caesar's III Gallica, or the Capricorn for Augustus' XIV Gemina), or to their battle honours (the elephant of V Alaudae or the dolphin and warship of X Fretensis). The annual birthday feast celebrating the foundation of the legion (*natalis aquilae*, lit. 'birthday of the eagle'), parades and training exercises were of fundamental importance in fostering mass unit identity and maintaining morale at the level of the legion, because these might be the only times outside of war when the full unit gathered together.

Opposite:
Marble statue of Augustus as *imperator*, from the Villa of Livia at Prima Porta. The decoration of the cuirass features the symbolic return of an *aquila* captured by the Parthians at Carrhae (53 BC). No soldier himself, Augustus was the commander-in-chief of a 'new model' army of his own making. (Fields-Carré Collection)

to the group of fellow soldiers was crucial to his performance in battle. The legionary fought first for his comrades, his century and legion, then for prizes and glory, and lastly for the often distant Emperor and the *Res Publica* (Roman state).

The close bonds between the eight men of the *contubernium* would have been strong simply by virtue of having to share a cramped single room together in barracks, or a tent on campaign. The other crucial bonding aspect of the *contubernium* was that it was a mess group. The Roman Army had no general messes for its soldiers, no dining halls in its fortresses or mass catering facilities when on campaign. Roman soldiers were expected to prepare their own meals and had to pay for food by deductions from their wages. As well as the pleasure of eating together, we can imagine the soldiers discussing (or complaining about) the day's duties: this was also essential to the fostering of group identity.

These bonds, created within the fort or camp, in training, daily duties, and at leisure and meal times in the close proximity of the barracks, initially bound men together as comrades. War and battle solidified them. The legionaries in the century fought effectively because they were well known to each other as friends and comrades – the century was not such a large unit that it became faceless and impersonal. Moreover the legionaries took pride in their collective centurial identity. They were their own elite within the legion and were driven by the bonds of comradeship not to let their fellow soldiers down in battle, to stand and fight for the men around them.

The terms for comradeship in the Roman Army are notable. *Contubernalis*, meaning tent- or mess-mate within the *contubernium*, expressed not only the most basic group and social ties within the legion, but also the dependency of *contubernales* upon each other in battle. *Commilito* (fellow-soldier) was perhaps the most binding term, for it was applied across the spectrum from the ordinary soldier (*miles*) to the general and, most importantly, the emperor. *Commilito* spoke of the unity of the army and of respect for fellow soldiers whatever their rank.

Manipularis or *commanipularis* (soldier in the same maniple) implied the reliance of legionaries upon each other, and century upon century, for success and survival in battle. The most poignant term, regularly inscribed on tombstones, was *frater* (brother). On many such monuments it is clear from the different family names of the deceased and the heir(s) that they could not have been actual brothers, but the term expresses with great eloquence and simplicity the fundamental bonds between comrades. If the legion can be described as a society, the *contubernium* was the family of the legionary.

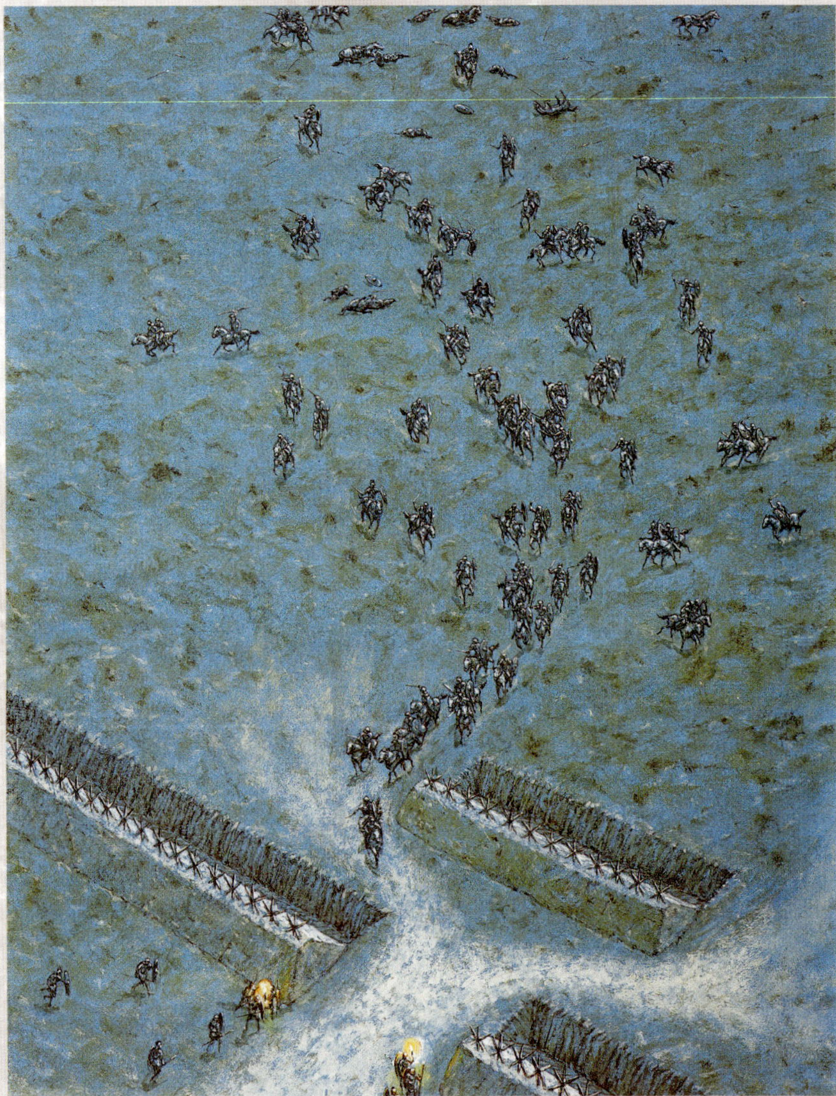

A RECONSTRUCTION DEPICTING THE AFTERMATH OF THE BATTLE OF SECOND CREMONA, 24/25 OCTOBER 69 AD

The critical engagement that decided the outcome of the 'Year of Four Emperors'. Here the victorious Flavian cavalry is hotly pursuing the fleeing Vitellian cavalry who are attempting to reach the safety of their camp outside the town of Cremona. (© Adam Hook, Osprey Publishing)

For those who served unit and state well, decorations might follow. The highest decoration available to the legionary, irrespective of rank, was the *corona civica* – the civic crown of oak leaves awarded for saving the life of a fellow-citizen in battle. No act of bravery in battle was viewed as so important or so selfless as forcing back the enemy to save a fallen comrade. It was the epitome of comradeship, illustrating for whom the legionaries really fought: each other. This was the essence of the effectiveness of the army.

Polybius notes that the Romans encouraged valour by the awarding of decorations, and ensured that soldiers were conspicuous to their commanders on the battlefield by the wearing of animal skins (skirmishers), or crests and feathers (regular legionaries)

AWARDS AND DECORATIONS

A legionary centurion being awarded with *torques* and *armillae* by Marcus Aurelius. Traditional awards of *dona militaria* (military decorations) were still made by Marcus Aurelius and the chaotic Marcomannic and Sarmatian wars provided numerous recipients. This winter scene is inspired by Dio's account of the defeat of the Iazyges on the frozen river Danube in AD 172–73. Here Marcus Aurelius comes forward with hand outstretched to greet a surprised legionary centurion as a fellow-soldier (*commilito*). Aurelius' senior advisor, Claudius Pompeianus, carries the soldier's awards – *torques* and *armillae*. (© Angus McBride, Osprey Publishing)

(Polybius, *The Histories*, 6.22–23, 39). Decorations for valour available to all ranks included *torques* (neck-bands or collars) and *phalerae* (metal disks, serving as medals) worn on a harness, and *armillae* (bracelets/armbands) of precious metal, as well as grants of money and promotions. The awarding of other crowns, spears and flags were increasingly restricted to centurions and higher officers. On parade and in battle Roman soldiers wore their decorations with pride.

If decorations were the carrot to bravery, discipline was the stick. Discipline was enforced with severity. Cowardice in battle and other derelictions of duty, such as falling asleep on guard duty, were punished by *fustuarium* (being beaten to death by comrades whose lives had been endangered), floggings and demotions. If a complete unit displayed cowardice in battle it might suffer decimation, when every tenth man was selected by lot and executed. This was a rare and extreme punishment but occurred as late as AD 18 (Tacitus, *Annals*, 3.21). Other punishments were more symbolic, intended to shame offenders, such as putting soldiers on rations of detested barley or ostracizing them from military life by making them camp outside the ramparts. They might be stripped of their military belts (i.e. their military identity) and forced to parade outside the headquarters wearing heavy helmets and holding out long, heavy staffs or sods of turf. Only when soldiers had redeemed themselves in battle might these punishments be revoked.

Altar (RIB 2092) dedicated to Disciplina Augusti by soldiers of *cohors II Tungrorum milliaria equitata* stationed at Birrens-Blatobulgium (Edinburgh, National Museums of Scotland). The cult links two concepts, namely, obedience to the Emperor and military efficiency. The top of the altar is hollowed out to form a focus where offerings of fruit or grain may be deposited. (Fields-Carré Collection)

DRESS AND EQUIPMENT

Compared to the Republican period, the dress and equipment of the imperial legionary showed the usual mix of continuity and change. The military identity of individual soldiers was conferred not by a uniform – the soldier's clothing of tunic and cloak was little different to that of the civilian – but by the military belt (*balteus*) and boots (*caligae*).

The *balteus* took the form of either a single waist belt decorated with silvered, sometimes embossed, bronze plates, or two crossed belts slung from the hips. The date of the introduction of the cross belts is not certain; they may have appeared during the close of the reign of Augustus, to which the apron of studded straps belongs. It was probably during the reign of Tiberius that *niello*, a black alloy of sulphur and silver, lead or copper, began to be widely used to decorate belt plates with intricate inlaid designs. Such belts identified a man as a soldier; Juvenal characterized soldiers as 'armed and belted men' (*Satires*, 16.48). The removal of the *balteus* stripped a soldier of his military identity; it was confiscated if a soldier was dishonourably discharged (Herodian, *History of Roman Empire*, 2.13.10). In Rome in AD 69, civilian pranksters used razor-sharp knives to slice through the belts of unassuming soldiers in a crowd. The soldiers went on the rampage when they realized what had happened and numerous civilians were killed, including the father of one legionary (Tacitus, *Histories*, 2.88).

Military boots, *caligae*, were the other key item of identification. The date of their introduction is uncertain, but they were certainly the standard footwear for the Roman soldier from the reign of Augustus until the early 2nd century AD. Really a heavy-duty sandal, the crunch of the iron-nailed sole identified the presence of a soldier as much as his jingling belts (Josephus, *Bellum Judaicum*, 6.85). Archaeological finds from across the Empire indicate that there was a major degree of standardization in the form of *caligae* and the nailing pattern of soles, suggesting that pattern books for this, and perhaps other items of military equipment, were issued by the emperors. The nailing patterns, giving support to the ball, arch and heel of the foot, are viewed as the precursors of the sole patterns on modern training shoes.

The colour of military tunics is much disputed. Evidence for centurions parading in white could refer to the wearing of fine linen tunics, or perhaps to the colour of crests and *pteruges* (fabric-strip defences for the upper arms, abdomen and thighs). Otherwise, the suggestion that centurions normally wore woollen tunics dyed red, and lower ranks wore off-white tunics is plausible. In terms of armour and weaponry, the imperial legionary carried the familiar trio of *gladius*, *pilum* and *scutum*. During the Augustan period, the shield was modified, eventually becoming a curved rectangular board.

Regarding the sword, some Roman troops continued to employ the *gladius Hispaniensis* until about 20 BC (a notable example comes from Berry-Bouy in France), but it was quickly superseded in Augustus' reign by the Mainz/Fulham-type *gladius* (named after prominent find-spots). This sword was a clear development of the *gladius Hispanienis*, but had a shorter and broader, waisted blade

Reconstruction of an oval *clipeus*, the typical flat shield carried by auxiliary infantrymen and cavalrymen alike). An oval *clipeus* was only slightly lighter than a cylindrical *scutum*, its greater height compensating for the latter's greater width. (Fields-Carré Collection)

'Sword of Tiberius'. Found in the Rhine at Mainz, this is another example of the long-pointed 'Mainz'-type *gladius*. So-called because its scabbard bears a relief of Tiberius receiving Germanicus in AD 17 on his 'heroic' return to Rome following his Germanic campaigns. (The Trustees of the British Museum)

(*c*.40–56cm long, up to 8cm across the shoulders) with a notably long tapering point. Examples weigh between 1.2kg and 1.6kg. The metal scabbards of these swords could be tinned or silvered and finely embossed with various motifs, often derived from Augustan propaganda.

The short Pompeii-type *gladius* was introduced during the mid-1st century AD. It was a sword quite different from the Spanish and Mainz/Fulham *gladii* with its parallel edged blade and short triangular point (*c*.42–55cm long, 5–6cm wide), but legionaries clearly maintained the same cut-and-thrust fighting technique. This sword weighed about 1kg. The fine embossed scabbard of the Mainz/Fulham *gladius* gave way to a wood and leather construction with metal binding and chape, to which punched, engraved or embossed decoration was applied. All Roman swords in this period were attached to the belt or baldric via a four-ring suspension system.

The majority of legionaries in the imperial period fought in heavy body armour, though some troops fought without armour at all. Caesar made use of such legionaries to fight as *antesignani*, that is lightly equipped legionaries (*expediti*) who probably skirmished with light missiles in front of the standards of the main battleline or reinforced the cavalry. A relief from the legionary headquarters building (principia) at Mainz shows two legionaries fighting in close order, equipped with *scuta* and *pila*, but apparently without body armour, suggesting that even the 'heavy' legionaries could fight *expediti*.

Two other reliefs from Mainz reveal the regular armours employed by legionaries. In one scene, a *legionarius* marching behind a *signifer* wears a cuirass of *lorica segmentata* (the term is modern), an articulated armour of iron plates and hoops. The cuirass offered substantial protection, especially to the shoulders and upper back, but terminated at the hips, leaving the abdomen and upper legs exposed. It is probable that some kind of padded garment was worn underneath to absorb the impact of blows, protect the skin from chafing and ensure that the armour was properly settled, so that the chest and other plates lined up correctly. Reconstructions of this armour suggest it weighed about 9kg. Another relief from Mainz portrays a centurion (his sword is worn on the left) in what at first sight appears to be a tunic. However, the splits at the arms and thighs indicate that this was a ring mail shirt (*lorica hamata*), the splits necessary to facilitate movement. On many such monuments the actual details of the rings were originally painted in. Mail was probably the armour most widely used by the Romans. In the imperial period shirts were sleeveless or short-sleeved and could extend far down the thighs, though lengths varied. Most legionaries wore shirts with a doubling over the shoulders of leather faced with mail, modelled after the shoulder guards of the Greek linen cuirass. Such shirts weighed 9–15kg, depending on the length and the number of rings (at least 30,000). Other shirts had full shoulder capes and might weigh 16kg. Occasionally shirts were faced with fine scales. Scale was another common armour (*lorica squamata*), being cheaper and easier to produce than mail but inferior in defensive qualities and flexibility.

Such shirts were worn over an arming doublet known as a *thoracomachus*, probably made of linen stuffed with wool. This helped absorb the shock of blows and prevented the metal of the armour being driven into the body (Anonymous, *De Rebus Bellicis*, 15).

ROMAN PATTERN-WELDED SWORDS, 3RD CENTURY AD
It has been suggested that the sword became a secondary weapon in the 3rd century, legionaries relying on a thrusting spear until it shattered in combat and only using the sword as a reserve weapon. This is nonsense and the development of beautiful pattern-welded swords by Roman smiths in the late 2nd century AD indicates the continuing primacy of the *gladius* as the legionary's close-quarter weapon. Pattern-welded blades were formed around a core of multiple iron bars with differing carbon contents to produce different tones, twisted into a screw then hammered and folded countless times, providing a strong yet flexible core to which hard cutting edges were welded. The process meant that every sword was unique, while the mysteries of its production and the presence of *orichalcum* inlays of divine figures suggest a closer relationship with the sword, perhaps even a degree of veneration. The top three swords have also been forged with fullers, grooves running the length of the blade, imparting extra strength, while the hilt detail illustrates the typical Roman form, here decorated with silver bands after an example from Illerup in Denmark. (© Angus McBride, Osprey Publishing)

Full-size example of an auxiliary trooper at the Corinium Museum, Cirencester. A characteristic feature of imperial cavalry helmets is the extension of the cheek-pieces to cover the ears, commonly shaped as simulated ears. The model is also wearing a Gallic-type mail shirt with shoulder-cape. Note the *spatha* hangs at the right hip. (Fields-Carré Collection)

Pteruges, overlapping linen or leather strip defences for the upper legs and arms, were often attached to such garments, but could not prevent serious injuries to the limbs to which Roman soldiers were particularly susceptible (e.g. Caesar, *Bellum Gallicum*, 5.35). Greaves were regularly worn by centurions but not by lower ranks until the end of the 1st century AD and perhaps only against particular opponents such as the Dacians. Articulated arm defences (*manicae*) were certainly employed by gladiators in this period (Tacitus, *Annals*, 3.43–46, for the crupellarii fighting for Sacrovir in AD 21), but might not have come into widespread military use until the reign of Domitian (AD 81–96).

Legionaries wore a number of different types of helmet. At the beginning of the early Roman Empire bronze, occasionally iron, Montefortino helmets were common, the traditional legionary helmet since the 4th century BC. These had a single bowl with a very slight rear peak, and cheek pieces that covered the ears and protected the sides of the face. Later versions of the helmet, including the so-called Coolus-type, were in use until the late 1st century AD, and had substantial neck guards and cheek pieces with flanges to protect the throat and cut-aways to facilitate hearing.

Early in the Augustan period, perhaps even during Caesar's conquest of Gaul, Roman smiths began to adapt Gallic Port and Agen-type iron helmets for legionary use. These so-called Imperial Gallic helmets were high-quality, single bowled pieces, with embossed 'eyebrows' at the front of the bowl and ridges at the nape of the neck to break the force of downward sword blows. The Romans added a substantial neck guard (really a rear peak), a brow peak, increased the size and curvature of the cheek pieces and also added throat flanges. Towards the middle of the 1st century AD a variant of this helmet was produced in Italian workshops, using both iron and bronze (a progression from the Italic Montefortino-type), and known as the Imperial Italic type.

Legionary helmets were substantial pieces with bowls 1.5–2mm thick, weighing about 2–2.3kg. Helmets and cheek pieces were lined with woollen felt, and the fitting of some helmets may have allowed an air space between the skull and the bowl to dissipate the shock of blows. Montefortino-type helmets had broad cheek pieces that covered the ears, but the new Imperial Gallic helmets were soon made to incorporate ear holes. However, unless a soldier had a helmet specially made or adapted, the cheek pieces might still partially cover his ears. While cheek pieces gave good protection to the sides of the face they could obscure peripheral vision, and the exposed centre of the face made a tempting target for opponents. The Batavian and Tungrian auxiliaries fighting at Mons Graupius stabbed at the faces of their British opponents (Tacitus, *Agricola*, 36) and Caesar records how the centurion Crastinus was killed at Pharsalus by a sword thrust to the mouth (Caesar, *Bellum Civilia*, 3.99).

Late Roman parade helmet.
(AKG London)

Monumentul de la Adamklissi, dedicated to Mars Ultor, the Avenger, was probably the handiwork of soldiers. This is metope I, which depicts a cavalryman charging into battle, his *lancea* held horizontally in a relaxed position. The trooper wears a short-sleeved mail-shirt and carries a hexagonal *clipeus* but, curiously, is bareheaded. (Fields-Carré Collection)

LIMBS OF THE ROMAN ARMY: AUXILIARIES

As part of the military reforms of Augustus, the *auxilia* were completely reorganized and given regular status. Trained to the same standards of discipline as the legions, auxiliary soldiers were now long-service professionals like the legionaries and served in units that were equally permanent. Drawn from a wide range of warlike peoples throughout the provinces, especially on the fringes of the empire, they were *peregrini* (non-citizens) and would receive Roman citizenship on completion of their 25 years' service. Their senior officers, in contrast, were Roman citizens.

The imperial *auxilia* had the tasks of patrolling, containing raids, tax collecting, and the multitudinous duties of frontier troops – the legions were stationed within the frontiers, both to act as a strategic reserve and to intimidate potentially rebellious indigenous 'friendlies'. The *cohortes equitatae* (mixed cohorts) of the *auxilia*, which became increasingly common as the 1st century AD progressed, encapsulate this flexibility very well. As a combination of foot and horse in a ratio of about 4:1, they were especially suited to garrison and local policing activities, and could hold their own in small-scale warfare.

Drawn from peoples nurtured in the saddle, the cavalry of the *auxilia* continued to provide a fighting arm in which the Romans themselves were not so adept. The Romans therefore preferred to recruit former enemies such as the Gauls, Germans, Celtiberians and Thracians, all of whom were renowned for their equestrian skills. The Gauls were considered to be the most skilful riders and the three Gallic provinces provided some 44.5 per cent of the troopers serving in the cavalry of the *auxilia* during the Flavian period, AD 69–96. It has been estimated that in the time of Augustus the army had a total strength of some 300,000 men, of which around 30,000 were cavalry. By the turn of the 2nd century AD these figures had risen to approximately 385,000 and 65,000 respectively.

Following changes in the Republican command structure, the Imperial cavalry *alae* are thought to have consisted of 16 *turmae*, each with 30 troopers commanded by a *decurio* and his second-in-command the *duplicarius*, if they were *quingenaria* (16 × 32 = 512), or if *milliaria* 24 *turmae* (24 × 32 = 768). Drawn from the equestrian order, cavalry commanders were ranked as *praefectus alae* (*ala quingenaria*, *ala milliaria*). These were men who had already served as prefects of auxiliary *cohortes* (*praefectus cohortis*) and either as tribunes in legions (*tribuni angusticlavii*) or tribunes of *cohortes milliariae*. By the mid 2nd century AD there were some 90 posts as *praefectus alae*, and the commands of the *alae milliariae* devolved on a select group of about ten, consisting of the pick of the men who had already commanded *alae quingenariae*.

The organization of the *cohortes equitatae* is less clear, but according to the Roman engineer Hyginus (*De muntionibus castrorum*, 27), consisted of six centuries of 80 men, four *turmae* of 30 troopers if *cohors equitata quingenaria* as well as the *decurio* and the *duplicarius* (6 × 80 + 4 × 32 = 608); or ten centuries of 80 men, eight *turmae* of 30 troopers and both the *decurio* and *duplicarius* if *cohors equitata milliaria* (10 × 80 + 8 × 32 = 1,056). The pride of the Roman cavalry was obviously the horsemen of the *alae*, but more numerous were the horsemen of the *cohortes equitatae*. Having served for some time as infantrymen before being upgraded and trained as cavalrymen, these troopers were not as highly paid, or as well mounted as those of the *alae*, but they performed much of the day-to-day patrolling, policing and escort duties. The *alae* would spend times of peace on manoeuvres and training, and should hostilities break out they were deployed as a highly mobile strike force, supplemented, if the need arose, by the *cohortes equitatae*. In battle, according to the soldier-scholar Arrian, the mounted contingents of several cohorts were taken from their parent units and massed to form one composite force, roughly equivalent in size to an *ala*.

Like legions, auxiliary units had numbers and names. Those units originally raised in the western provinces generally took their names from a tribe or region, those in the east from a city. For example, there were five cohorts raised in Gaul, cohors I–V Gallorum. Equally, many auxiliary units had titles incorporating the name of an emperor, such as Augusta, Flavia, Ulpia or Aelia.

Again, like the names of legions, auxiliary names became interlinked with the unit's history, so emphasizing its distinct identity. *Ala Gallorum et Thracum Classiana invicta bis torquata civium Romanorum* was raised in support of Rome during the Gallic revolt of

Tiberius' reign (AD 21). It took the title *Classiana* from the name of its first commander, the Gallic nobleman Classicianus. The later addition of a contingent of Thracians gave it *et Thracum*. It gained the title *invicta* (invincible), and the honour of a *torque* twice (*bis torquata*), and the premature grant of citizenship to all of its serving men, *civium Romanorum* (of Roman citizens), through its achievements in battle. Henceforth the unit itself employed the designation c(ivium) R(omanorum), but all future recruits remained non-citizens until honourably discharged – citizenship went only to those serving at the moment of the battle honour. The first *torque* was possibly gained during the reigns of the Flavians (r. 69–96), and the second either during the reign of Trajan (r. 98–117) or that of Hadrian (r. 117–138), on both occasions in Britain.

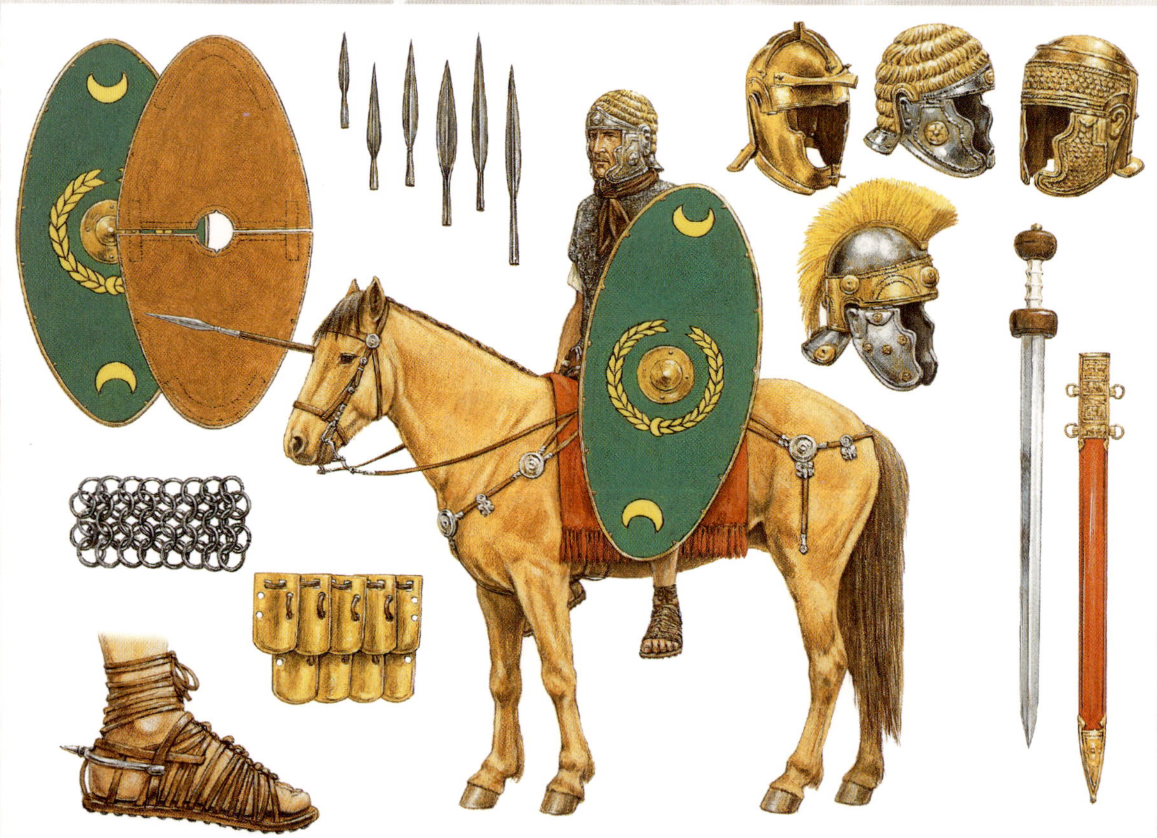

AUXILIARY TROOPER AND EQUIPMENT
This mounted trooper, fully armed and equipped for battle, represents a cavalryman from the time of Trajan's Dacian wars. Though manufactured in the early part of the 1st century AD, his helmet is of auxiliary cavalry type 'A', while his short-sleeved mail shirt is based on those worn by troopers on Trajan's Column. In addition he has a woollen scarf (*focale*) tied around his neck to prevent chafing from the mail shirt. Around him we see details of his equipment and armour, plus four helmet types seen in the 1st century BC. (© Adam Hook, Osprey Publishing)

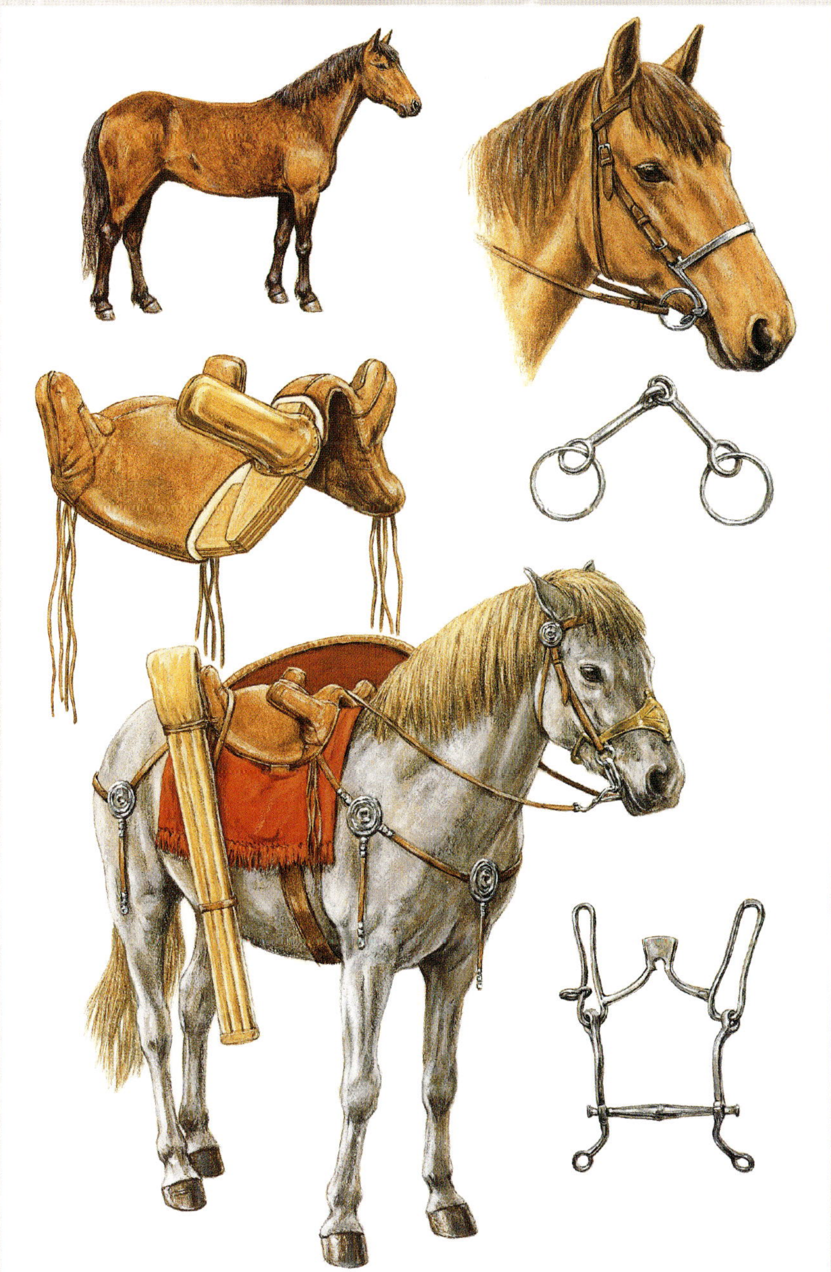

CAVALRY MOUNT AND EQUIPMENT, 1ST–2ND CENTURY AD

Horses of 14 to 15 hands would have been quite adequate for military purposes. The lack of stirrups tended to limit the desirable size of mounts, even if larger animals were available; riders had to vault into the saddle from the ground, clearing the tall saddle-horns. The metalwork on the right shows the Roman curb bit (bottom right) and the iron snaffle bit. (© Adam Hook, Osprey Publishing)

The arrival of the Roxolani Sarmatians along the Danube in the second half of the 1st century brought Rome face to face with a new type of horsemen. These were *cataphractarii*, first mentioned by Tacitus, heavily armoured horsemen wearing 'iron plating or toughened leather' (*Histories*, 1.79). Rome's response was, of course, to begin employing them. Although some units may have existed earlier, Hadrian formed the first regular unit of *cataphractarii*, *ala I Gallorum et Pannoniorum catafractaria* from Sarmatian settlers in Gaul and Pannonia.

Cataphractarii were armed with a heavy spear (Greek *kontos*, Latin *contus*) some 3.65m in length and held two-handed without a shield. It was a weapon for shock action, being driven home with the full thrust of the body behind it. The greater weight of men, horse, and equipment meant their charge was considered to be more powerful than that of ordinary cavalry. As the weight factor prevented *cataphractarii* from charging at anything much faster than a trot, a slow but steady advance by a dense armoured mass meant their impact was more psychological than physical.

At the other end of the scale, imperial Rome employed Numidians from Africa. These horsemen, who as we have seen had wreaked such havoc in the armies of Rome during the war with Hannibal, were completely un-armoured and rode bareback without even a saddlecloth or a bridle. If a harness was used it was of the simplest type, a rope around the neck and another noosed around the jaw to make a primitive bridle. But sometimes they dispensed even with this, the rider guiding his mount by tapping its neck with the butt of a spear. The weakness of this method was that the rider had no way to enforce his wishes. It might do well enough for skirmishing at a distance, but not for persuading a mount to charge into contact. Yet the Numidians' speed and agility allowed them to charge and withdraw before their opponents could react.

THE COMPOSITE BOW

The composite bow combined layers of sinew, wood and horn to create a weapon with a balance of strength under tensile and compressive forces that enabled an efficient transfer of the potential energy stored in the fully drawn bow. Its design took full advantage of the mechanical properties of the materials used in its construction. Sinew has great tensile strength, while horn has compressive strength. When released, the horn belly acts like a coil, returning instantly to its original position. Sinew, on the other hand, naturally contracts after being stretched, which is exactly what happens to the convex back of the bow as it snaps back to resume its original shape. This method of construction and the materials employed thus allows the bow to impart a greater degree of force to the arrow when fired, compared with the wooden self-bow of the same draw weight.

Rome also employed horse archers – the epithet *sagittariorum* in the title of a cavalry unit denoted the men as such – specially drawn from peoples renowned for their skill in this field. Mounted on swift, nimble horses, their prime tactical role was to demoralize and disorganize the enemy by inflicting losses from a distance. Nevertheless, horse archers were probably equipped with shafted weapons as well as the formidable composite bow.

Roman auxiliary cavalrymen carried a *clipeus* (flat shield), either oval or hexagonal in shape. To be light enough to be held continually in battle, shield-boards were usually constructed of double or triple thickness plywood made up of thin strips of birch or plane wood held together with glue. The middle layer was laid at right angles to the front and back layers. Covered with linen and rawhide on both sides, they were edged with copper-alloy binding and had a central iron or copper-alloy boss (*umbo*) covering a horizontal handgrip and wide enough to clear the fist of the bearer. When not in use the shield was carried obliquely against the horse's flank, hung from the two side-horns of the saddle and sometimes under the saddlecloth. It was protected by a leather shield-cover, which was tightened round the rim of the shield by a drawstring.

In terms of spears, the cavalry generally used a *lancea* (light spear) approximately 1.8m long. It was suitable for throwing or thrusting over-arm as shown in the figured tombstones of the period. Even though such funerary carvings usually depict troopers either carrying two *lancae*, or *calones* (grooms) behind them holding spares, Josephus (*Bellum Judaicum*, 3.96) claims that Vespasian's eastern cavalry carried a quiver containing three or more darts with points as large as light spears. He did not say specifically where the quiver was positioned, but presumably it was attached to the saddle. Arrian (*Tactica*, 40.10–11) confirms this in his description of the cavalry exercises in which horsemen were expected to throw as many as 15, or, in exceptional cases 20 light spears, in one run.

For swords, the cavalry used a *spatha* (a long, narrow, double-edged broadsword), with a blade length of 64.5–91.5cm and width of 4–6cm. The middle section of the blade was virtually parallel-edged, but tapered into a rounded point. It was intended primarily as a slashing weapon for use on horseback, though the point could also be used.

The *spatha* was worn on the right side of the body, as numerous cavalry tombstones show, suspended from a waist belt or baldric whose length could be adjusted by a row of metal buttons. From the 2nd century onwards, however, the *spatha* started to be worn on the left side, although not exclusively so.

ROMAN IMPERIAL TACTICS

THE TRADITION OF THE REPUBLIC had been that a senator should be prepared to serve the state in whatever capacity it demanded, and be proficient in his role. A practical people, the Romans believed that the man chosen by the competent authority would be up to the task in hand. In the Republic that authority had been the electorate, under the Principate it would be the Emperor. In other words, there was no training for the job, thus the man sent to command an army would have to learn the skills himself, from the leisure of reading books or the harder lesson of the battlefield.

It is interesting that handbooks on military tactics and the art of generalship continued to be written under the emperors, notably by Onasander (under Claudius), Frontinus (under Domitian), Aelian Tacticus (under Trajan), Arrian (under Hadrian) and Polyaenus (under Antonius Pius). All these authors claimed to be writing with a principal purpose, namely to elucidate military matters for the benefit of army commanders, and even the Emperor himself. Thus Frontinus, in the prologue of the *Strategemata*, explains his intentions:

> For in this way army commanders will be equipped with examples of good planning and foresight, and this will develop their own ability to think out and carry into effect similar operations. An added benefit will be the commander will not be worried about the outcome of his own stratagem when he compares it with innovations already tested in practice.
>
> (Frontinus, *Strategemata*, 1 praefatio)

As under the Republic, the imperial emperors saw no need to establish a system to train future commanders. On the contrary, it was still believed that by using handbooks and taking advice, a man of average ability could direct a Roman Army.

Traditionally the Romans had an organized but uncomplicated approach to tactics. The principles were: the use of cavalry for flank attacks and encirclement; the placing of a force in reserve; the deployment of a battleline that could maintain contact, readiness to counterattack and flexibility in the face of unexpected enemy manoeuvres. As the disposition of forces and the tactical placing of reserves were vital elements of generalship, the Roman commander needed to be in a position from where he could see the entire battle. The underlying rationale of this style of generalship is well expressed by Onasander when he says the general 'can aid his army far less by fighting than he can harm it if he should be killed, since the knowledge of a general is far more important than his physical strength' (*Stratêgikos*, 33.1). To have the greatest influence on the battle the general should stay close to, but behind his fighting line, directing and encouraging his men from this relatively safe position.

This was certainly what Antonius Primus did at Second Cremona (AD 69). In bright moonlight the Flavian commander rode around urging his men on, 'some by taunts and

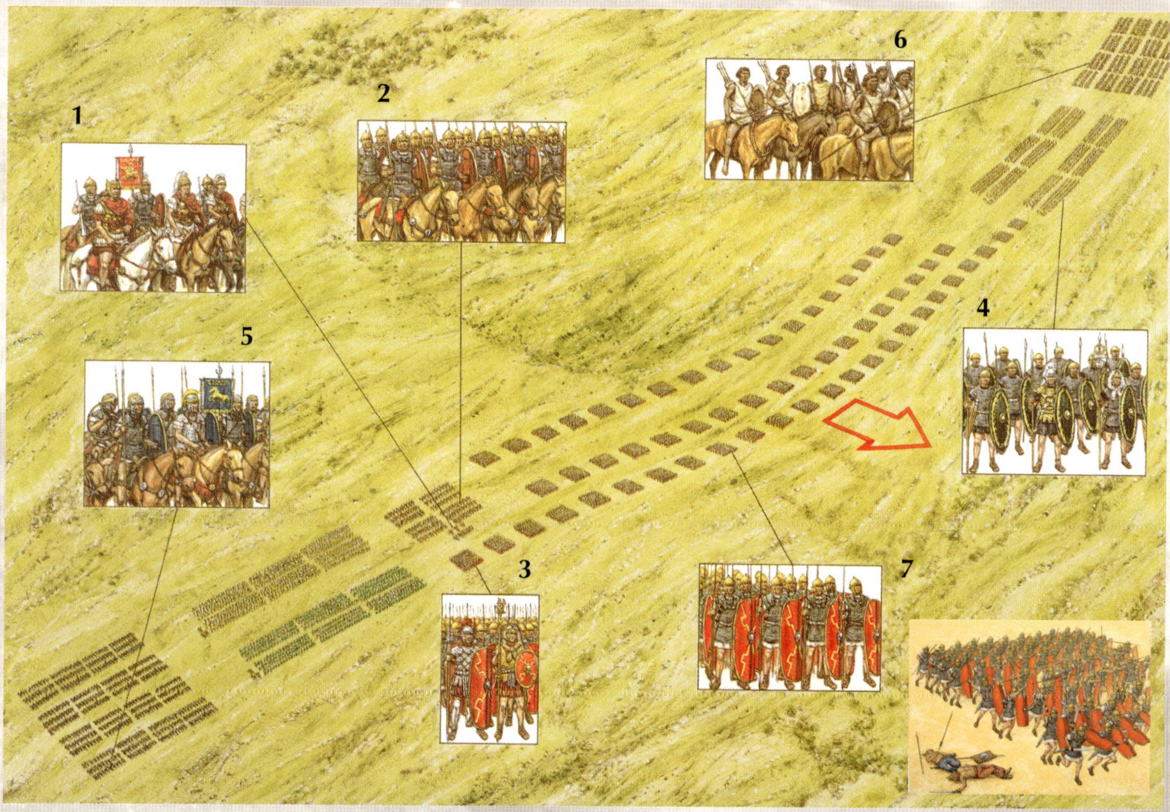

LEGIONARY FORMATION

This reconstruction is based on the formation with which legio III Augusta and auxiliaries defeated the African rebel Tacfarinas in AD 17. Here we see a legion (centre) of 60 centuries and ten cohorts drawn up in triplex acies using a 4-3-3 arrangement of cohorts. The legate (legion commander), his vexillum standard and his six tribunes are positioned behind the first cohort, with trumpeters to sound tactical signals (inset 1). The 120 legionary cavalry behind him (inset 2) serve both as a bodyguard and a reserve. We can guess that the legion's aquilifer (standard-bearer) and its *primus pilus* – the senior centurion of the first cohort, a soldier of great prestige and authority – would be stationed in the front rank of that cohort (inset 3).

The legion is supported on each flank by two cohorts of auxiliary light infantry, with *c*.480 soldiers per cohort – we have placed the auxiliary centurions and standard-bearers of the centuries in their front ranks (inset 4). On each flank an ala of auxiliary cavalry, *c*.500 strong in 16 turmae or troops, completes the battle array. Inset 5 shows the command group of a European unit, Gallic or Thracian, and (inset 6) troopers of a Numidian unit. While the legionaries (inset 7) make a frontal assault, the light infantry will add missile support; the cavalry will attempt to knock out the light troops and cavalry of the enemy army, preventing any envelopment by enemy flanking attacks, and will then swing inwards to assault the enemy main body from the flanks and rear. (© Adam Hook, Osprey Publishing)

appeals to their pride, many by praise and encouragement, all by hope and promises' (Tacitus, *Histories*, 3.24.1). Another renowned Flavian general, Quintus Petilius Cerialis, is depicted during the rebellion of Civilis (AD 70) doing the same thing, which occasioned no small risk.

During his governorship of Cappadocia, Arrian had to repel an invasion of the Alani. Arrian wrote an account of the preparatory dispositions he made for this campaign, the *Ektaxis katà Alanon*. This unique work, in which the author represents himself as the famous Athenian soldier-scholar Xenophon, sets out the commands of the governor as if he were actually giving them. He had two legions, XII Fulminata and XV Apollinaris, and a number of *auxilia* units under his command, in all some 20,000 men. Arrian himself took charge of the dispositions and recognized the need for personal, hands-on leadership:

> The commander of the entire army, Xenophon [i.e. Arrian], should lead from a position well in front of the infantry standards; he should visit all the ranks and examine how they have been drawn up; he should bring order to those who are in disarray and praise those who are properly drawn up.
>
> (Arrian, *Ektaxis katà Alanon*, 10)

Trajan's Column is outstanding, not only for its size, but also in the idea of recording in detail the progress of an imperial campaign. Naturally, throughout the story the emperor has a dominant position, not only in artistic portrayal, but also in the frequency of his appearance. (Fields-Carré Collection)

To carry out his orders, Arrian could look to the legionary legate, the military tribunes, centurions and *decuriones*. Nonetheless, it is interesting to note that the tactics advocated by Arrian are safe and simple, competent rather than brilliant.

Surprising as it may seem, there is no history of the imperial Roman Army by any ancient author and little detailed examination of military practices. Amongst the Roman historians, Tacitus has some detached references to the arms and equipment of legionaries and auxiliaries, and to formations adopted by such generals as Domitius Corbulo and Julius Agricola. It is indeed curious that Joseph ben Matthias, better known to history as Josephus (Flavius Iosephus), wrote the best descriptions of the army in war and peace. An aristocratic priest chosen by the Sanhedrin, the Jewish council of state, to defend Galilee in the revolt of AD 66 against Rome, Josephus witnessed first-hand the legions of Vespasian and his son Titus in action against his Jewish countrymen. Like Polybius before him, as a defeated foreigner Josephus was very much interested in seeking the primary factors that contributed to the superiority of Roman arms.

ROMAN TACTICAL DOCTRINE AND PRACTICE

Much about imperial Roman Army tactics remains similar to the tactical arrangements already discussed for the late Republican army, but with necessary adaptations to suit changing environs and enemies. What hadn't changed at all was the grit required to deliver those tactics. 'It would not be far from the truth to call their drills bloodless battle, their battles bloody drills' (Josephus, *Bellum Judaicum*, 3.75), so runs the most celebrated line of Josephus. The patriot-turned-partisan, writing in the 1st century AD, presents a rather idealized view of the Roman Army's efficiency, but he is not far wrong when he puts the revolt's failure down to the effectiveness of the arduous training given to the legions. The imperial legionary had to be both physically and mentally stronger than his 'barbarian' adversary. As Josephus points out, 'military exercises give the Roman soldiers not only tough bodies but determined spirits too' (*Bellum Judaicum*, 3.102).

Although referring to a battle fought between the armies of Otho and Vitellius, rivals for the imperial purple, Tacitus' description of First Cremona (AD 69) is well worth a look at:

> 42. At this moment, the enemy [i.e. the Vitellians] advanced with unbroken ranks. In fighting qualities and numbers he had the advantage. As for the Othonians, scattered, outnumbered and weary as they were, they went into action gallantly. Indeed, as the battle was fought over a wide area thickly planted with a maze of vines and vine-props, it presented a variety of aspects. The two sides made contact at long and short range, in loose or compact formation. On the high road, Vitellians and Othonians fought hand-to-hand, throwing the weight of their bodies and shield-bosses [*umbonis*] against each other. The usual discharge of *pila* was scrapped, and swords [*gladii*] and axes [*secures*] used to pierce helmets and armour. Knowing each other [i.e. the praetorians and legio I Italica] and watched by their comrades, they fought the fight that was to settle the whole campaign.
>
> 43. As it turned out, two legions made contact in open country between the Padus [Po] and the road [Via Postumia]. They were Vitellian legio XXI Fulminata, long known and famous, and on the Othonian side legio I Adiutrix, which had never fought before, but was in high spirits and avid of distinction in its first action. Legio I Adiutrix overran the front ranks of legio XXI Fulminata, and carried off their eagle (*aquila*). Smarting under this humiliation, the latter got their own back by charging legio I Adiutrix, who lost their legate, Orfidius Benignus, and a great number of standards [*signa*] and flags [*vexilla*]. In another part of the field, legio V [Alaudae] punished legio XIII [Gemina], while the

vexillatio from legio XIIII [Gemina Martia Victrix] was outnumbered and rolled up. Long after the Othonian commanders had fled, Caecina and Valens [i.e. the Vitellian commanders] were still bringing up reinforcements to strengthen their men. Then, at the eleventh hour, came the Batavi [*cohortes*], after routing the force of gladiators. These had crossed the Padus in their ships only to be done to death in the very water by the cohortes confronting them. As a sequel to this success, the Batavi now delivered their onslaught on the Othonian flank.

(Tacitus, *Histories*, 2.42–43)

PRIOR CENTURY IN BATTLE, 1ST CENTURY AD
Here we see a *prior* (front) century formed in four ranks of 20, with the centurion, identified by his transverse helmet crest, positioned on the extreme right of front rank. The *signifer* is at the centre of the formation to prevent him from being killed during the first clash and stop the standard from falling into enemy hands. The inset reveals the regular 'chessboard' formation of the legionaries. (© Angus McBride, Osprey Publishing)

When imperial Roman armies were pitted against each other we might expect sophisticated tactics skilfully applied. But Tacitus' brief but dramatic account tells us this was far from the case. Roman tactics were basically aggressive, with the doctrine of the offensive a dominant feature. This did not make the Romans invincible – they did suffer some terrible reverses – but they believed that defeat in one battle did not mean defeat in war.

For the first century of the Principate, we possess no order of battle with a detailed description of the dispositions adopted, but Tacitus' account of Domitius Corbulo's campaigns against Parthia suggests that such matters on the field of battle were very much the same in Caesar's day. In one of his encounters with the Parthian king Tiridates in AD 58, Domitius Corbulo placed the *auxilia* on the flanks and legio VI Ferrata, reinforced with 3,000 men from III Gallica to give the impression of strength, in the centre (Tacitus, *Annales*, 13.38.6).

For the legion, a favourite battle formation would likely be the venerable triple line of cohorts, the *triplex acies*. Some caution is required here, however. The *triplex acies* is absent from the battle descriptions of the early Empire but the sources for the imperial period are admittedly usually vague when it comes to the fine details of deployment in battle. It is entirely possible that the *triplex acies* gradually fell out of general use, for it was best suited to large legionary armies, and not all battles were on the same scale as Pharsalus for example. One might assume that the formation was still widely employed

Formed in 1972, the Ermine Street Guard is, in every sense of the meaning, the mother of all Roman experimental history groups. Best known for their portrayal of legio XX Valeria Victrix, the members of the Guard have contributed enormously to our knowledge of Roman military equipment. Here the Guard are putting on an educational display for the general public. (Ancient Art and Architecture)

during the Augustan conquests, i.e. while the generals of Augustus were veterans of the civil wars in which the *triplex acies* had played such a decisive role.

The very flexibility of the cohort structure, with its sub-divisions of *centuriae* and *contubernia*, would allow almost any variation of line and composition. The most basic was the *simplex acies*, the 'simple' or single line of cohorts. During the late Republic this was often a battleline of necessity, used when an army was too small to deploy into two or more lines, or when faced with a larger and more mobile opponent – for example, Caesar's army at Ruspina in 46 BC. Yet sometimes a large imperial army might have to fight in a *simplex acies*, in order to deploy rapidly and meet a surprise attack.

Regarding the two-line *duplex acies*, we know that this formation was used in earlier times both by and against Caesar. At Ruspina, although Caesar was initially deployed in a *simplex acies*, he converted this into a *duplex acies* when surrounded by the forces of Labienus. The *duplex acies* was also employed against him by a Pompeian general during the final stage of the Ilerda campaign (49 BC) in Spain. Lucius Afranius confronted Caesar with five legions in *duplex acies*, each legion presumably in a 5-5 formation of cohorts – 25 cohorts in each of the two battlelines. Afranius also had a third reserve line of Spanish auxiliary cohorts, but this was presumably some distance behind the legionary formation; Caesar clearly did not consider Afranius' army as being drawn up in a triple battleline. If the third line of auxiliaries was a reserve – and presumably a static one, whereas the legionary formation was to be mobile – then the second line of legionary cohorts must have been intended to support, reinforce and, if necessary, to relieve/replace the first line. The second line could also turn about or wheel to face an enemy coming at the rear or flanks, and so fight as a *simplex acies*.

The late 4th or early 5th century AD writer Vegetius applies the *duplex acies* 5-5 formation of cohorts to his description of the *legio antiqua* – 'the ancient legion'. It has been suggested that this element of his problematical description was derived from an early imperial source and therefore represents the typical battle array of the imperial legions. In Vegetius' *duplex acies*, the more powerful first cohort is positioned on the right of the first line. The fifth cohort holds the left, and accordingly has stronger soldiers than cohorts two, three and four. The sixth and tenth cohorts hold the right and left of the second line respectively, and also contain the strongest soldiers because of the potential vulnerability of the flanks.

However, the *duplex acies* does not receive ready confirmation in the battle accounts of the first three centuries AD, although it is likely to have remained a tactical option or reality. The fact remains that we are generally much more poorly served by the surviving imperial sources for battle arrays. Tacitus' account of the battle of Mons Graupius (AD 84) seems fairly clear: a *simplex acies* of auxiliary cohorts, and the legions held back in reserve (*Agricola*, 35). From Tacitus' accounts of the two battles of

Cremona during the civil war of AD 69, we are again left with the impression of the opposing armies in *simplex acies*, though the use of reserves is mentioned at the first battle (*Histories*, 2.43).

Tacitus goes into some detail about the marching order of Germanicus' army as it proceeded to the battle of Idistaviso (AD 16). The marching column (*agmen*) was arranged so that the legions, praetorian cohorts and auxiliary units could simply turn or wheel into battleline; however, the brief description of the battle itself does not suggest anything other than a *simplex acies*. Admittedly, the descriptions of all the above battles are essentially so vague about cohort deployment that, for all we can tell, the cohorts of Germanicus' legions might have been arranged in more than one line.

When the soldier-emperor Maximinus marched into rebellious Italy in AD 238, he advanced on the city of Emona in an *agmen quadratum*. This was a hollow square or rectangular marching formation, with the baggage protected in the centre; but such marching formations were also designed to deploy readily into battlelines. Maximinus' formation was a shallow rectangle: legionary infantry formed the front; Maximinus was at the rear with the praetorians and other guard units; and the sides were formed by cavalry and light troops, including *cataphracts* and horse archers. Maximinus' *agmen quadratum*, like all such formations, was therefore effectively a *duplex acies* with cavalry wings; however, it clearly was not a *duplex acies* based on 5-5 arrangements of legionary cohorts.

In Arrian's description of the battleline that he drew up against the migrating Alani (AD 135), he tells us that the legionaries were formed in eight tight ranks. Yet the legionaries had marched to the battlefield four abreast, and when in battle formation the leading four ranks were armed with *pila* while the rear four ranks had *lanceae* or light javelins. Perhaps we have here the normal components of a legionary *duplex acies*, but closed up immediately one behind the other so as to form a strong single line?

The cohort was to remain the basic tactical unit and the century the basic administrative unit. In his description of the defeat of Boudicca at Mancetter (AD 61), Cassius Dio picks out the contrast between the contending sides:

> Thereupon the armies approached each other, the barbarians with much shouting, mingled with menacing battle songs, but the Romans silently and in order until they came within a javelin [*akóntion* in Dio's Greek] throw of the enemy. Then, while their foes were still advancing against them at a walk, the Romans rushed forward at a signal and charged at full speed, and when the clash came, easily broke through the opposing ranks.
>
> (Cassius Dio, *The Roman History*, 62.12.1–2)

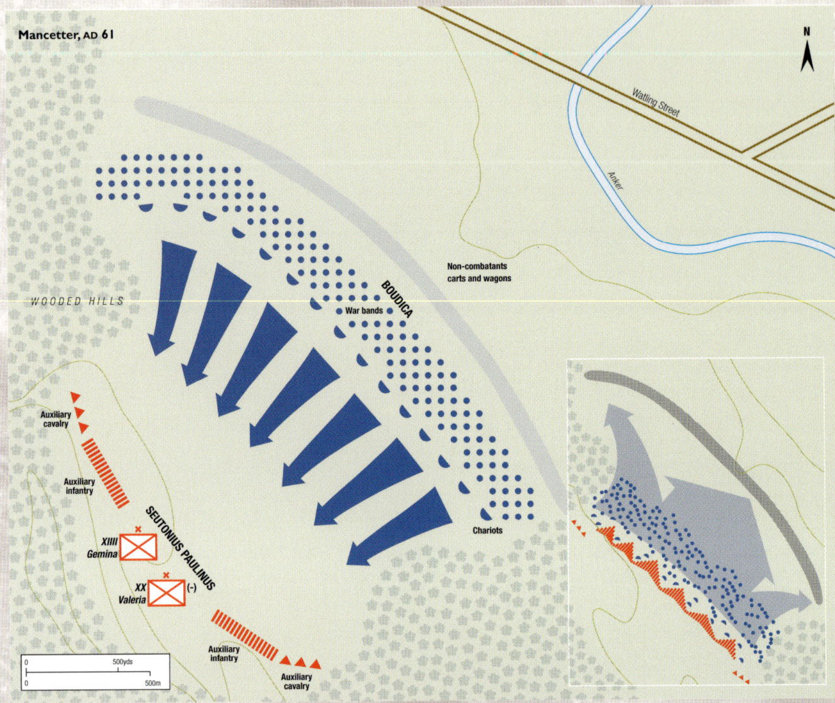

MANCETTER, AD 61

In AD 60 Prasutagus, the client king of the Iceni, died leaving half his possessions to the Emperor. He had hoped this would protect his kingdom and family, but the Romans decided otherwise and incorporated his kingdom, which covered large parts of today's East Anglia, into the province. When his queen Boudicca protested, she was flogged and her daughters raped. Boudicca raised the Iceni in revolt, and they were quickly joined by their neighbours the Trinovantes, a tribe that inhabited parts of today's Suffolk and Essex. The underlying cause of the revolt was the harsh and oppressive Roman occupation and administration of Britain: licentious soldiers, voracious tax collectors and 'noble savages' are commonplace themes in Tacitus, but the commonplace is often true.

Silently executed, the Roman advance was a slow, steady affair, culminating in a close-range barrage of *pila* and an explosive charge of armoured men. The enemy often gave way very quickly. In AD 14, for example, Germanicus led XXI Rapax in an assault, which swiftly scattered the Germans in a single, decisive charge (Tacitus, *Annales*, 1.51.2).

Having discussed the Roman cavalry in the previous chapter, they are a useful point from which we can feel our way deeper into imperial battle tactics. As noted, we do not have a manual describing the drills and tactics of the Roman Army in detail, although Arrian's *Tactica* covers many aspects of cavalry manoeuvres. The sources, however, occasionally provide some details and it appears that the imperial Romans had an organized but uncomplicated approach to tactics, as previously discussed. Cavalry was

LEGIONARY FORMATION

Two legionary centuries, one *prior* (front) and one *posterior* (rear), are depicted in close and open order respectively. The *prior* century is formed in eight ranks and ten files, each legionary occupying a space 3ft wide and probably 3ft deep (0.91m2). The *posterior* century is depicted in open formation, the legionaries drawn up in four ranks and 20 staggered files. (© Adam Hook, Osprey Publishing)

unsuitable for holding ground because of its tendency to advance and retreat rapidly, so it was primarily used for flank attacks and encirclement. For large-scale actions during the early imperial period, the favourite formation had likely remained the *triplex acies*, with auxiliary cohorts stationed on either side of a centre formed by the legions, and *alae* deployed on the wings with an additional force kept in reserve. This was the formation, albeit without the luxury of reserve *alae*, adopted by Suetonius Paulinus against Boudicca (Tacitus, *Annales*, 14.37). Alternatively, the auxiliary infantry could form the first line and be supported by the citizen soldiers, as demonstrated by Julius Agricola at Mons Graupius. Again, cavalry formed the wings, but here they were supported by more *alae* behind the main line. However, if the enemy was overwhelmingly superior in horsemen the Roman cavalry was then either placed behind a dense infantry line or closely supported by strong detachments of auxiliary infantry.

Cavalry formations are somewhat obscure in our sources. In *Tactica* (18.2) Arrian deals largely with the tactics and formation used by a double-*turma* of 64 troopers. On cavalry formations for larger units he recommends, without going into too much detail, that these should be considerably wider than they were deep (*Tactica*, 16–17). Even so, a very deep formation might be employed to break through an enemy line (*Tactica*, 17.3). If one of the wings of an army was anchored on a natural or man-made obstacle, i.e. something that would prevent enemy outflanking manoeuvres, then cavalry would form only on the exposed flank of the infantry.

When the army deployed for battle it was the infantry who were expected to form up in the centre to fight the main action and deliver the crushing blow. However, the success of the cavalry in protecting the flanks and defeating the enemy cavalry could decide the outcome. The cavalry of the Principate employed a mix of skirmish and shock tactics and was effectively trained and equipped for both. Arrian, in his description of the *hippika gymnasia*, devotes four chapters in the *Tactica* (36–39) to the use of the javelin: 'throwing their javelins in as heavy and continuous a rate of fire as possible' (36.3), 'they must carry as many javelins as they can throw … provides nothing more than a continuous rate of fire and incessant din' (37.1).

As horses refuse to collide into an oncoming line of horsemen, encounters between opposing cavalry units would have been very fluid, fast-moving affairs. When combats occurred, it was either because the two lines had opened their files, allowing them to gallop through each other's formation, or they had halted just before contact, at which point individuals would walk their mounts forward to get within weapon's reach of the enemy.

The cavalry of the Principate was highly confident, and, because it was well trained and led, was able to rally more easily after a pursuit or flight and keep its formation. Cavalry were not normally expected to charge well-ordered infantry, as the results would have been mutually catastrophic to the opposing front ranks. Besides, a horse, especially one being ridden, will not in normal circumstances collide with a solid object if it can stop or go around it. Tacitus (*Histories*, 4.33) describes loyal Roman cavalry refusing to charge home on a solid line formed by the rebel Batavian cohorts.

Cavalry, therefore, would employ typical skirmishing tactics, that is, riding up, shooting, wheeling away, and then rallying ready to try again. Arrian describes these tactics against a simulated infantry target in the *hippika gymnasia*: 'Charging straight on, they veer to the flanks, as if turning in a circle. Their veering is to the right, that is, to the spear. Thus nothing stands in the way of the javelin throwing and, in the charge, shields have been set over those throwing' (*Tactica*, 36:5).

Portrait statue of Claudius as Iuppiter, from Lanuvium (Vatican City, Musei Vaticani). In his capacity of censor, this far-sighted emperor not only allowed prominent Gauls into the Senate but also pushed through a resolution to grant civil rights to the provinces as a whole. Taking its cue from the Prima Porta Augustus, this portrayal of Claudius depicts him as a benign cosmocrat. (AKG)

The object of shooting at an enemy infantry unit was to weaken it, so that it would be unable to withstand a mounted charge. Many *alae* under the Principate carried *lancae*, but were still armoured and equipped for close combat. When the battle had been won, the cavalry naturally came to the fore, pursuing and harrying the broken foe.

Looking at the broader Roman Army, the Romans had a consistent and practical approach to the battle array of their armies. The formation employed against the African rebel Tacfarinas in AD 17 was typical: light infantry cohorts were arranged on either side of legio III Augusta, while cavalry formed the wings. This formation was still current in the 3rd century, for example at the battle of Nisibis (AD 217). Sometimes the formation was simply cavalry on the flanks and heavy infantry in the centre, as at Mons Graupius (AD 84), where the fearsome Batavian and Tungrian auxiliary cohorts formed the centre of the line. A variation on this basic theme was to mix light and heavy infantry in the centre; this was achieved by simply placing the light troops in the intervals that separated the sub-units of heavy infantry, as at Nisibis. Light troops, or at least soldiers equipped with long-range missile weapons, could also be posted behind the heavy infantry in order to keep up a continuous 'fire' over the heads of the men in front – as in Arrian's battle against the Alani in AD 135, or by both Roman armies at Issus in AD 194.

As we have seen, intervals in the battlelines were necessary to maintain the cohesion of the units and to prevent them dissolving into a disorganized mass. It was easier for battlelines to advance and maintain formation if this was carried out by small mobile units acting in unison, rather than by a huge and unwieldy continuous line. Intervals allowed light troops to make sallies against the enemy and then retreat to safety. Intervals could also allow cavalry to pass through the ranks of the infantry and make frontal charges against the enemy. At Nisibis, the non-continuous battleline allowed the heavy infantry units (legions, praetorian and auxiliary cohorts) to maintain a strong defensive formation, while the light troops positioned between them were free to make opportunist 'marauding sorties' against the Parthian archers and armoured *cataphracts*, some of whom were mounted on camels.

It might be wondered if an army maintaining gaps in its battleline did not run the risk of the enemy pouring through the gaps and surrounding individual sub-units. However, enemies who charged into an interval might find themselves caught in the 'crossfire' of missiles thrown by light troops, and – because legionaries were trained to fight as individuals, and to turn and meet attacks from all directions – the files on either side of the penetration could simply turn inwards to face the danger and attack its flanks. Also, if the Roman Army was drawn up in more than one battleline, the penetrating enemy would face an immediate counter-charge from the front. Of course, this all depended on the Romans holding their nerve and fighting back in an orderly fashion; if an enemy succeeded in establishing a penetration amongst the ranks, panic could quickly take hold. Even veteran legionaries found it disconcerting to be threatened on their unshielded (right-hand) side. Sometimes the enemy were actually lured into entering the intervals in the battleline, which would close up behind and trap them.

The conventional lines of Roman battle formations were supplemented by a range of more localized tactical formations, with an ancestry stretching back into the Republican period. The *cuneus*, for example, was a dense formation employed for crashing through thin battlelines, or exploiting gaps in formations. The Latin word means 'wedge'; but the formation according to some ancient sources seems to have had four sides – which is why translators normally render *cuneus* as 'square' or 'column'. Tacitus describes legionaries fighting in *cunei* at the first battle of Cremona (AD 69), but there the term is used of those soldiers who could not form a regular extended battleline because of obstacles such as trees, ditches and vineyards in the agricultural landscape (*Histories*, 2.42). Tacitus' use of *cuneus* suggests that it was a term that could broadly be applied to any deep but narrow-fronted formation. Yet Vegetius says that late Roman soldiers nicknamed the *cuneus* the 'pig's head' (*caput porcinum*), and describes it as narrower at the front than it was at the rear. The name suggests that this kind of formation did not taper to a point but, like a pig's snout, had a flat front; one imagines that a literally triangular formation would have its point rapidly blunted by enemy missiles. It has also been suggested that a wedge-like *cuneus* was achieved by two dense columns advancing obliquely at converging angles, so that the heads of the columns would meet, or nearly so, and strike the enemy battleline at the same point. Once the heads struck the enemy line, the two columns could swing forward like gates around this pivot, to fight as a regular line. Of course, such a tactic would also have had a huge psychological impact on those soldiers directly in its path; the *cuneus* would be vulnerable to volleys of missiles and to envelopment, but it would not be surprising if soldiers facing it lost their nerve before the actual physical impact.

Orbis means 'world' or 'circular' but, like the *cuneus*, when used to describe a formation the term was not necessarily literal. The *orbis* was usually formed in emergencies, when a unit or complete army was surrounded by the enemy, and it was clearly designed for all-round defence. Some modern scholars have suggested that the *orbis* was in fact similar to the *agmen quadratum* – such as Crassus' formation at Carrhae; Vegetius refers to the hollow square as the *acies quadrata* – the four-sided battleline (*De Re Militari*, 1.26). From this perspective, it is perhaps easier to imagine the *orbis* as roughly square rather than circular. Whatever its shape, the *orbis* could facilitate successful retreats, or enable soldiers to hold out against superior enemy forces for considerable lengths of time. During Caesar's first invasion of Britain (55 BC), 300 legionaries were

TESTUDO BATTLE

At the battle of Issus (AD 194), the army of the Roman governor of Syria, Pescennius Niger, was formed high up in the Cilician Gates pass. His main battleline was composed of legionaries, but behind them were ranks of javelineers, stone-throwers and archers, so that the front ranks could hold the enemy in close quarters battle, while the missile troops behind fired over their heads. The opposing army of Emperor Septimius Severus (r. 193–97) had a similar array, legionaries at the front and light troops following (perhaps both armies could be described as being in *duplex acies*), but they had to climb and endure bombardment. When they advanced into missile range, the Severan legionaries formed *testudines*, and so eventually came to close quarters with Niger's line, but in the hand-to-hand fighting the Severans had the worst of it – no doubt weary from their advance, and still under a missile barrage from Niger's light troops. Lobbing their weapons downhill, Niger's javelineers and stone-throwers would have had the advantage over the Severan light troops. A timely thunderstorm, driving rain into the faces of Niger's troops, but only onto the backs of the Severans, lessened the resolve of Niger's men, and the cry went up in the Severan army that Jupiter had sent the storm to aid them. Modern readers might scoff at such a reaction, but divine intervention was very real to the Romans. The Severan legionaries redoubled their efforts, and the enemy began to fall back. Then the Severan cavalry – detached earlier in the day to find a way round Niger's position – slammed into the rear of his army, and this decided the battle.

gradually surrounded by some 6,000 Morini warriors; but by forming an *orbis* they managed to fend the Morini off for four hours until Caesar's cavalry came to the rescue, and sustained remarkably few casualties. The formation in which the Romans defeated the Sarmatian Iazyges on the frozen River Danube in the winter of AD 173/174 was presumably some form of *orbis* or *acies quadrata*. Pursued across the river, the Iazyges – all cavalry – halted on the thick ice and waited for the Romans to catch up; they had long experience of negotiating the ice, and expected to defeat the Romans on the treacherous surface. When the Romans got near the Iazyges attacked, some coming straight on, others moving to envelop the Romans' flanks. In response, the Romans formed into a 'compact body that faced the enemy in every direction' (Cassius Dio, *The Roman Histories*, 71:7). This close formation received the charge of the Iazyges with ease (it was presumably not at the speed usual for a charge on land), and soldiers scrambled forward to grab the horses' tack and haul riders from their saddles. The battle dissolved into a mêlée, with men and horses slipping and falling as they struggled on the ice. The Romans – who were apparently not above using even their teeth as they grappled with the enemy – prevailed.

We have already encountered another battle formation, the *testudo* ('tortoise'), the archetypal Roman formation which was widely employed in both sieges and pitched battles to protect soldiers from hails of missiles. The *testudo* consisted of interlocking *scuta* creating a protective wall and roof encapsulating the formation and it could be formed by any number from a mere handful of soldiers to a complete army. The interlocked roof of shields of a large and properly formed *testudo* was supposed to be strong enough for a horse-drawn chariot to be driven across it (Cassius Dio, *The Roman History*, 49.39.3). It was strongest when it was static, but was frequently employed for an advance on enemy fortifications or battlelines. When a *testudo* reached an enemy wall the formation could be sloped down by the ranks kneeling and stooping from the rear, thus forming an assault ramp, or at least reducing the distance to the top of the wall. The rebel Batavian cohorts used this tactic when attacking the legionary fortress of Vetera in AD 69.

The fundamental tactics of the Roman Army were disciplined and coherent, and combined with bravery and hardened souls they made the imperial Roman Army a force perfectly suited to Rome's expanded frontiers. They bolstered tactical skills, however, with other abilities critical to imperial growth.

ENGINEERING

IT IS A TRUISM THAT a Roman soldier's *raison d'être* was to wage war, to kill without being killed. However, it is important to remember that the Roman soldier was a builder as well as a fighter, and the most common and simplest engineering task carried out by him was building roads. These enabled troops to move more swiftly and supplies to be delivered more efficiently, and were especially important additions to newly acquired territories. The units involved often put up milestones, commemorating the Emperor or their legate:

> To the Emperor Caesar, son of the divine Nerva, Nerva Traianus Augustus Germanicus Dacicus [i.e. Trajan] pontifex maximus, tribunicia potestas XV, imperator VI, consul V, pater patriae, having reduced Arabia to form a province, he opened and paved a new road from the borders of Syria as far as the Red Sea, by Gaius Claudius Severus, *legatus Augusti pro praetore*.
>
> (ILS 5834)

In addition to their famous roads, however, the Romans faced a variety of other engineering challenges. Josephus says that whenever the Romans entered hostile territory, they would 'first construct their camp' (*Bellum Judaicum*, 3.76). Marching camps, to which Josephus is referring, were overnight halts for armies or units on campaign. These camps, 'constructed more quickly than thought' (*Bellum Judaicum*, 3.84), provided a simple measure of security for troops camped under canvas.

Marching camps each had a low earth rampart (*agger*), about five Roman feet (1.48m) in height, topped with some form of timber obstacle. The examples of the square-section wooden stakes (*pila muralia*) for this that have survived are sharpened at both ends, and have a narrower 'waist' in the middle for tying together. They may not, therefore, have been set vertically in the *agger*, as hammering them in would have damaged the sharp ends. Besides, such a palisade would hardly have been very effective as the surviving examples are only five Roman feet in length. It seems more likely that sets of three or four *pila muralia* were lashed together with pliable withies or leather ties at angles and placed on the rampart crown as giant caltrops – what Vegetius (*De Re Militari*, 3.8) calls *tribuli*. Although this was never considered a defensive structure, tangling with such an obstacle in an attack would have caused chaos and blunted the impact of an onrush. Whatever the exact employment of the *pilum muralis* – it was probably a very versatile device – each legionary carried one or two *pila muralia*, preferably in oak, as part of his regulation marching order.

Outside the defences was a single V-shaped ditch (*fossa*), usually not more than five Roman feet (1.48m) wide and three Roman feet (89cm) deep, the soil from which went to form the *agger*. The entrances of marching camps, there were no gateways as such, were of two types. First, those defended by *tituli*, namely short stretches of rampart and ditch set a few metres in front of the gap in the main rampart spanning its width (Hyginus, *De muntionibus castrorum*, 49). In theory these detached obstacles would break the charge of an enemy. Second, those defended by *claviculae* (lit. 'little

MARCHING CAMP, 1ST CENTURY AD

Marching camps were fundamental to Roman military practice, giving armies on the march a secure campsite each night, as well as a position to retire to if a battle was unsuccessful. The illustration shows the waterproof goatskin tents of a century that are visible behind the rampart. Tents would normally be further back, out of missile range. (© Angus McBride, Osprey Publishing)

keys'), namely curved extensions of the rampart (and sometimes its ditch), usually inside the area of the camp, although external and double *claviculae* are also known from aerial photography. They would force an oblique approach towards the entranceway, usually so that an attacker's sword arm faced the rampart, denying him the protection of his shield.

Within a marching camp, the tent-lines were deliberately laid out, each line in its customary space so that every unit knew exactly where to pitch its tents and each man knew his place. Each tent (*papilio*) measured, exclusive of guy-ropes, ten Roman feet (2.96m) square and housed a *contubernium* and their equipment. They were made of best-quality cattle hide or goatskin with access back and front and enough headroom inside to enable a man to stand up. Made of at least 25 shaped panels, which were sewn together, they could be rolled up into a long sausage-shape and in this form were carried by mule. This shape may have given rise to the nickname *papilio* ('butterfly') as it rolled up like a grub and with its wings probably reminded the soldiers of the insect emerging from the chrysalis. The length of a centurion's tent was twice that of a *papilio*, while those of tribunes and above were taller, box-like structures paved with cut turf.

Two main axes, starting from the entrances, crossed at the centre of the camp; one of them, the *via praetoria*, led from the entrance of the same name to the *porta decumana*, so named because at the time of the manipular legion the tents of the tenth maniples stood nearby; the other, at right angles to it, was the *via principalis*, interrupted at midpoint by the *praetorium*. This was the tent of the general, 'which resembles a temple' (Josephus, *Bellum Judaicum*, 3.82). The tribunes' tents ran the length of the *via principalis*, and the surrounding areas were occupied with the soldiers' tents each in its appointed place. Between the rampart and the tent-lines was a wide open area known as the *intervallum*, which ensured all tents were out of range of missiles thrown or shot from outside the camp. More importantly, this space allowed the army to form itself up ready to deploy into battle order. The *intervallum* also allowed full access to the defences. Calculating the number of troops each marching camp would have housed is fraught with difficulties. As a rule of thumb, however, it is usually thought that a full legion could be accommodated under leather in about 12 hectares.

Frontinus, onetime governor of Britain (73–77) and engineer of note, wrote several technical treatises. In one he quotes with approval the maxim of Domitius Corbulo, a commander renowned for his realistic training methods: 'Domitius Corbulo used to say that the pick (*dolabra*) was the weapon with which to beat the enemy' (*Strategemata*, 4.7.2). This can only be a reference to the proven ability of the Roman Army to build marching camps for itself. Obviously recruits would have to be instructed in these military techniques, whereas fully trained soldiers would have to be exercised at fairly frequent intervals so as to maintain standards.

Britain easily provides the largest number of practice camps in the Empire, the most common size being around 30.5m^2. Often a kilometre or two away from the site of a fort and close to a Roman road, these sites are where troops trained in constructing marching camps and in particular the most difficult sections of the camps, the corners and gateways. A practice camp has been recognized at Cawthorn, where the legionaries from VIIII Hispana based at nearby York (Eburacum), practised not only the art of entrenchment but also the construction of bread-ovens (*clibani*).

FORTS AND FORTRESSES

Augustus appointed legions and auxiliary units to individual provinces where he perceived a need, either because of inadequate pacification (e.g. Iberia), or because he intended a province to be a platform of aggrandizement (e.g. Germania). Before the Varian disaster, Augustus greatly extended Roman territory in directions that suited him, enhancing his own reputation, acquiring revenue in the form of booty and bringing prestige to the state. During the winter months, the troops were scattered and stationed in winter quarters (*castra hiberna*), before being assembled in camps (*castra aestiva*) for summer campaigns. Of course the latter installations would also include the camps built at the end of every day during campaigns. Equally, winter quarters were not permanent – the Augustan ones on the Rhine show evidence of frequent modifications – and in more urbanized provinces, such as Syria, the troops could be billeted in towns and cities.

As noted, when an army was on campaign it constructed marching camps to provide security at night, but once an area was conquered the army laid down a network of smaller turf and timber forts roughly a day's march apart. Under Claudius, when a belated recognition came that the Roman Army was no longer poised to continue the Augustan expansion of the empire, these winter quarters and wayside forts became permanent. Britain's garrison, for instance, fluctuated between three and four legions during the 1st century AD, depending on the demands of other provinces, but from the late 80s the number remained at three, though not always the same three, with their permanent camps, or what are conveniently labelled legionary fortresses, at Isca Silurum (Caerleon), Deva (Chester) and Eburacum (York). Likewise, some auxiliary units were beginning to be stationed in separate forts; the earliest known auxiliary fort is that at Valkenburg in southern Holland, constructed in AD 40 or thereabouts.

It should be emphasized that there is no such thing as a typical Roman fortress or fort. The layout of a fortress, for instance, was standardized, but a close examination of fortress layouts shows that there were considerable differences in detail between individual fortress plans, and between the same types of building at different sites.

All the same, their plan and design preserved the main defensive features of the marching camp from which they had evolved. The shallow ditch and palisade of the latter were, however, replaced by more substantial earthworks in permanent camps, often with two or more V-shaped ditches and an earth or turf rampart surmounted by a timber parapet. The four gateways were retained, but towers now defended them, and further towers were added at the four angles and at intervals between.

Roman commanders favoured large concentrations of soldiers and generally, prior to Domitian (r. 81–96), fortresses were permanent camps accommodating two legions. This was a concentration of some 10,000 legionaries in a single spot, and we find two such places on the Rhine where in AD 69 Vetera (Xanten-Birten) was garrisoned by V Alaudae and XV Primigenia, and Mogontiacum (Mainz) by IIII Macedonica and XXII Primigenia.

However, as the result of the rebellion in AD 89 led by Lucius Antonius Saturninus, governor of Germania Superior, who induced the two legions (XIIII Gemina Martia Victrix and XXI Rapax) based at Mogontiacum to support his cause, Domitian issued a

The multiplication of defensive ditches (five in all) on the north and east sides of Ardoch fort is the result of successive reductions in its size and not of anxiety over its security. Initially the Flavian fort had an area of some 3.5 hectares, but that of the Antonine period had been reduced to about 2.3 hectares. (Fields-Carré Collection)

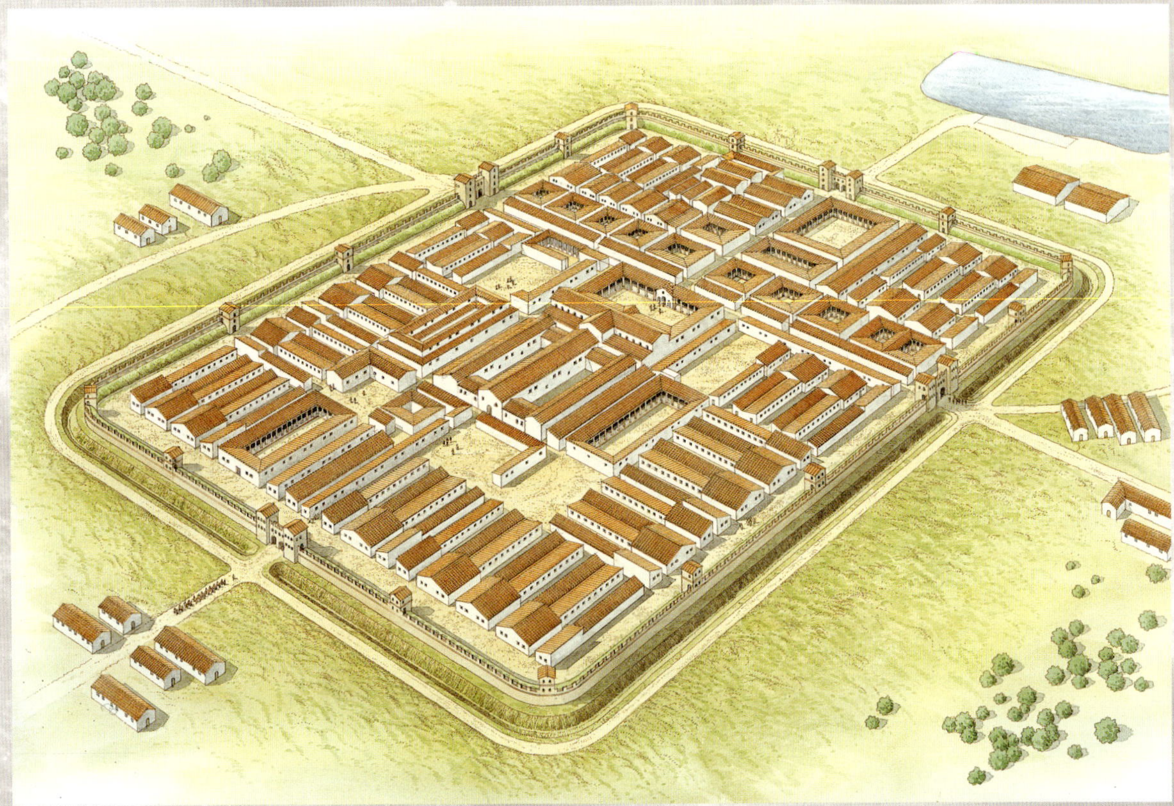

FLAVIAN FORTRESS AT NOVAESIUM (NEUSS), c.AD 80
Strategically placed on a high ground near the west bank of the Rhine, the site at Neuss was occupied by Roman troops from the reign of Augustus onwards. Ten distinct chronological periods have been identified. The earth-and-timber fortress that succeeded earlier encampments was destroyed in AD 69, and rebuilt in stone by legion VI Victrix. But it remained in occupation for only around 35 years, after which it was demolished to make room for an auxiliary fort. Of the fortress, sometimes known as the Koenen-Lager after the excavator, nothing now remains, but its layout is known from extensive excavations carried out in the late 19th century. The ramparts enclosed an area of 24.7 hectares, which is fairly standard for a legionary camp. The *principia* occupied its usual position at the crossroads. The building flanking the commander's house to the left is thought to have been the *valetudinarium*. (© Brian Delf, Osprey Publishing)

regulation forbidding more than one legion to occupy the same camp (Suetonius, *Domitianus*, 7.4). Thus the two legions at Mogontiacum were separated, and the fortress cut to one legion (XIIII Gemina Martia Victrix), and in general fortresses were reduced in size (*c.*20–25 hectares) to house a single legion. The one exception to Domitian's regulation was Egypt, where the two legions that formed its garrison (III Cyrenaica and XXII Deiotariana) were concentrated in one camp at Nikopolis just outside Alexandria, continuing to do so till at least AD 119, when one was transferred to reinforce the garrison of troublesome Judaea.

As the army began to adopt a primarily defensive role and surveillance of the frontier itself began to assume greater importance, the auxiliary units were gradually spaced out, garrisoning forts between and beyond the legionary fortresses. Indeed, the framework of Roman occupation and control was firmly based on the fort (*c.*1–5 hectares), a permanent camp accommodating an auxiliary unit. The layout of the auxiliary fort was essentially a miniature of the legionary fortress plan. During our period a fort was protected by an earth rampart – revetted with either timber or turf and founded upon a corduroy of logs or a stone base – surmounted by a spilt-timber breastwork or woven wattle-work hurdles and fronted by one or more V-shaped ditches. The rampart was pierced by four gateways, each with a timber tower above the gate passage itself or towers to either side. Further towers, set within the body of the rampart, stood at the angles as well as being spaced at regular intervals around the perimeter.

Tacitus rightly calls the fort the 'soldiers' hearth and home' (*Histories*, 2.80.4), the objective being to provide a permanent and tolerably comfortable quarter for its

FLAVIAN LEGIONARY FORTRESSES, AD 86

garrison. As such, it was hardly inferior in its facilities to the fortress of the legions. It must also be secure from the possibility of surprise attack. Yet a fort was not designed as an impregnable stronghold; on the contrary it was a jumping-off point, a base for wide-ranging activities. In wartime the enemy was engaged at close-quarters in the field, while at other times the garrison would have patrolled well beyond the frontier either to support allied tribes or to conduct punitive campaigns.

SIEGEWORKS

Siege warfare was a haphazard affair at the best of times and not undertaken lightly. However, if a Roman commander chose to conduct a siege, he had three modes of action at his disposal: well-trained troops, machines and siegeworks.

A siege normally followed a recognized pattern of events. The first and obvious phase was to impose a blockade, with the aim of starving the besieged into submission. The second phase provided a natural corollary to this: a line of entrenchments, known as a contravallation, was dug and erected around the objective, out of range of missile weapons, mechanical or manpowered, with the dual purpose of denying access to or issue from the objective and of providing the besiegers shelter from surprise attacks. In its simplest form the contravallation was no more than an *agger*, though more often than not the earth rampart was reinforced by a ditch and palisade. The third phase of a siege comprised the development of a further line of entrenchments, known as a circumvallation, which faced away from the objective and protected the rear of the besiegers from possible attack from without. Of course this was an optional expedient, the Romans besieging Masada (AD 73–74) opted to encircle the target only with a contravallation (see below).

Naturally, the circuit wall itself was the chief obstacle to the besieger. A breach could be achieved by attacking it under cover of a *testudo* with a battering ram (*aries*), or by digging a mine into the wall which would collapse, or else digging a tunnel underneath the wall. As well as going through or under the wall, it was also possible to go over it by employing a siege tower suitably fitted with a boarding-bridge. Jotapata (Mizpe Yodefat) in Galilee was 'perched on a precipice, cut off on three sides by ravines of such extraordinary depth' (Josephus, *Bellum Judaicum*, 3.158). The only access was from the north, where a wall had been built to prevent such a thing, and it was here that Vespasian pitched his camp sometime early in AD 67. Several days followed during which the Jewish rebels made a number of sorties against the Romans. Vespasian now decided to prosecute the siege with vigour, throwing up a ramp of earth and timber against the wall. Though the soldiers forming the work-parties were protected by sheds (*vineae*), timber and wickerwork structures sheeted in fire-resistant rawhides, they were greatly impeded by the missiles hurled at them by the defenders.

Vespasian now set 160 two-armed torsion machines (*ballistae*), of various calibres and firing either arrows or stones, to work to dislodge the enemy from the wall. The Jews retaliated by making swift sallies in 'guerrilla-fashion' and demolishing the sheds. However, the work on the siege ramp continued, and Josephus, the rebel leader, decided to build the wall higher, accomplishing this by having a screen of rawhides of newly slaughtered oxen strung along the top of the wall to protect the workers. The hides broke the impact of the incoming missiles, and being moist, they quenched those that were on fire.

The besieged had plenty of grain but little water, so Josephus rationed water at an early stage. The besiegers got wind of this and took heart, believing the siege almost

THE NEW-STYLE ROMAN ARROW-FIRER

The iron-framed ballista first appears on Trajan's Column, where one scene depicts the machine on a timber platform and surrounded by a timber construction. It is thought that this scene represents a response to the vulnerability of artillerycrews. Housing the ballista in a protected emplacement would have provided the twin necessities of a firm base for the machine, and a shelter from the elements as well as from enemy fire. (© Brian Delf, Osprey Publishing)

over. But the people of Jotapata confounded them by washing out their clothes in their precious water. These being hung out to dry on the battlements, the walls soon ran with water. The Romans thought they must have some secret source of supply.

Josephus now decided to quit Jotapata, believing it would draw the Romans away, but the people pleaded with him not to leave them, and so he stayed and organized many sorties. The Romans counteracted with their artillery, which was now augmented with Syrian slingers and Arab bowmen, but all this made the Jews even more determined to resist.

Vespasian now brought up a battering ram, and at the very first strike the wall was shaken 'and piercing shrieks were raised by those within, as if the town had been captured already' (*Bellum Judaicum*, 3.220). Josephus tried to defeat the ram by ordering sacks to

The BBC ballista, a one-talent stone-projector built in 2002 under the direction of Alan Wilkins, following Vitruvius' specifications. The 26kg-stone missile can be seen behind the machine. The historian Josephus claims a range of 400m for this ballista, but Philon suggests that its effective range was nearer 160m. The reconstructed machine achieved only 90m before teething troubles forced it to retire. (A. Wilkins.)

Top:
Catapult arrowheads with tangs for insertion into the arrow shaft are less common than the socketed variety. These examples from Qasr Ibrim (Egypt) date from the late 1st century BC; their length (*c*.48mm tip) and weight (*c*.15g) are not excessive, but their pyramidal points suggest artillery projectiles. It is presumed that the tang was fitted into a short, hardwood foreshaft, which was then attached to a longer shaft of soft wood. (The British Museum)

Bottom:
Wooden foreshaft (*c*.13cm) for a catapult arrow. Wind tunnel tests indicate that, fitted with an arrowhead, this object would have performed well as a short crossbow quarrel. However, studying similar hardwood objects from Haltern (Germany), Schramm suggested that they were components of composite arrow-shafts. Fitted with a tanged arrowhead, the foreshaft could be slotted into a longer soft-wood shaft, just like the more familiar socketed arrowheads. (The British Museum)

be filled with chaff and lowering them down over the wall so that they would weaken its blows. Each time the Romans moved their ram to a new spot, so the defenders did likewise with their bales of chaff (*Bellum Judaicum*, 3.223). In the end the Romans managed to cut the bales off the ropes and so continued their battering of the wall. Three parties of the rebels then rushed out of the gates and, armed with dry wood mixed with bitumen and pitch, made a bonfire of the ram. While this was going on, a Jew, renowned for his might, cast a huge stone down from the wall and on to the ram and broke off its iron head. Before the Romans could respond, the Jews torched many of the other machines, but this did not prevent the besiegers from erecting the ram again and continuing their battering of the wall (*Bellum Judaicum*, 3.227–28).

It was about now that Vespasian was wounded in the foot by an arrow, which so incensed his soldiers that they renewed their attack on the city regardless. Incidentally, Tacitus describes the future Emperor as 'a worthy successor to the commanders of old' (*Histories*, 2.5.1), that is to say, leading from the front and setting an example to his 'fellow soldiers' (*commilitones*). In the meantime the defenders still clung stubbornly to Jotapata's crumbling battlements, and Josephus recounts how one of the men standing close to him was decapitated and his head flung hundreds of metres from the body. Even more shocking was the fate of a pregnant woman obviously caught up in the horrors of the siege. She was shattered by an incoming stone just as she stepped out of her house at sun-up, and the unborn child was flung some distance away (*Bellum Judaicum*, 3.245–46).

That same daybreak, having finally breached the wall, the Romans prepared for the final assault, but were forestalled by the rebels charging out to meet them. While a furious fight ensued, the Romans attempted to scale the unbreached part of the wall, but this move was checked by the stratagem of scalding oil, the first recorded use of this weapon. The defenders then quickly resorted to a second ruse: they poured boiled fenugreek (*faenum graecum*, 'Greek hay') upon the boards which the Romans were using in their attempt to scale the wall, thus making them so slippery as to be unusable (*Bellum Judaicum*, 3.275–78).

BATTLE: JEWISH-ROMAN WARS AND THE BATTLE OF MASADA

WHEN WE LOOK AT THE PRINCIPATE, the period of Roman history that covers the reigns of the emperors down to AD 284, few sieges are known in detail. Although Augustus continued to employ encircling tactics, for example at the mountain stronghold known as Mons Medullius, greater emphasis was again given to the storming assault. In AD 9, while campaigning in Dalmatia (an area now encompassing Croatia, Bosnia and Yugoslavia), the armies of Germanicus and the future Emperor Tiberius stormed a succession of strongholds. At Splonum, there is the curious case of the cavalryman who terrified the defenders by knocking down a section of parapet with a stone; and at Raetinum, the townsfolk waited for the Romans to break in before setting fire to the place and fleeing to safety.

A generation later, Domitius Corbulo, Nero's successful general (so successful that the Emperor had him killed), was famous for saying that 'the pickaxe was the means of vanquishing the enemy'. As discussed, Corbulo was probably advocating the protection of a campaigning army by carefully entrenching a camp each evening. His dynamic style of siegecraft is typified, not by earthworks, but by the kind of storming assault unleashed at Volandum in AD 58. Having set up a long-range barrage from catapults, slingers and stonethrowers, he sent one task force to undermine the defences, protected by a *testudo* shield-formation, while another moved ladders up to the wall; 'the attack was so energetic', writes the historian Tacitus, 'that within a third of the day the walls were stripped of their defenders, the barricades at the gates were overthrown, the fortifications were scaled and captured, and every adult was butchered' (*Annals*, 13.39). When his army subsequently arrived outside Artaxata, the townsfolk immediately surrendered, thereby saving their lives, although nothing could stop Corbulo demolishing their town.

The readiness of Roman armies to storm fortifications is again apparent from the events at such towns as Joppa, Gabara, Japha and Gerasa, during Rome's First Jewish War. (The first of three major revolts against Roman rule in the province of Judaea.) Typically, once the defences were scaled, all males of sword-bearing age were slaughtered and the legionaries were given free rein to plunder and destroy. But these rapid actions have been overshadowed by the detailed accounts of more elaborate operations at Jotapata, Gamala and Jerusalem, and the spectacular archaeological remains at Masada.

As already seen in the previous chapter, after the defenders of Jotapata (AD 67) had endured a week of assaults and had beaten each one back, the future emperor Vespasian decided to construct an embankment up to the walls. His intention, like Caesar's at Avaricum, was to enable his legionaries to storm across onto the battlements, but the defenders foiled his plan by heightening the town wall at this point. The historian Josephus, who was present as the defending general, records that Vespasian then brought up a battering ram, under cover of a missile barrage. But, although the wall was finally breached, the Roman attack was repulsed and Vespasian had no option but to increase the scale of the operation, yet again. This time, three 15m iron-clad siege towers were constructed to overlook the town walls, while the embankment was again heightened. Finally, writes Josephus, 'on the forty-seventh day, the Roman embankments overtopped the wall' (*Bellum Judaicum*, 3.316); that night, the legionaries silently crossed over into the town and began the slaughter, sparing only the women and children to be sold into slavery.

Some months later, at Gamala, Vespasian again countered difficult terrain by building an embankment for battering rams. But when the legionaries eagerly burst into the town, they were hindered by the steep, narrow streets, and presented a static target for the missiles of the defenders, huddled high on the hillside. They withdrew as rapidly as

ROMAN ARTILLERY, c.AD 69

The machines depicted here follow the descriptions of Vitruvius as far as possible. The ballista is a medium-heavy 40-pounder with 24cm-diameter springs. Some details remain controversial, such as Vitruvius' omission of the long, diagonal support struts that Heron mentions. Likewise, the arrow-firers follow Vitruvius' description and differ from earlier models in their taller springs and curved bow-arms. (© Brian Delf, Osprey Publishing)

possible, but a second attack succeeded, after one of the towers on the town wall was undermined. The legionaries set about their usual business, and according to Josephus (perhaps exaggerating only a little) 'blood, pouring downhill, flooded the whole town' (*Bellum Judaicum*, 4.72).

The war reached its climax in AD 70 when, yet again, a Roman army arrived outside Jerusalem. Vespasian's son, Titus, orchestrated a full-scale siege, no doubt fully aware of previous Roman operations here. As Tacitus later commented, 'all the devices for conquering a town, known from the ancients or newly thought up, were assembled' (*Histories*, 5.13). Three embankments were constructed to carry battering rams against the outer wall, a new defence since the days of Pompey and Herod; a second wall was breached and taken; then two pairs of embankments were thrown up against the Temple platform. When one pair collapsed to undermining, and the other went up in flames, Titus briefly flirted with the idea of blockading the city, and had his men construct a 40-stade (7km) encircling wall, complete with 13 forts. As usual with major construction projects, the work gangs vied with one another to be first finished; Josephus writes 'the whole thing was built in three days ... for work worthy of months, the speed defied belief' (*Bellum Judaicum*, 5.509). But, as so often in the past, no sooner was the encirclement complete than the assault began again in earnest. A new embankment carried rams up to the formidable Antonia fortress, which sat at the corner of the Temple platform; the demolition of the fortress opened up a broad ascent onto the platform itself, where the Temple was finally destroyed, despite Titus' protestations. In the days and weeks to follow, the looting and slaughter spread down into the city.

Although the fall of Jerusalem signalled the end of the war, rebels still held three of the fortified palaces originally built by Herod. We know nothing of the siege at the first of these, Herodium. At the second, Machaerus in present-day Jordan, Josephus records that, 'after reconnoitring the vicinity, [the Roman commander Sextus Lucilius Bassus] decided to make his approach by heaping up [an embankment] in the eastern ravine, and set to work, hurrying to raise the embankment swiftly and thereby make the siege easy' (*Bellum Judaicum*, 7.190). The archaeological remains show that, on the contrary, Bassus planned his assault from the west. It is on this side that the unfinished siege embankment can still be seen, and some way behind it a small camp of 0.18 hectares, which might have accommodated 100 or so men within its 2.9m-thick ramparts. Another nine or ten camps, most of them much smaller, are dotted around the site, linked by the disjointed lengths of a 3km circumvallation. However, it was not by assault that Bassus conquered the place, but by a ruse: having captured one of the rebels trying to attack the Roman lines, Bassus threatened to crucify him, whereupon the defenders surrendered.

THE SIEGE OF MASADA, AD 73

The third of Herod's palaces provided the setting for the most famous siege of the Jewish War, perhaps the best-known siege of all, at Masada; along with Numantia and Alesia, it offers that rarest of opportunities, the combining of historical narrative with archaeology. Bassus had died in office, so a new Roman commander, Lucius Flavius Silva, was sent out; the evidence of inscriptions suggests that he was given the Judaean command in AD 73, and must have arrived late in the year to begin preparations for the siege. Josephus describes in some detail Silva's initial actions around Masada, which in many ways are similar to Scipio's actions at Numantia:

> For now it was that the Roman general came, and led his army against Eleazar and those Sicarii who held the fortress Masada together with him; and for the whole country adjoining, he presently gained it, and put garrisons into the most proper places of it; he also built a wall quite round the entire fortress, that none of the besieged might easily escape; he also set his men to guard the several parts of it; he also pitched his camp in such an agreeable place as he had chosen for the siege, and at which place the rock belonging to the fortress did make the nearest approach to the neighboring mountain, which yet was a place of difficulty for getting plenty of provisions; for it was not only food that was to be brought from a great distance [to the army], and this with a great deal of pain to those Jews who were appointed for that purpose, but water was also to be brought to the camp, because the place afforded no fountain that was near it.
>
> (Josephus, *Bellum Judaicum*, 10.1)

Having encircled the enemy fortress, Silva began the next phase of assault by constructing an embankment. Again, these were tried and tested tactics, but the logistical feat seems incredible to the present-day visitor. Josephus says that Silva found only one place capable of supporting an embankment, namely *Leuke* ('the white place'), which he describes as a 'very broad rocky prominence which ran far out, 300 cubits [135m] below the height of Masada' (*Bellum Judaicum*, 7.305). When Schulten explored the site in 1932, he was accompanied by General Adolf Lammerer, who suspected that the Romans had simply built the framework of their embankment onto an existing spur, jutting from the side of Masada. This has now been proven by the geologist Dan Gill, who has estimated that the bulk of the present-day ramp is a natural chalk outcrop, topped by 4–5m of compacted debris. The striking colouration of the chalk spur suggests that this was Josephus' *Leuke* (although its base lies 100m below the plateau, not 300 cubits).

'Ascending onto it and occupying it,' writes Josephus, 'Silva ordered his army to pile up an embankment. Working eagerly and with many hands, the embankment was firmly

THE ROMAN EMPIRE, AD 117

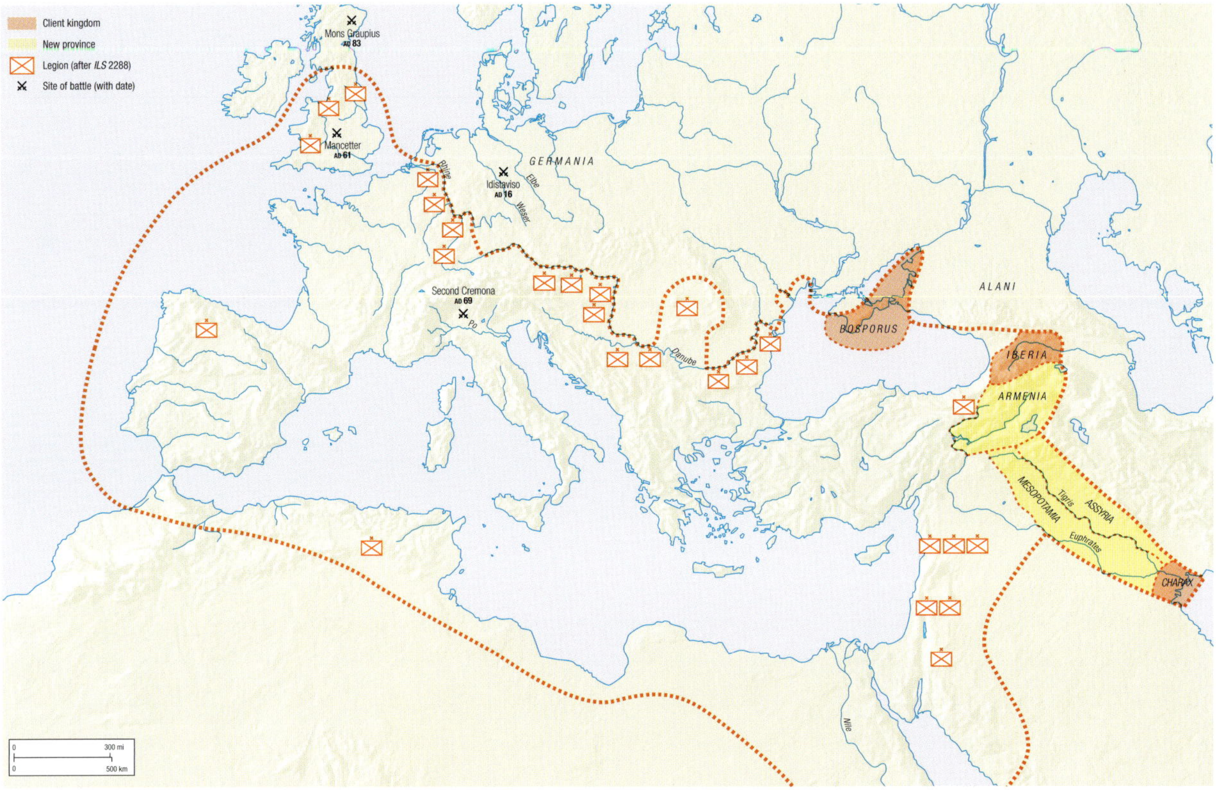

raised up to 200 cubits [90m]. But he thought that it was neither firm enough nor sufficiently large to be a foundation for machinery, so a layer of large stones was fitted together on top, 50 cubits [22m] in breadth and height' (*Bellum Judaicum*, 7.306–7). No vestiges of this extra layer have ever been found. It is sometimes interpreted as a separate platform at the head of the embankment, but Silva's siege tower required a smooth runway right up to the wall. Hawkes' suggestion of a stone causeway running up the crest of the embankment is the most plausible, but Josephus' measurements are problematic, unless his '200 cubits' refers to the original spur, and his '50 cubits' to the material piled on top by the Romans. However, Gill has suggested that, originally, this material averaged only 8m in thickness (6m along the crest, 10m on the sloping flanks), creating a smooth runway which, at its apex, fell 12m short of Masada's summit. Certainly, this would explain the extreme height which Josephus attributes to Silva's siege tower; but at 60 cubits (27m), the top 10m of the tower would still have overlooked the fortress battlements.

The iron-clad tower was reportedly equipped with catapults, and probably also held the battering ram which Silva finally deployed against the wall. However, it was well

LEGIONARIES, MID-2ND CENTURY AD

This plate is based on a relief of three legionaries carved on a sandstone slab from Croy Hill on the Antonine Wall in Scotland. All three legionaries carry heavy flat-tanged *pila* and their cylindrical shields (*scuta*) are decorated with rosettes and Capricorn emblems derived from distance slabs set up on the Antonine Wall by legio II Augusta to commemorate completed sectors of rampart, *c.*142. The men wear heavy hooded *paenula* cloaks, secured by buttons at the chest. Their *caligae* sandals are represented on victory monuments of the later 2nd century, but this traditional legionary footwear might actually have gone out of use in the years before the Antonine Wall was built. (© Angus McBride, Osprey Publishing)

known that rams worked most successfully against stone fortifications, by dislodging individual blocks and shaking the wall apart, so when the Romans breached Masada's wall, the defenders threw up a timber-laced earthwork, against which the ram was powerless. Josephus again provides the details, and extends the narrative of events:

> The other machines that were now got ready were like to those that had been first devised by Vespasian, and afterwards by Titus, for sieges. There was also a tower made of the height of sixty cubits, and all over plated with iron, out of which the Romans threw darts and stones from the engines, and soon made those that fought from the walls of the place to retire, and would not let them lift up their heads above the works. At the same time Silva ordered that great battering ram which he had made to be brought thither, and to be set against the wall, and to make frequent batteries against it, which with some difficulty broke down a part of the wall, and quite overthrew it. However, the Sicarii made haste, and presently built another wall within that, which should not be liable to the same misfortune from the machines with the other; it was made soft and yielding, and so was capable of avoiding the terrible blows that affected the other. It was framed after the following manner: They laid together great beams of wood lengthways, one close to the end of another, and the same way in which they were cut: there were two of these rows parallel to one another, and laid at such a distance from each other as the breadth of the wall required, and earth was put into the space between those rows. Now, that the earth might not fall away upon the elevation of this bank to a greater height, they further laid other beams over cross them, and thereby bound those beams together that lay lengthways. This work of theirs was like a real edifice; and when the machines were applied, the blows were weakened by its yielding; and as the materials by such concussion were shaken closer together, the pile by that means became firmer than before.
>
> (Josephus, *Bellum Judaicum*, 10.5)

Confronted by this new ingenuity, and the frustration of his siege engines, Silva opted to apply a different method of siege resolution. He ordered that his men throw burning torches onto the wooden wall, and the resulting fire was aided by nature:

> Now, at the very beginning of this fire, a north wind that then blew proved terrible to the Romans; for by bringing the flame downward, it drove it upon them, and they were almost in despair of success, as fearing their machines would be burnt: but after this, on a sudden the wind changed into the south, as if it were done by Divine Providence, and blew strongly the contrary way, and carried the flame, and drove it against the wall, which was now on fire through its entire thickness. So the Romans, having now assistance

> from God, returned to their camp with joy, and resolved to attack their enemies the very next day; on which occasion they set their watch more carefully that night, lest any of the Jews should run away from them without being discovered.
>
> (Josephus, *Bellum Judaicum*, 10.5)

Accordingly, Silva resorted to the age-old expedient of setting fire to the woodwork, but next day when his troops, fully armoured for the assault, entered Masada they found that the defenders had committed mass suicide.

Masada illustrates that the Roman way of war was not simply a matter of unthinking discipline and unbroken lines. The empire Rome built during the first two centuries AD was a territory of enormous contrast and varied enemies, and intelligence as much as force was required to hold on to such an expanse of land.

THE LATER ROMAN EMPIRE, AD 200–6TH CENTURY

INTRODUCTION: SURROUNDED BY ENEMIES

In the early 3rd century AD, the Roman Empire stretched confidently from Scotland to the Sahara and the upper Tigris, an enormous imperial enterprise and the most powerful state in the world. The following centuries saw the Romans pitted against enemies in the traditional three main frontier sectors: along the Rhine against the Alamanni, Franks and other Germanic tribes; on the Danube against first the Sarmatians and Goths, then the Hunnic tribes, and finally the Avars and manifold Slav groups; in Armenia and Mesopotamia with the Sassanid Persians. Eventually, just beyond our period, Arab tribes erupted from the Arabian peninsula to sweep through the Levant.

Identification of turning points is an understandable temptation, and acceptable provided that the qualifications for each particular date are not forgotten. After the murder of Severus Alexander in 235, the Roman Empire experienced 50 years of instability, commonly termed the '3rd-century Crisis', a period which marks the transition to the later Empire. The conversion of Constantine (r. 306–12) to Christianity in 312 initiated the Empire's transformation from polytheism to Christianity, and prompted the development of the Church as a powerful and wealthy institution. For some scholars the Church was yet one more substantial group of idle mouths for Roman tax-payers to support, with unfortunate long-term consequences, but the Church also served imperial goals beyond the frontiers and reinforced loyalties within. In 363 Julian's grand invasion of Persia ended in death for himself and near disaster for the Roman Army, but this set-back ushered in 140 years of almost unbroken peace in the east. In 378, the Eastern Emperor Valens (r. 364–75) was killed in battle at Adrianople in Thrace (see p.241), and many of his Gothic opponents had to be allocated lands for settlement, but thereafter successive eastern Emperors generally managed the 'Gothic problem' to their advantage. In 395 the last sole Roman ruler, Theodosius I (r. 378–95), died, the Empire was split between his young sons, and Emperors ceased to campaign regularly in person, but such divisions had occurred in the past, often beneficially, and there were advantages in withdrawing the Emperor from the battlefield.

'Immortal' Rome was captured by Alaric's Visigoths in 410, but it had long ceased to be an imperial capital so that the event was largely of symbolic importance: Augustine in Africa wrote *City of God* to demonstrate the superiority of the heavenly over the terrestrial city, but in Italy the Visigoths withdrew and emperors continued to rule from Ravenna. In the 440s, Attila challenged imperial authority in both east and west, threatening even

Previous page: 'Alaric's Entrance Into Rome.' Alaric (370–410), King of the Visigoths, invaded and raided Piraeus, Corinth, Megara, Argos, Sparta, and sacked Rome in 410. (Corbis)

to reduce emperors to vassal status, but his Hunnic federation disintegrated after his death in 453 so that within a decade his heirs were seeking Roman help.

In 476, the last Roman Emperor in the west was deposed by a 'barbarian' general, but the authority of the Eastern Emperor was still acknowledged, a Western consul was annually nominated to share the chief titulary magistracy with Eastern colleagues, and under Theoderic the Ostrogoth a regime which carefully maintained a Gotho-Roman façade dominated the western Mediterranean from Ravenna.

Individually the significance of each of these 'key' dates must be qualified, but cumulatively they contributed to diminishing imperial authority and undermining the fiscal and military structures that permitted the imperial machine to function. By the late 5th century, an emperor had become irrelevant in the western Mediterranean, although the Eastern ruler was accepted as a figurehead by some.

* * *

During the late Empire, only in the east did the Romans face an enemy with a sophistication comparable to their own. The Iranian Sassanids supplanted the Parthian Arsacids during the 220s, imposing themselves as a new military elite on a heterogeneous population, which included substantial groups of Jews and Christians in densely populated lower Mesopotamia. Persian kings did not maintain a large standing army until at least the 6th century: there were garrisons in frontier cities and fortresses, but for major campaigns kings instructed their nobles to mobilize provincial levies. Minor gentry of free status served as mounted warriors providing a backbone, and they probably brought along their own retinues. The system was feudal, with royal land grants carrying an obligation to serve or send troops on demand; campaigns inside the Persian kingdom seem to have been unpaid, on the assumption that soldiers could support themselves from their estates, but payment was given for foreign expeditions. Feudal arrangements could be extended to attract troops from outside the kingdom – who worked for specific terms – but mercenaries were also recruited, sometimes from the Hunnic and Turkic tribes beyond the north-east frontier, sometimes from specific internal groups such as the Dailamites who inhabited the mountains south of the Caspian.

Bronze head of Constantine with his eyes characteristically gazing to heaven. (Ancient Art and Architecture)

Persian armies are often associated with heavily mailed cavalry, but their most potent element were mounted archers: Roman tactical writers advised that the Persians could not withstand a frontal charge, but that any delay in engaging at close quarters would permit them to exploit their superiority at archery. The Persians were heirs to a long Middle-Eastern tradition of siege warfare and they had a formidable capacity to organize sieges, dig mines and deploy a variety of engines

EASTERN FRONTIER IN THE 4TH CENTURY AD

to capture even the most strongly fortified positions. In the 6th century there was a substantial overhaul of the tax system as well as a redistribution of land, which was intended to bolster royal power by permitting the payment of some permanent units, an imitation perhaps of the Roman *comitatus*. But the feudal link between king and nobility remained crucial, dictating that military prestige was essential for royal authority: kings might embark on foreign campaigns to acquire booty and prestige for internal consumption.

The personal prestige of the war leader was also vital for Rome's various tribal enemies in Europe. These groups ranged from small war bands from an extended family or single village, through more complex clan and tribal bands into which the family units would be subsumed, to the occasional but mighty international federation.

Most of the German and Gothic groups who challenged the Empire were collections of smaller clan or village units, united under the authority of a king. The right to lead depended ultimately on success, especially in warfare; although leading families (such as the Gothic Balti and Amali) attempted to create dynasties, these could not survive the shock of prolonged failure or the absence of a suitable war-leader. There was some instability in these groups, and units – such as the Carpi, who were prominent until AD 300 – might disappear permanently; others such as the Lombards are absent from our sources for several generations before re-emerging in the 6th century. Such changes did not represent the elimination of these people, but their subjection to a different elite that imposed its identity on its followers. Powerful German kings might be able to mobilize 10,000 warriors, and larger forces – such as those that confronted Julian at Strasburg in AD 357 – could be produced through alliances. On rare occasions German leaders commanded larger numbers – the Amal-led Ostrogoths fielded 25,000–30,000 warriors after subsuming a rival Gothic group in the Balkans – but this was exceptional, the product of Roman power that forced tribes to coalesce or face defeat.

The most powerful Roman enemies were the supranational federations, represented by the Huns in the 5th century and the Avars in the 6th and 7th. These groupings swallowed the variety of smaller tribal units within their sphere of action, with terror and booty providing the cement; their existence required regular warfare, and their ruthless leaders had the manpower to overrun the defences of even major cities. Both Huns and Avars posed serious challenges to Roman authority, but their inherent instability was their undoing: Attila's death in 453 led to fatal dissension amongst his potential heirs, while the Avars never recovered from their failure at Constantinople in 626, since

Aurelian's wall at Rome. (Ancient Art and Architecture)

weakness at the top permitted constituent sub-groups to rebel. The image of the Huns is of nomadic warriors whose attachment to their horses was such that they could scarcely walk, and it is true that the various warrior elites will have fought as cavalry, but all these groupings could also field substantial infantry forces which would have been provided by less prestigious elements, for example the Slavs within the Avar federation.

Collectively Rome's enemies rivalled, or surpassed, its military strength, but the Romans could usually hold their own, partly through superior organization and training, partly through strong defences, but above all by the strategy of trying to avoid simultaneous conflict on different frontiers. Along the Danube or Rhine tribal groupings might cooperate in the short term, but Roman diplomacy was adept at exploiting potential splits. Possession of a small but powerful navy was a factor which distinguished the Romans from all their opponents, with the exception of Saxon raiders in the North Sea and the Vandal kingdom in North Africa which took over part of the western Roman fleet.

Of the Roman world only Africa, the Iberian Peninsula and, to a lesser extent, Britain, were spared invasion. The cumulative nature of the frontier pressure during the late Empire is evident, with emperors unable to divert troops from one sector to another and instead constrained to confront invaders in conditions which led to defeat. The consequences for imperial prestige are obvious, and by the late 260s the Empire was virtually split into three units that attended separately to their own security, a problem made worse by a rapid turnover of emperors (21 between 235 and 284 alone). The Empire was only reunited by Aurelian (r. 270–75) in a series of energetic campaigns, which were helped by instability in Gaul following the murder of Postumus in 269 and by the death of Odaenathus; also, he was prepared to abandon the exposed province of Dacia and redeploy Roman troops along the lower Danube. Perhaps most significantly, the energetic Shapur died in 270 and it was to be 50 years before the Persians had a comparable leader. Yet if military failure guaranteed overthrow in the late Empire, success did not ensure survival: both Aurelian and Probus (r. 276–82), who continued Aurelian's re-establishment of the Empire, succumbed to plots in military camps, and Carus (r. 282–83) died while invading lower Mesopotamia, allegedly struck by lightning.

Prolonged warfare inside the frontiers, regular defeat, and the rapid turnover of emperors cumulatively had major economic consequences. Emperors required more money to pay donatives and salaries to their troops, and the available supplies of bullion had to be squeezed in order to produce the necessary precious metal coins. Under Gallienus (r. 253–68) this resulted in the silver content of the *denarius*, the standard coin for military pay, declining to 5 per cent; subsequently there were issues of bronze washed in arsenic to provide a short-lived silvery brightness. The declining value of coinage triggered an offsetting rise in prices which resulted in an inflationary spiral, particularly during the last third of the third century.

One victim of inflation was the government, whose tax revenues declined in value; granted the inflexibility of the tax system, it was difficult to raise large new sums of cash. A consequence was an increasing reliance on taxation in kind: troops needed to be supplied and, rather than extracting increasingly worthless coin from rural taxpayers to permit units to purchase food and other necessities, the cycle was short-circuited by the transfer of goods directly to the troops. This development might have been accidental and haphazard, with armies gradually adopting the practice of securing their own supplies and leaving provincial administrations to acknowledge that their appropriations could be offset against tax demands. Other victims of inflation were the cities, where the spectacular building developments of the previous 150 years ceased.

Another consequence of crisis was the marginalization of the Senate and a professionalization of military command. In 238 the Senate and armies had contested the imperial succession, but under Gallienus senators were effectively removed from military commands. This development had begun earlier, since the Severans had sometimes preferred trustworthy non-senators for important commands, but the insecurity of Emperors furthered the change while troops also demanded reliable leaders rather than aristocratic amateurs. When Aurelian came to power with the backing of the upper Danube legions and then used these troops to restore the Empire, it transpired that Pannonians, and other officers of Balkan extraction, became prominent. These were professional soldiers, at whom civilian intellectuals might sneer for their lack of culture, but they proved to be solidly committed to the idea of Rome and its traditions, as well as effective generals.

The crisis also had a religious impact, since a natural inference from repeated misfortune was that the gods had to be placated. At first this took the form of intensified supplication to traditional deities: in 249 Decius issued a general instruction to all citizens to offer prayers and sacrifices on his behalf. A consequence, probably unintended, of this order was that Christians were faced with the choice of disobedience or apostasy; some abandoned the faith, many more probably found means to evade the ruling, but there were enough martyrs to identify Christians as traitors to the Empire. Persecution lapsed with Decius' death, but was restarted in 257 by Valerian who specifically targeted the Christians, with attention focused on the priestly hierarchy; his defeat in battle terminated proceedings. The successful Aurelian advertised his devotion to the traditional divinities, especially Victoria, Mars, Hercules and Jupiter who were all connected with success in war, and to these he added a special devotion to the cult of the Unconquered Sun, Sol Invictus, after the defeat of Palmyra in 273. Devotion to the correct divinity did bring success, as Diocletian and Constantine would continue to demonstrate in their different ways. In the long run, however, Rome's deep-seated imperial over-commitment and its spreading internal factions would undo its integrity, although as we shall see its army was still capable of greatness and innovation.

DEVELOPMENT OF THE ROMAN ARMY

The twilight of the Roman Empire saw a revolution in the way that war was waged. The drilled infantryman, who had been the mainstay of Mediterranean armies since the days of the Greek hoplite, was gradually replaced by the mounted warrior. This change did not take place overnight, and in the 3rd and 4th centuries the role of the cavalryman was primarily to support the infantry. However, by the time of Justinian's reconquest of the west, in the 6th century, the situation had been completely reversed, and it was the infantryman who found himself in the supporting role.

The late-Empire *eques*, or ordinary cavalryman, was, in many ways similar to his infantry counterpart. He was more likely to have been a German, Sarmatian or Hun than an Italian, and he had probably never seen Rome. He fought for pay or booty, and did not particularly feel any great loyalty or sense of duty to the empire he was defending. Unlike the infantryman, however, he formed the elite of the army, and as time progressed his equipment and status improved as that of the infantryman declined. He was the precursor of the medieval knight who was to rule the battlefield for centuries to come.

As we have seen, the 3rd century AD was a period of chaos in the Roman world. Civil war and economic decline had greatly weakened the Empire, at a time of increasing pressure on the frontiers. Previously the Empire had been defended primarily by infantry-based armies protecting the *limes*, or frontier zones. The problem with this system was that when the frontier defences were penetrated, as happened with increasing frequency in the 3rd century, there were no troops in reserve to deal with the invasion. Another problem was that such breakthroughs were often by fairly small, fast-moving bands of raiders (particularly the Goths along the Danube and the Franks and Alamanni along the Rhone): by the time temporary task forces, or *vexillationes*, had been drawn from the frontier defences and dispatched to the troubled areas, their foes had long since moved on.

One of the results of this pressure on the Empire's defensive system was an increase in the cavalry arm. This was not because cavalry had proved themselves tactically superior to infantry, but rather because fast-moving cavalry had a better chance of deploying quickly to trouble-spots. Gallienus took this one step further and created all-cavalry reserve forces, which were based at strategic locations in northern Italy, Greece and the Balkans. These reserves were probably created by withdrawing the old 120-man cavalry detachments from the legions and brigading them into new units called *equites promoti*.

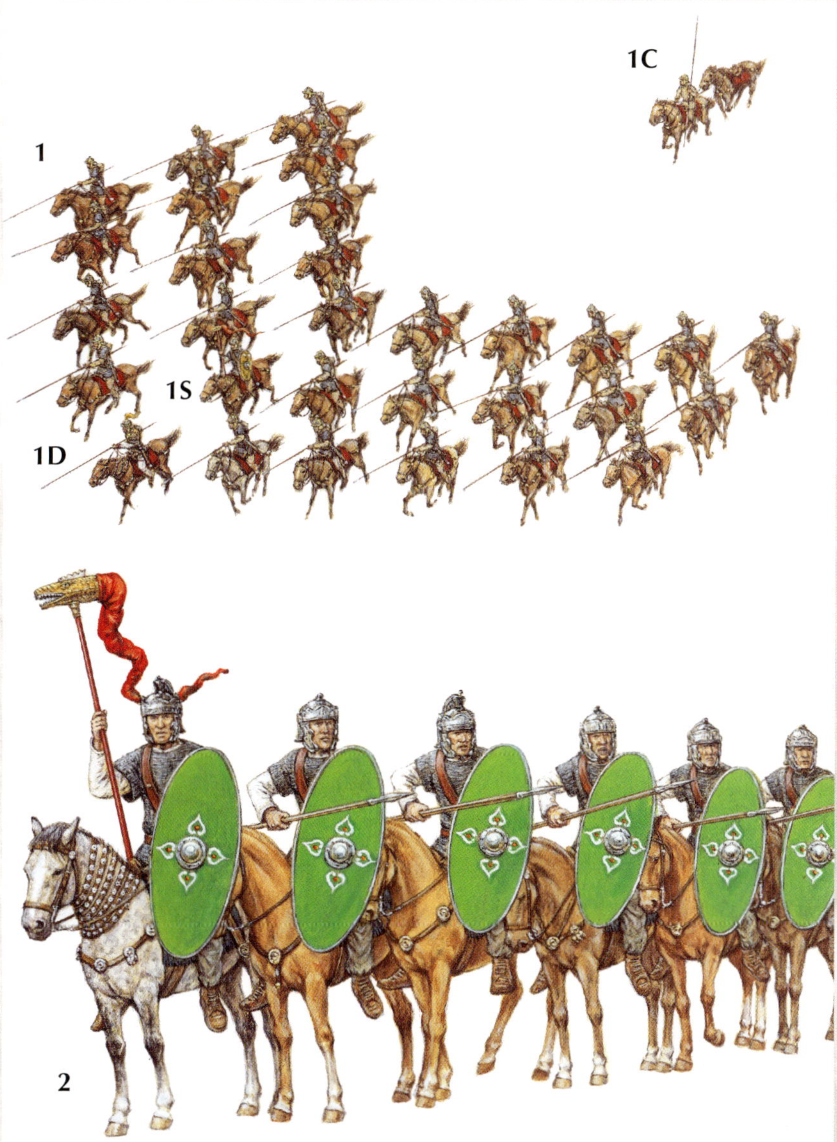

CAVALRY WEDGE AND *TESTUDO*

This plate presents (1) a 3rd-century *turma* of 30 *contarii* (lancers) in a hypothetical wedge or *cuneus* of three ranks. The decurion (1D), commander of the *turma,* forms the point, and the *draconarius* standard-bearer (1S) rides in the rank behind him. Behind the *turma* the decurion's servant – *calo,* often a slave (1C) – follows on one of the decurion's remounts and leads the other on a long rein. At (2) we show another variation of the *testudo,* here a loose shield wall formed by 3rd-century cavalrymen, who have formed up in a slightly oblique rank, with the horses' heads turned in, so as to present their shielded side to the enemy. (© Adam Hook, Osprey Publishing)

These in turn were supplemented by light skirmishers recruited in Illyricum (*equites dalmatae*) and North Africa (*equites mauri*), possibly together with heavier units of *equites scutarii*. Eventually these new units came to be collectively referred to as *equites illyriciani* or as *vexillatio*, a term which had originally meant a detachment drawn from the frontier legions. The new *vexillationes* also enjoyed higher status than the old auxiliary cavalry. A unit at full strength was about 500 men.

The central cavalry reserve was instrumental in the success of the Illyrian emperors (Claudius, Aurelian, Probus, Carus and Diocletian) in restoring order in the latter part of the 3rd century. However, in the relative calm of Diocletian's reign (284–305) there was a partial return to a forward defensive strategy along the frontiers. Diocletian probably maintained a small central field army (*comitatus*) which included two *vexillationes* (*promoti* and *comites*) and three legions (*lanciarii*, *ioviani* and *herculiani*), but the bulk of the *equites illyriciani* were distributed along the eastern frontiers, and never quite regained their former status.

The 4th century saw a complete reorganization of the army. Constantine enlarged the *comitatus* to include five cavalry *vexillationes*, five legions and ten new small infantry units called *auxila*. The *comitatus* was given higher status and privileges than the static frontier forces. In keeping with a trend that had been established by Gallienus in the mid-3rd century and reflecting the increasing importance of their role, the cavalry were ranked as senior to the legions and *auxilia*. Constantine also disbanded the Praetorian Guard and replaced it with the *scholae*, an all-cavalry force which included units of *scutarii* and *gentiles*.

A single centralized field army could not, however, cope with the frequent emergencies that erupted simultaneously at various points throughout the Empire. Constantine's successors, therefore, increased and divided up the *comitatus* to form several regional field armies (*comitatenses*) to act as reserves in Gaul, Illyricum, Thrace and the east, and gave a new designation (*palatini*) to the units of the Emperor's central field army. Before long, units of *comitatenses* and *palatini* became mixed in the same armies, although the *palatini* continued to have higher status.

At some point the field army was split between the Eastern and Western halves of the Empire. This probably occurred in 365, when the Empire was divided between Valentinian and Valens. Many units were divided in two, keeping their original names but adding the designation *seniors* or *iuniores* to distinguish between them. It is quite possible that the two halves of a unit were not recruited up to their former strength, but remained at a strength of about 300 – a unit size which carried through into Byzantine times.

We have a fairly good idea of how the army was organised from the *Notitia Dignitatum*, a contemporary document that lists all units at the end of the 4th century for the west and the beginning of the 5th century for the east. Frontier forces, descendants of the old legions and auxiliaries, dropped in status and became stationary garrison troops known as *limitanei* (guarding the *limes*) or *ripenses* (based along the river frontiers). Eventually these troops became little more than a part-time militia, and they were rarely called on to take part in major campaigns. When this did occur and *limitanei* were transferred to the field army, they were given the title *pseudocomitatenses*.

The new units created for the field armies were markedly smaller than the old 6,000-man legions: probably no more than 1,000–2,000 men. The majority of the army's foot soldiers, however, were provided by new-style units called *auxilia*, which had an establishment strength of about 500 men. As is the case in all armies, actual strengths were probably much lower, particularly on campaign.

A mosaic in the Basilica of Moses, Mount Nebo, Jordan, dating from 530–31, includes this cavalryman; he wears a light brown tunic, red cloak, and broad white trousers with yellow trim at the bottom of the legs. The figure can perhaps be identified with the barbarian *foederati* under the orders of the *Dux Palaestinae* in 536. (Studium Biblicum Franciscanum)

The old distinction of legionaries being citizens and auxiliaries non-citizens disappeared with the general enfranchisement of all inhabitants of the Empire in 212. Furthermore, by the 4th century AD both legions and *auxilia* were accepting recruits from beyond the Empire's borders – primarily Germans. At the battle of Strasbourg (357), the Cornuti, Bracchiati and Batavi (all *auxilia*) are described fighting with spears, javelins and swords.

The 5th-century writer Vegetius says that the legions were more heavily equipped and more strictly disciplined than the *auxilia*. It may be that the *auxilia*, all of whom were higher status *palatini*, were trained to operate with a greater degree of flexibility than the legions: one day acting in small units in commando-style raids, the next day brigaded together in a larger formation, fighting in the line of battle. While there is no conclusive proof of this, contemporary writings suggest that whenever a tough job came up, the

THE BATTLE OF STRASBOURG, AD 357
This scene captures the moment just before the opposing sides come into contact. The two sides are trying to intimidate each other and build up courage. The front ranks are closed up ready for the clash, the rear ranks are throwing javelins and the whole formation is supported by a unit of archers firing overhead. (© Gerry Embleton, Osprey Publishing)

generals turned to the *auxilia palatina* to find their men. An indication that the legions were not this flexible can be found in an incident at the siege of Amida in 359, where two legions are described as bring excellent fighters in open country 'but quite useless, indeed a positive nuisance' in more specialized operations.

SOLDIER FROM LEGIO HERCULIANI, 3RD CENTURY AD

This man represents one of the many Illyrian soldiers that formed the core of the Roman armies in the chaotic 3rd century. The soldier's bronze scale armour or *lorica squamata* has replaced the more familiar segmented plate armour of the early legionaries. His shield design marks him as a member of the legio Herculiani, one of the new elite, smaller legions. (© Gerry Embleton, Osprey Publishing)

Both legions and *auxilia*, therefore, should be looked upon as heavy infantry, performing basically the same task on the battlefield and being similarly equipped. The writings of Vegetius, however, imply that a portion of the men in each unit – legion and *auxilia* – were trained as light infantrymen. This is borne out in battle descriptions, where groups of skirmishers are usually formed by selecting men from various units, rather like 18th-century light companies.

There were also a number of specialist light infantry such as *sagittarii* (archers), *exculcatores* (probably javelinmen), *funditores* (slingers) and *balistarii*. The *balistarii* are normally assumed to be artillerymen who manned small field catapults. While this is a logical assumption on the basis of their name, the one example we have of them in action sees them escorting a general and acting as skirmishers. An alternative explanation is that they were light infantry crossbowmen. In spite of the view that the crossbow was a medieval weapon, later Roman crossbows are known to have existed from archaeological finds, further supported by Vegetius who mentions troops 'who annoyed the enemy with arrows from the *manubalistae* or *arcubalistae*'.

As the cavalry increased in importance in the 5th and 6th centuries, the infantry began to decline. By the 6th century the *Strategikon* recommends:

> The general would be well advised to have more cavalry than infantry. The latter is set only for close combat, while the former is easily able to pursue or to retreat, and when dismounted the men are all set to fight on foot.
>
> (*Strategikon*, 8.2.85)

Writing when Roman fortunes were at their lowest ebb, Vegetius says that 'the name of the legion remains to this day in our armies, but its strength and substance are gone' (*De Re Militari*, 2.3). Yet while this degradation of the infantry may have started earlier, the 4th-century *pedes* was as capable as his predecessor of standing firm in the line of battle, even if he was no longer looked upon as the elite of the army.

Several different types of cavalry are listed in the *Notitia Dignitatum*, and in many cases we can deduce their role and equipment from the unit name. Units of *mauri*, *dalmatae* and *cetrati* were probably light, fast-moving javelin-armed skirmishers. The many *equites sagittarii*, or horse archers, were probably also light cavalry, although some would have been heavily equipped. Fully armoured lancers, modelled on Sarmatian, Parthian and Palmyran lancers, also formed part of the 4th-century army and were called *catafractarii* or *clibanarii*.

Statuette of a Roman cavalryman, minus his horse, 4th–5th century. He wears a lamellar cuirass and thickly padded Iranian-style trousers. (Metropolitan Museum of Art, New York)

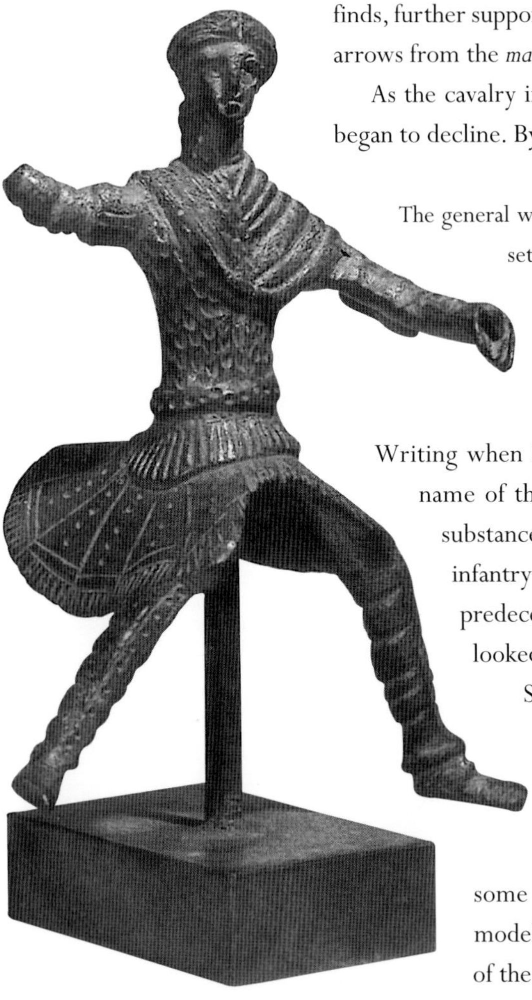

The majority of cavalry, however, were probably little different from the auxiliary cavalry of the earlier Empire, and were trained and equipped for close combat and for skirmishing from a distance with javelins. Such conventional heavy cavalry probably included units styled as *promoti*, *scutarii*, *stablesiani*, *armigeri*, and *brachiati* as well as those bearing Germanic or Gallic tribal names or named after reigning emperors. A few senior cavalry units were *comites* rather than *equites*, and some of these were further distinguished by a descriptive name (*Comites Alani* or *Comites Clibanarii*, for example); the title was probably honorific.

All of these cavalry types could be found in the static frontier forces (*limitanei* and *ripenses*) as well as in the field armies. Some were the descendants of the old auxiliary *alae*; others included *illyriciani*, conventional *equites*, *catafractarii* and *sagittarii*. These were further supplemented by 'native' cavalry or *equites indigenae*, of which both *sagittarii* and *promoti* are recorded on the eastern frontier. Elsewhere, particularly on the Danube frontier, could be found units called *cunei equitum*, who may also have been semi-irregular, locally recruited cavalry.

By the 6th century, the *bucellarii* – private armies employed by imperial warlords – had been institutionalized and Roman field armies had evolved into large followings of mounted warriors who owed allegiance to powerful warlords – direct ancestors of the

ARMIES OF THE WARLORDS

The aftermath of the disastrous Persian and Gothic campaigns of 363 and 378 respectively saw the increased transfer of many units of *limitanei* to the *comitatus* (as *pseudocomitatenses*). This probably resulted in a weakening of the frontier defences as well as a degradation in the quality of the field army. More and more Roman commanders turned to bands of barbarians to fill the ranks of their mobile field forces. Theodosius, for example, is reported to have employed 20,000 Goths at the battle of Figidus in 394. These barbarian allies (*foederati*) were given land to settle in return for military service; however, they fought together under their own leaders and were nominally Romanized.

Increasingly, as the reliability of the regular field armies decreased, military commanders and even wealthy individuals began to hire bands of private retainers or *bucellarii*. The great warlords of the 5th century, such as Stilicho, Aetius and Aspar, all maintained large personal followings and came to rely on them almost exclusively. In 444 Valerian, a wealthy magnate in the east, is recorded as overpowering the local governor with a 'great horde of barbarians', and in the 6th century Belisarius employed as many as 7,000 *bucellarii*. Attempts were made to limit such private armies, including a law of 476 that made it illegal for individuals to maintain 'gangs of armed slaves, *bucellarii* or Isaurians'. However, it seems that the practice remained fairly common.

feudal host. The old *comitatenses* were reduced, like the *limitanei*, to strategic garrisons, and the cavalry had become the arm of decision. Weapons too had changed: the typical Roman cavalryman now carried a bow as his principal weapon (probably as a result of Hunnic and Persian influences). Shock cavalry was provided primarily by the German *foederati*, who by the mid-6th century had evolved into regular units of lancers.

The size of late Roman armies is a complex game for which most of the pieces are missing. In the 3rd century army units probably numbered upwards of 350,000, with a further 40,000 in the navy. Numbers increased significantly under Diocletian and Constantine, so that the total military establishment exceeded 500,000 – perhaps even 600,000. But paper strength will always have surpassed disposable strength, and many troops were committed to particular assignments so that only a small proportion of the total establishment could be deployed for individual campaigns. In the 4th century, an army of 50,000 was large, and by the 6th century mobile armies rarely exceeded 30,000.

In spite of complaints about discipline, Roman training appears to have remained tough. A succession of military manuals indicates that attention was devoted to training

The Emperor Theodosius and his family receive tokens of submission from barbarians while seated in the imperial box at the hippodrome. From the base of the obelisk at the Hippodrome in Constantinople. (Ancient Art and Architecture)

and tactics, at least in the Eastern Empire, although it is probably correct that organization, rather than basic military skill, increasingly emerged as the way in which Romans surpassed their opponents. The Romans had the capacity to coordinate troops over long distances to build up complex armies, with artillery units as well as infantry and cavalry, and then keep these supplied on campaign: the infrastructure of roads, warehouses, granaries, arms factories and the billeting arrangements generated a complex body of law, and enabled the Romans to move their men wherever they were needed.

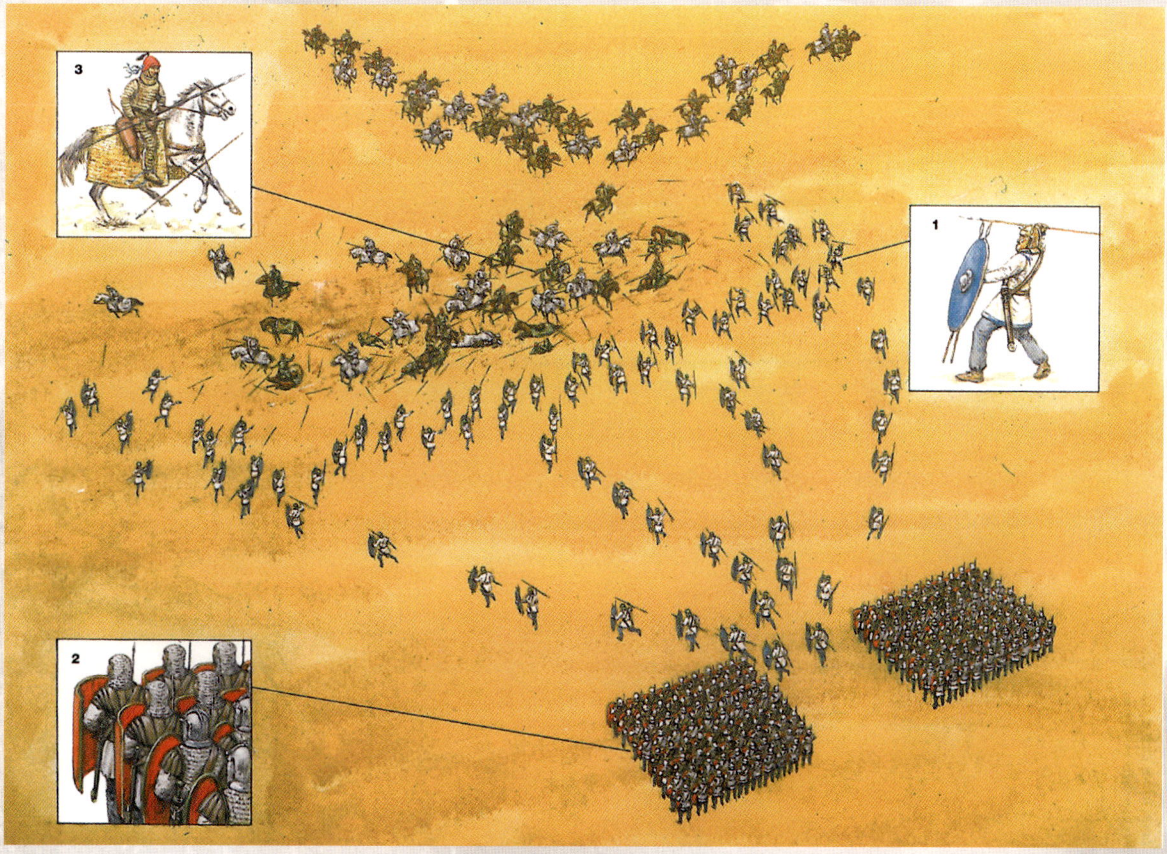

LANCIARII* ATTACKING PARTHIAN *CATAPHRACTS

Here we see a century of *lanciarii* (inset 1) – light-armed legionaries equipped with *lanceae* – deploying from the interval between two centuries of heavy legionary infantry (inset 2), to swarm around a squadron of Parthian *cataphracts* in a battle of the 3rd century AD. Fooled by the tempting gap between the centuries of heavy infantry, the *cataphracts* – fully armoured cavalry (inset 3) – have charged on to a line of caltrops, leg-breaking pits and other booby-traps hidden in the sandy grassland before the Roman battleline. As the *lanciarii* bombard the stricken cavalry with their light javelins, another Parthian squadron wheels away before it hits the booby-traps. (© Adam Hook, Osprey Publishing)

APPEARANCE AND EQUIPMENT

It is well known that the imperial Roman Army was equipped and supplied by the state. State-run factories produced weapons, clothing and armour, the state provided rations and medical services, and it ran stud farms to raise cavalry mounts. The *Notitia Dignitatum* lists 35 state factories or *fabricae* across the Empire at the start of the 5th century, producing everything from catapults to armour. There were also state-run clothing mills and boot makers.

It has been assumed, therefore, that the late Roman soldier was uniformly equipped, and modern reconstructions usually present such a view, even on campaign. Many modern authors have studied the available evidence and come up with theories on uniform distinctions for legions, cavalry and *auxilia* based on the assumption that all units of similar name would have the same uniform.

Such theories are probably grossly inaccurate: by the end of the 4th century, uniform issues were beginning to be replaced by a clothing allowance, and by the 6th century even weapons and armour were expected to be purchased by the soldiers from an allowance. A record from 423 states that five-sixths of the amount raised to clothe the army should go directly to the troops as a cash allowance, and only one-sixth be allocated to state clothing factories to produce uniforms for recruits.

Troops of the *limitanei* probably bought their clothing from stores attached to their fort. Even if such stores were furnished by state suppliers, we can assume that a certain amount of 'local flavour' would have crept into the soldier's appearance. Since many soldiers in the 5th-century *limitanei* had other occupations, it is unlikely that a high

Military cloaks: by the 3rd and 4th centuries the rectangular *sagum* appears to have been the cloak most associated with the army. Fringes, as well as applied decorations, can be seen on many examples. From left to right tombstone of Aurelius Lucianus, Rome; fresco, Luxor, Egypt; mosaic, Piazza Armerina, Sicily; mosaic, Cologne, Germany.

CLOTHING ON CAMPAIGN

Taking as an example a unit of Julian's army assembled for the invasion of Persia in 363, we can visualize them in Antioch, before they set off, presenting a fairly uniform appearance, at least within the unit. Even though the soldiers might have purchased their clothing themselves, chances are that a certain style would have predominated, even if colours and details varied according to individual taste and wealth. However, we would expect some of the veterans of Julian's Gallic army, having arrived in north European clothing, to have bought new clothes locally that were more suitable for the hot southern climate.

Once the campaign had begun, hot heavy items from the north would have been discarded. After the first few engagements, bits and pieces of Persian equipment would have started to appear: hacked shields, damaged helmets and armour would all have been replaced. On its return to Antioch, the army would have had a completely different appearance from when it left, and probably would have lost any semblance of uniformity. The same would hold true for almost any campaign, particularly those fought away from home.

degree of uniformity could have been imposed on them once issue uniforms had been replaced by a clothing allowance.

It is generally assumed that the clothing of the field army would have shown more consistency that that of the *limitanei*, however, because field units had no fixed base, and were nearly always on campaign, regular supply from a fixed source would have been more difficult. In fact, the clothing allowance probably came about to ease the logistical difficulties of re-supplying these mobile troops. It is easy to picture such units after a long campaign presenting a very motley appearance; clothing does not last very long in the field and the soldier would have had to make local purchases fairly regularly.

The campaigns of the 5th century, in particular, were notorious for the participation of barbarian allies, and we can assume a fair deal of 'cross cultural' exchanges between the soldiers of different nationalities that served side by side. We would be very hard pressed indeed to distinguish between a 'Roman' soldier (perhaps born a Goth) serving in the army of Stilicho and a 'Gothic' soldier (perhaps born a Roman) in Alaric's army.

To identify such units in the field, the *Strategikon* says that shields should be of the same colour and it implies that helmet plumes were also in a uniform colour. Such simple details could provide a degree of uniformity.

The *Notitia Dignitatum* lists unit shield patterns in the same way as a modern equivalent might list unit cap badges. This does not guarantee that all men in the unit would have carried well-painted shields. After a battle, damaged shields would have been replaced from battle salvage or perhaps from a central reserve. It is highly unlikely that a soldier on campaign with such a replacement shield would have the time, or the paint, to reproduce some of the highly detailed designs shown in the *Notitia* before his next

SOLDIERS OF THE SEVERAN ARMY, LATE 2ND AND EARLY 3RD CENTURIES
From right to left we have a legionary, a soldier of the Praetorian Guard and a Roman phalangite. According to Cassius Dio, the population of Rome was shocked by the appearance of the Danubian Army of Septimius Severus when he marched on Rome in 193; we can only assume that it was the barbarian practice of wearing long-sleeved tunics and trousers that caused the outrage. (© Graham Sumner, Osprey Publishing)

This figure follows the funerary portrait of Aurelius Justinus of legio II Italica, who was killed during a war against the Dacians. The details include the plank construction of the shields, which had iron reinforcing bards and stitched-on rawhide edging, and one socketed and two tanged *pila* shanks from Saalburg in Germany, dating to *c.*260. The dagger detail illustrates a typical 3rd-century *pugio*. (© Angus McBride, Osprey Publishing)

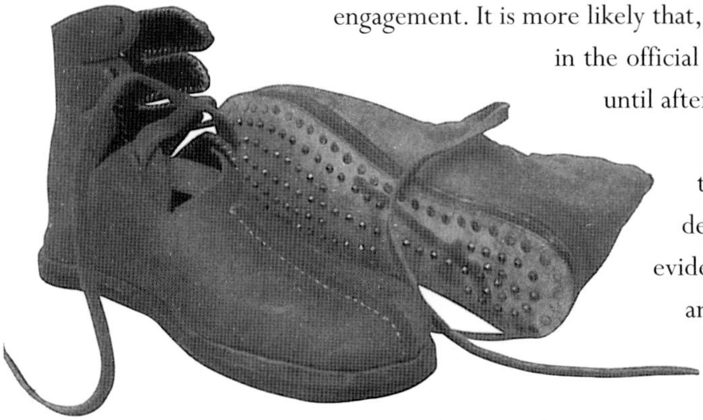

engagement. It is more likely that, at best, he would have given it a quick coat of paint in the official unit colour, leaving the job of fixing it up properly until after the campaign.

The question of how much armour was worn by the late Roman infantryman has been a matter of debate. Both before and after Vegetius there is strong evidence that the Roman infantryman wore metal body armour and helmet. Ammianus Marcellinus, who was a soldier himself, makes frequent reference to 4th century infantry in 'gleaming' armour, and describes the infantry at Adrianople as 'weighed down by the burden of their armour' (*The Later Roman Empire AD 353–378*, 31.13). Egyptian carvings from the 5th and 6th centuries clearly show Roman infantrymen wearing scale and mail armour. The 3rd-century Arch of Galerius also shows infantrymen in scale armour.

Reconstructed 3rd-century boots by Mark Beaby, based on finds from Dura Europos. The integral laces distinguish this type of boot, and the soles came in either nailed or flat versions.

Some monumental evidence appears to depict 3rd- and 4th-century infantry in leather muscled cuirasses. While it is possible that such armour was worn, it is far more likely to have been a classical convention employed by artists, and should not be taken at face value. There are numerous examples of artistic renditions of soldiers in heroic classical and pseudo-classical dress, continuing through to modern times. While leather muscled cuirasses may have been worn occasionally, archaeological and literary records indicate that iron mail or bronze scale was the most common body armour of the period.

Vegetius' claim that infantry armour was abandoned in the mid-4th century can be partially accounted for by the obvious material losses sustained in the Persian and Gothic disasters of the time. It is also consistent with the increase in use of federate troops and the introduction of allowances in place of issued equipment. If the main field armies of the 5th century were composed of barbarians and a few elite Roman cavalry units, it is quite likely that an infantryman would not have been willing to pay for expensive armour out of his allowance, nor have any real need for it. A large shield would probably have been sufficient protection for troops who only had a static supporting role.

For most of the soldier's service he would have no call to wear armour, for example when on routine guard duty, foraging expeditions or skirmishing. Marches were conducted with armour carried in wagons. Only when called on to fight in line of battle did the late Roman infantryman seem to need such added protection. The *Strategikon* calls for 'picked men … to have mail coats, all of them if it can be done, but in any case the first two in the file' (Maurice, *Strategikon*). This seems to imply that mail armour was kept in reserve rather than as part of an individual soldier's kit, and was issued as required. The same may even have been true of helmets, with soldiers usually wearing the characteristic pill-box shaped 'Pannonian leather cap' which Vegetius says was introduced to accustom the men 'to having the head covered so they might be less sensible of the weight of the helmet' (*De Re Militari*).

It is difficult to say when, or to what degree, body armour for the infantry was re-introduced. It is quite probable that in some areas or units it never completely dropped out of use. Troops in richer areas, in more stable posts, or in higher quality units may have used armour, while others abandoned it. This is consistent with the fact that most of the evidence for 5th- and 6th-century infantry armour comes from Egypt. Later Byzantine manuals all call for the infantry to be armoured, but whether such recommendations were always carried out is a matter of conjecture.

On balance, it seems reasonable to assume that until at least 378 the Roman infantryman wore metal body armour and a helmet when fighting in line of battle, whether he served in a legion or *auxilia*. When on patrol, on the march, on guard duty, or acting as a skirmisher, he probably left most of it off, as would specialist light infantry. The use of body armour may have been less common, as the role of infantry declined, but by the time of Justinian, at least some units were wearing full armour again, and its use probably never completely died out.

LATE IMPERIAL TACTICS

The most common formation of the late imperial Romans remained the battleline. This was, as Vegetius (*De Re Militari*) tells us, 'solely designed to repulse' an attack. It was used because infantry were usually being deployed defensively in this period, with cavalry providing the army's offensive capability. The line could be formed up in either four, eight or 16 ranks. The *Strategikon* says that fewer than four ranks did not have enough staying power and more than 16 added nothing to the unit's strength. It was easier to reduce the frontage than expand, because of the accordion effect such a manoeuvre would have had on flanking units. It seems that in most cases an eight-rank formation was used, striking a balance between increasing staying power through depth and getting as many men as possible into action.

Arrian describes an actual battle order for a legion preparing to face cavalry, and gives us a good idea of how such a formation would have looked:

> The legionaries will be formed in eight ranks and deployed in close order. The first four ranks will consist of men armed with the spear [probably *pilum*]... The men of the first rank will present their spears at the approach of the enemy ... those of the second, third and fourth ranks will be in a position to throw their spears. They will be directed to aim their strikes accurately at the right time in order to knock down the horses and throw the riders... The four ranks immediately behind will consist of men armed with the *lancea*. Behind these there will be a ninth rank composed of archers, those of Numidians, Kyreneans, Bosporians and the Ituraeans.
>
> (Arrian, *Ektaxis katà Alanon*)

Although from before the later Roman Empire, this order of battle is consistent with the rather confused description of Vegetius. It also matches the *Strategikon*, although a 16-rank formation is more common in that work. This may mean that the infantry of the later period needed increased depth to compensate for lower morale, or it may mean nothing more than that the author of the *Strategikon* plagiarized old Hellenistic manuals which used a 16-rank formation.

One thing clear in all the descriptions is that the various ranks in a formation performed different tasks. The first four ranks were expected to do the real fighting and consequently were more heavily armed. The file closers in the rear rank had a supervisory role, while the men in the intervening ranks were to provide depth to the formation and

BATTLEFIELD MEDICS

One area in which the Roman Army stood apart from its opponents is the way in which it was able to provide medical care to its soldiers. Procopius describes some amazing operations after a skirmish during the siege of Rome, and the *Strategikon* advises that after any battle commanders should deliver prompt medical treatment to the wounded and oversee the burial of the dead. Not only is this a religious duty, but it greatly helps the morale of the living. In fact, the *Strategikon* gives detailed instructions on the use of battlefield medics, recommending that eight to ten men per *bandon*, 'alert, quick, lightly clothed and without weapons' should follow behind their units 'to pick up and give aid to anyone seriously wounded in the battle, or who [has] fallen off his horse, or is otherwise out of action, so they may not be trampled by the second line or die through neglect of their wounds' (Maurice, *Strategikon*, 11.9).

throw light javelins over the heads of the front ranks. Attached archers from other units would be drawn up behind and also fire overhead. The *Strategikon* says that mail armour should ideally be provided for all men in the unit, but concedes that this may not be possible, in which case at least the first two and last ranks should have armour.

Vegetius has each man in the formation occupying a frontage of 1m and a depth of 2m. This can be corroborated by a 3rd-century shield found at Dura Europos which is about 1m wide. This frontage would have allowed the men to present a solid shield wall to the enemy, while the depth would have given room for the men to throw their javelins. Prior to contact, however, the ranks would move closer together, and the file closers 'should order those in the rear to close in forcefully on those to the front ... if necessary to prevent some from hesitating and even holding back' (*Strategikon*, 12.16).

Owing to the unpredictabilities of frontier and imperial warfare, the late imperial Roman soldier would be more likely to engage the enemy in a skirmish than formal battle. Although the *Strategikon* advises against drawing men from different units for such actions, the accounts of Ammianus Marcellinus clearly show that, in the 4th century at least, this was the normal practice. If heavy infantrymen were to engage in a skirmish or to fight in rough terrain, the *Strategikon* says they 'should not have heavy armament such as helmets and mail coats' (Maurice, *Strategikon*) and they should be issued with smaller shields and short spears. In such irregular warfare the men would naturally have fought individually rather than in formation. The *Strategikon* says that they 'ought not be drawn up in close order ... but in irregular groups, that is three or four armed with javelins and shields so they may protect themselves if necessary while hurling the javelin. They should also have one archer to provide covering fire for them.'

Infantry are predominant in this siege scene from the Arch of Constantine. During sieges the cavalry would usually be deployed on foraging and scouting duties. The helmets worn by the men on the left are the late Roman-style Attic helmets of single bowl construction. They are similar to the classical Attic style, but different enough to make artistic convention unlikely. (Deutsche Archaologische Institut, Rome)

Late Roman cavalrymen also fought using skirmishing tactics, and although they might have worn armour, they could be considered as 'light cavalry'. On the march they might act as scouts, forage for food, lay enemy territory to waste or protect the flanks and rear of the column. When the army formed up for battle the cavalry would be called on to screen the deployment, hamper enemy deployment, protect the flanks of the infantry, defeat enemy cavalry and pursue broken opponents. They were not expected to deliver the crushing blow that would defeat the enemy army; that was the job of the infantry.

The best surviving account of 3rd-century cavalry in action comes from Zosimus, who clearly describes the skirmish tactics employed by Aurelian's cavalry against Palmyran *cataphracts* in 272:

> He [Aurelian] ordered his cavalry not to engage immediately with the fresh cavalry of the Palmyrans, but to wait for their attack and pretend to flee, and to continue so doing until excessive heat and the weight of their armour had so wearied men and horses that they had to give up the chase. This stratagem worked, as the cavalry adhered to the order of the Emperor. When they saw their enemy tired and that the horses were scarcely able to stand under them, or themselves to move, the Romans drew up the reins of their horses and, wheeling around, charged the enemy, trampling them as they fell from their horses. A confused slaughter ensued, some falling by the sword and others by their own and their enemies' horses.

(Zosimus, *The New History*, 1.25)

Zosimus goes on to describe the several follow-on engagements in which the infantry formed the main battleline 'with shields close to each other and in compact formation' while the cavalry employed the same hit-and-run light cavalry tactics, but this time with less success:

> At the commencement of the engagement, the Roman cavalry made a partial withdrawal, in case the Palmyrans, who outnumbered them and were better horsemen, should surround the Roman Army unawares. But the Palmyran cavalry pursued them so fiercely, though their ranks were broken, that the outcome was quite contrary to the expectation of the Roman cavalry. For they were pursued by an enemy much superior in strength and therefore most of them fell. The infantry had to bear the brunt of the action. Observing that the Palmyrans had broken their ranks when the cavalry commenced their pursuit, they wheeled about and attacked them while they were scattered and in disarray.
>
> (Zosimus, *The New History*, 1.27)

Accounts of cavalry tactics from the 4th century present a similar picture. Ammianus Marcellinus describes a cavalry action as 'not a pitched battle but a succession of quick skirmishes' (*The Later Roman Empire AD 353–378*, 15.4.8). When the army deploys for battle it is still the infantry who are expected to form up in the centre to fight the main action – 'their flank covered by squadrons of cavalry' (*The Later Roman Empire AD 353–378*, 16.12.3). This is how the Roman Army deployed for the battle of Strasbourg in 357 and at Adrianople in 378. Although the infantry were expected to bear the brunt of the heavy fighting, the success of the cavalry in protecting the flanks and defeating the enemy cavalry could decide the action.

In terms of the actual formations used by Roman cavalryman, according to Asclepiodotus:

> There are various formations of cavalry of many kinds, some square, some oblong, some rhombus-shaped, while others are brought together in a wedge. All these formations are good when adopted at the right time, and one would not pick out one of them and judge it superior to the others, since in another spot against different enemies and on a different occasion one might find another formation more useful than the one for which it had adopted.
>
> (Asclepiodotus, *Tactics*, 7.1–2)

The wedge and the rhomboid, a diamond-shaped formation, were particularly suited to a fast skirmish action. With the leader and standard bearer at the point, command and control of the unit became simple, as all the troopers had to do was conform to the movement of the standard. These formations allowed 'the carrying out of sharp wheeling

SKIRMISHERS

Much, perhaps most, of the Roman soldier's combat experience would have been gained in small engagements as skirmishers rather than pitched battle. This scene recreates a description by Ammianus Marcellinus of such an action that took place in the upper Rhine valley in 357 AD, prior to the battle of Strasbourg. (© Gerry Embleton, Osprey Publishing)

movements ... for it is hard to wheel about with square formations' (Arian, *Ars Tactica*, 16.8). Furthermore, as Vegetius tells us, a wedge 'pierces the enemy line by a multitude of dart directed to one particular place' (*De Re Militari*). The cavalry wedge, therefore, was naturally a preferred formation of light horse archers such as the Scythians and

CAVALRY IN PURSUIT, MILVIAN BRIDGE, AD 312

This plate, based on a relief from the Arch of Constantine, shows the pursuit and destruction of Maxentius' Praetorians by Constantine's heavy cavalry supported by horse archers. The Praetorians are retreating over the bridge which has suddenly collapsed in the middle, throwing many of them into the water. (© Christa Hook, Osprey Publishing)

Huns, and should not be confused with the Germanic wedge which was more like an attack column.

The square and oblong formations would be used when complicated manoeuvre was less important than the ability to deliver an effective charge. A square was usually four ranks deep. Arrian tells us:

> Cavalry drawn up in depth do not afford the same assistance as do infantry in depth, for they do not push on those in front of them, since one horse cannot push against another in the way that infantry push on with their shoulders and flanks. Nor when they are contiguous with those drawn up in the front do they constitute a single massed weight for the whole body of troops; on the contrary, if they mass and press against each other, they rather cause the horses to panic.
>
> (Arrian, *Ars Tactica*, 16.8)

The author of the *Strategikon* made the same point, saying that four ranks was enough and that extra depth added nothing. However, he conceded that the number of good soldiers capable of fighting in the front rank were limited in his day, making it 'necessary to regulate the depth of the formation according to the type of unit' (Maurice, *Strategikon*, 2.6). The better units could be formed five or seven deep and the worst up to ten deep.

Regarding the cavalry of the 5th and 6th centuries, when fighting from a distance with bows, their tactics would not have changed much from those described by Zosimus. They would ride up to their opponents in open order and probably in wedge formation to facilitate manoeuvre. They would discharge their arrows and, if they made no impression or if faced with a stronger opponent, would wheel away, conforming to the movement by their standard, to withdraw beyond bowshot and then wheel back to face the enemy again. If, on the other hand, their charge and arrow volley caused their opponents to flinch, they would continue to charge forward into close combat.

* * *

We can attempt to reconstruct how late imperial formations and tactics might actually have been used from the writings of Ammianus and Procopius. Taking an example from an engagement with Gothic infantry in 377, we find a Roman battleline deployed and ready to meet the enemy charge. The Romans would probably have been called to attentions with the enemy beyond maximum bow range – about 300 paces. Two ranks of archers, firing from behind the eighth rank, would probably open fire shortly after this. Firing at maximum range, at the dense target presented by the Gothic *cuneus*, the archers would be hoping to reduce the enemy's will to charge home rather than inflict serious casualties.

As the Goths drew closer to the Roman battleline, archery fire would become more effective, causing the advance to slow down and even halt before it came within close range. The two sides would now be between 50 and 100m apart. Casualties would have been relatively light, perhaps a few flesh wounds from arrows and a few faint-hearted men finding the opportunity to slip away. Ammianus describes the Romans as standing fast and remarks that no one 'strayed about or left the ranks' (*The Later Roman Empire AD 353–378*, 31.7.7). They would still be well spaced out as the javelin volley would not yet have been delivered.

Ammianus goes on to tell us that 'when both sides had advanced cautiously and halted ... the opposing warriors glared at each other with mutual ferocity. The Romans raised their morale by striking up their battle cry; this begins on a low note and swells to a loud roar, and goes by the native name of *barritus*' (*The Later Roman Empire AD 353–378*, 31.7.1). The *barritus* was of German origin and no doubt the Goths would be doing the

Model of the rear gate (*porta decumana*) of an Augustan camp at Haltern (Germany), one of several such camps along the River Lippe. At this early date, fortresses frequently display some irregularity in their internal layout. Here, in order to take advantage of the terrain, the gate is offset some 50m west of the via *decumana* (left side of photo). (Westfalian Museum of Archeology, Münster. Photo: S. Brentführer)

same thing. Both sides would be trying to intimidate each other with their battle cries and by clashing their spears on their shields. Tacitus gives a detailed description of the *barritus* and its effect.

> They either terrify their foes or themselves become frightened, according to the noise they make on the battlefield... What they particularly aim at is a harsh intermittent roar; and they hold their shields in front of their mouths, so the sound is amplified into a deeper crescendo by the reverberation.
>
> (Tacitus, *Germania*, 3)

Eventually, perhaps after only the briefest of checks, the Goths would begin moving forward again. When they were within 50m, the Roman archery fire might begin to cause actual casualties and then the front ranks would let loose with volleys of *plumbatae* (lead-weighted darts). At this point one of three things could happen: the Goths could hesitate and begin to draw back; the Goths could look as if they were about to charge home which might prove too much for the Romans' nerves, causing them to break; or with neither side intimidated, the Goths could close the last few paces and crash into the Roman formation. Ammianus tells us that the latter was the case and 'after an exchange of javelins and other missiles at long range, the opposing sides clashed and fought foot to foot in *testudo* formation' (*The Later Roman Empire AD 353–378*, 31.7.7).

Just prior to the clash, the fifth, sixth and seventh ranks would loose a volley of javelins and then the file closers would push them forward to support the front ranks, while the archers continue to fire at high trajectory, dropping arrows on the rear of the enemy formation. According to the *Strategikon*, the men in the front two ranks, having thrown their darts, would crouch down, lock shields and then:

> fix their spears firmly in the ground, holding them inclined forward and straight out using their shields... They also lean their shoulders and put their weight against the shields to resist any pressure from the enemy. The third man, who is standing nearby upright, and the fourth man, hold their spears like javelins, so when the foe gets close they can use them either for thrusting or for throwing and then draw their swords.
>
> (Maurice, *Strategikon*, XII)

Now a shoving match would ensue. Casualties resulted from the exchange of missile weapons by the men behind the front ranks; others fell to the spears and swords of the enemy at the first clash. Now it was more a trial of stamina. As long as the soldier kept his footing and did not slip, he was unlikely to receive serious injury. In the tight press there would have been little room to use weapons effectively.

Eventually, one side would begin to feel that things were not going well, either because they were being pushed back by a stronger formation or because of a sudden

PARADE, CLIBANARII, ROME, 357 AD

The unit of armoured cavalry depicted here is the *Scola Scutariorum Clibanariorum*, one of the new guards unit created by Constantine to replace the Praetorians, who were disbanded after the Milvian Bridge disaster. Given the occasion and the status of the unit, the soldiers' equipment, which shows Persian origin, is far more uniform and elaborate than one might find in a line unit on campaign. (© Christa Hook, Osprey Publishing)

disaster, like a new enemy hitting them in the flank or rear. As morale began to crumble, men in the rear ranks would start slipping away, defying the efforts of the file closers to keep them in line. This would further weaken the formation, hastening their demise. Eventually the whole formation gave way and the real casualties were inflicted. Ammianus vividly describes what happened to men who broke and ran. 'The fugitives on either side were pursued by the cavalry, who hacked at their heads and backs with all their strength, while at the same time men on foot hamstrung those who had got away but were checked by fright... The whole field was strewn with corpses, amongst whom were some only half dead who still nursed a futile hope of survival' (*The Later Roman Empire AD 353–378*, 31.7.7).

Shock tactics were used by the *foederati* and other primarily Germanic troops in the Roman Army. The soldiers, the ancestors of the medieval knight, did not skirmish at a distance; armed with lances and shields and perhaps supported by Roman or Hun horse archers, they would charge directly at the enemy and attempt to destroy him in close combat. Such a charge is described in the *Strategikon*:

> At the command '*Junge*' [Close ranks], the soldiers close up from the rear for the charge. With the troops marching in close formation, particularly after they have closed in tightly from the flanks, the archers open fire and the command is given: '*Percute*' [Charge]. The *dekarch* and *pentarchs* [experienced men in the front two ranks] then lean forward, cover their heads with their shields, hold their lances high as their shoulders in the manner of the fair-haired races, and protected by their shields they ride in good order, not too fast but at a trot, to avoid having the impetus of their charge breaking up their ranks before coming to blows with the enemy, which is a real risk.
>
> (Maurice, *Strategikon*, 3)

Facing a cavalry attack would have been much the same as facing a German infantry charge. In almost all cases, the Roman foot soldiers would have held their ground to receive such a charge at the halt. A frontal cavalry charge on infantry, however, would have been a very rare thing, for the simplest reason that while you can drive men on to do foolish things, you cannot do the same to horses. Modern re-enactments have found it nearly impossible to get horses to charge a shieldwall, particularly if the infantrymen are noisily clashing spears on their shields and raising the *barritus*. When this was attempted the horses stopped between 5 and 10m from the enemy. Some would just halt, some would rear up, while other would turn sideways or step backwards. Riding them hard did nothing to help, and it was even worse if the infantry charged the horses.

The Persians discovered the same thing at the battle of Sura in 531 when they went up against Belisarius' infantry, who were not exactly the same calibre as those of the 3rd and 4th centuries. It is worth reading Procopius' account of this engagement in full:

> The foot soldiers, and a very few of them, were fighting against the whole Persian cavalry. Nevertheless the enemy were not able either to rout them or in any other way overpower them. For standing shoulder to shoulder they kept themselves massed in a very small space, and they formed with their shields a rigid, unyielding barricade, so that they shot at the Persians more conveniently than they were shot by them. Many a time after giving up, the Persians would advance against them, determined to break up and destroy their line, but they always retired again from the assault unsuccessful. For their horses, annoyed by the clashing of the shields, reared up and made confusion for themselves and their riders.
>
> (Procopius, *The Secret History*, 1.18)

In the 4th century, when the infantry were more capable of aggressive action, Julian's soldiers quickly charged the Persian mounted archers on two recorded occasions. This accomplished two things: it reduced the amount of archery fire the Romans had to sustain and, as the modern tests confirmed, threw the enemy horses into confusion.

As long as the Roman infantry held their nerve, therefore, they had reason to be confident in the face of cavalry. Far greater a danger was the cavalry's mobility which allowed them to get around the front or flanks of the infantry. The infamous defeat of the Roman Army at Adrianople was brought about due to such an attack by the Gothic cavalry on the Roman flank while they were frontally engaged.

With most armies based on cavalry by the end of our period, battles took on a much more fluid appearance than when infantry had formed their backbone. Procopius' battle descriptions are full of fast-moving actions by small groups of mounted men, so much so that they take on an almost 'heroic' flavour, with individual champions challenging one another and performing deeds of daring. The character of these cavalry engagements is brought out by Procopius when he describes a battle against the Persians: 'And both sides kept making advances upon their opponents and retiring quickly, for they were all cavalry' (*The Secret History*, 1.15).

While Procopius' battle descriptions seem to emphasize heroic individual deeds, there may be a certain amount of author's licence as he tries to portray his warriors in a Homeric light. The *Strategikon* presents a more disciplined view of 6th-century action, and constantly stresses the importance of maintaining order. For example, it recommends against using trumpets and battle cries:

> The better silence is observed, the less disturbed will the younger men be and the less excited the horses... The battle cry 'Nobiscum', which it was customary to shout when beginning the charge, is in our opinion extremely dangerous and harmful. Shouting it at that moment may cause the ranks to break up. For because of that shout, the more timid soldiers in approaching really close combat may hesitate before the clash, while the bolder, roused to anger, may rashly push forward and break ranks. The same problem occurs with the horses, for they too differ in temperament. The result is that the battleline is uneven and without cohesion; in fact, its ranks may well be broken even before the charge, which is very dangerous.
>
> (Maurice, *Strategikon*, 2)

Roman soldiers of the 5th and 6th centuries employed a mix of skirmish and shock tactics and were effectively equipped for both. Yet while the armies of the late Roman empire remained formidable, this did not mean that they were not vulnerable and subject to desperate defeat.

BATTLE: CRUSHED BY THE GOTHS – ADRIANOPLE, 378

One of the great difficulties for historians without military experience is understanding how the Roman Empire, with arguably 500,000 men under arms, could not raise enough troops to crush the relatively small number of Goths, Huns and Alans who had overrun the Danubian provinces in the 4th century. Surely, two years after the crossing of the Danube in 376, Valens and Gratian between them could have sorted it out?

There were two serious problems that made the task more difficult than appearances suggest. The first was that the number of deployable, high-quality troops was limited. There are modern parallels to this problem. One example is the great difficulty the NATO nations (collectively with several million men under arms) had in finding a mere 50,000 troops to deploy to the Balkans in the 1990s. Even then, about half the troops had to be drawn from non-NATO nations. The Roman field armies were supposedly mobile and deployable, but orders to move to a new area of operations resulted in mass desertions. Second, all troops were committed on other fronts and there was a very real danger that if a significant number were moved, a potential enemy would take advantage of this deployment and attack. This is exactly what happened in the first months of 378.

A Roman guardsman of Alamannic origin returned to his home across the Rhine in the winter of 377–78 and while there talked indiscreetly about Gratian's plans to lead western troops to the east, to engage the Goths. This intelligence enticed his countrymen (the Lentienses) to launch a number of probing raids across the frozen Rhine in February 378. Although these were beaten back by a brigade of Roman *auxilia palatina* (the Celtae and Petulantes), they confirmed the fact that much of the western field army had already marched to Illyricum in preparation for operations against the Goths. The Lentienses seized the opportunity to attack in force, crossing the upper Rhine near Argentaria (Colmar). Gratian was forced to recall the units he had sent east, mobilize the troops left in Gaul and call on the Franks for assistance. Although the Lentienses were defeated in a fast-moving campaign that demonstrated Gratian's courage and resourcefulness, the unexpected attack delayed the Western Emperor's plans to aid his uncle against the Goths by several months. It would also have greatly reduced the number of troops he would have been willing to send east.

Equally, even if Valens had been able to come to terms with the Persians in the dispute over Armenia, it was impossible to completely withdraw all the Empire's best troops from the eastern frontier. In the spring of 378 he personally moved from Antioch (which had been his headquarters for operations against Persia) to Constantinople, where he had to deal with an outbreak of popular discontent. This was partly a result of the Catholic population objecting to his Arian faith, no doubt aggravated by the proximity of the Goths and the dismal campaign so far.

Valens did not remain long in the city, preferring to establish his base at the imperial estate of Melanthias, about 20km from the capital. Here he gathered together his forces, while appointing the newly arrived western general Sebastian as *magister militum* (lit. 'master of soldiers', a senior theatre command position) to replace Trajan. Sebastian took a body of picked troops to carry on the guerrilla war against the Goths, buying time for the Emperor to marshal his main force. According to Ammianus, Sebastian selected 300 men from each available unit, while Zosimus says the whole force was 2,000 strong – a reasonable number for such special operations.

The Goths, meanwhile, were apparently mainly centred in the river valleys south of the Balkan mountains, around the towns of Dibaltum, Cabyle and Beroea, but bands ranged far and wide over most of the Thracian countryside. As Valens moved to Constantinople at least one band of Goths was operating in the region around Adrianople, but on learning of the approaching imperial forces they withdrew north-west along the Maritsa River towards Beroea 'laden with booty'. Other bands were still north of the Balkans apparently, since Ammianus mentions a fortified Gothic position at Nicopolis which is 90km due north of Beroea on the other side of the mountains.

Sebastian, with his picked force, apparently enjoyed greater success in hit-and-run operations against the Goths than his predecessors. Ammianus' account compresses several months of operations into a few days and makes it seem as though Sebastian was leading an advance guard of the main army. However, it is clear that throughout the spring and summer of 378 he and his men were actively engaged in chasing down small groups of Gothic raiders and clearing them from the area around Adrianople while Valens and Gratian gathered their forces. The strategy seemed to be to try to pick off the small bands of raiders one at a time while simultaneously containing them in a more closely defined area. To ensure that the Goths did not try to break out to the north-west, Frigeridus, a Roman general, and his western troops fortified the Succi Pass to prevent raiders from operating in the northern provinces.

A good idea of the kind of campaign being fought in the early months of 378 is provided by Ammianus, when he describes an action in which Sebastian engaged a group of Goths to the north-west of Adrianople: 'Towards evening he suddenly caught sight of some Gothic raiding parties near the Maritsa River. He concealed himself for a while behind dikes and bushes, and then crept forward quietly under cover of night to attack them in their sleep. His success was so complete that all perished except for a few who saved themselves by speed of foot' (*The Later Roman Empire AD 353–378*, 31.11.4).

This, and other similar actions, drove home to the Gothic leader, Fritigern, the danger of continuing to operate in small bands that could be engaged and defeated piecemeal while foraging or pillaging. He knew that the two emperors would soon make a move against him and therefore it became more important to concentrate his forces to engage them, rather than keep dispersed for logistical reasons. If he made the first move, he might be able to dictate the terms of the campaign, whereas if he waited he would be caught in a pincer movement and destroyed. Consequently he recalled all his followers and allies to the vicinity of Cabyle before evacuating the area, moving into open spaces where they would not suffer a surprise attack or lack of resources.

Meanwhile Gratian, having defeated the Lentienses, was proceeding eastwards. Not wishing to leave the west undefended, however, he apparently only had a small body of troops with him rather than an army. Ammianus calls them 'lightly armed' and they were few enough in number to move by boat down the Danube. He stopped for four days at Sirmium (Sremska Mitrovica, Serbia), suffering from fever, then continued on again down the Danube to the 'camp of Mars' (a frontier fortress near modern Kula on the Serbian/Bulgarian border) where he lost several men in an ambush by a force of Alans.

By this time Valens' army had been assembled at Melanthias. We do not know much about its composition since very few units are named in the sources. It probably contained a sizeable portion of the eastern praesental army and the *scholae*, although some units would have been left in the east. Several other units had been engaged in the Balkans for much of the previous year and by now would have been seriously depleted. These included the unnamed legions that fought at Ad Salices, the Cornuti who were engaged at Dibaltum, some elements of the *scholae*, the 300 men from each unit selected to form Sebastian's force and no doubt others who are not identified. Valens probably had 15,000–20,000 men with him. Ammianus says that it was a varied force, presumably containing a mix of troop types and a high proportion of veterans.

Valens marched from Melanthias towards Adrianople. He would have known that the Goths had been concentrating in the region around Beroea and Cabyle and he probably intended to take the obvious route along the Maritsa River, following the retreating Goths that Sebastian had cut up as they tried to fall back to Beroea. His intention was probably to move west, past Adrianople, through the Maritsa Valley towards Philippopolis, cutting north when he reached the Sazliyka River, which runs south from the Balkans about half-way between Beroea and Cabyle. In this area he would be certain to encounter the Goths. Meanwhile, Gratian would move through the Succi pass to Philippopolis, and follow the Maritsa in the opposite direction to link up with him.

Unfortunately for the Romans, Fritigern moved first, striking directly south from Cabyle following the Tundzha River towards Adrianople with the intention of getting behind Valens' army and cutting his supply route from Constantinople. Their apparent target was the way station of Nike, about 24km from Adrianople on the road to Constantinople (probably near modern Havsa). Ammianus says that Roman reconnaissance found out that the 'enemy intended to intercept our lines of supply with a strong force' (*The Later Roman Empire AD 353–378*, 13.12.2), but what happened then is confusing. Valens apparently sent a body of foot archers and a troop (*turma*) of cavalry to 'secure the adjacent passes' and frustrate the Goths' intentions. This seems like a wholly inadequate force to do anything other than watch – especially as a *turma* was only about 30 men. It is also very unclear which route they guarded as it would have been impossible for a small force to watch several passes; probably they were sent up the Tundzha where they would have encountered the Goths moving south.

It seems likely that Valens had already marched west from Adrianople heading along the Maritsa valley when news reached him that the Goths were moving south from Cabyle along the Tundzha. He probably first thought it was only a small raiding party, but he soon realized it was a much larger force and he turned back towards Adrianople, establishing a fortified camp just outside the city. Now he had to make a decision. Should he engage the Goths or wait for Gratian to join him?

A number of factors influenced Valens' decision. First, his scouts reported the Gothic force contained only 10,000 fighting men. If Valens had at least 15,000 men, it would be very tempting to offer battle. Valens' political standing in Constantinople was very low at this point, as evidenced by the unrest he had to put down before embarking on this stage of the campaign. If he allowed a large Gothic army to take a position between Adrianople and Constantinople, he would not only find his supply lines cut off but the populace would feel abandoned by their Emperor. Finally if he did wait for Gratian, who presumably was only bringing a very small number of troops with him, Valens would have to share the glory, in exchange for only a limited amount of actual military support. With hindsight it is easy to fault Valens' decision to attack, but looking at the situation through Valens' eyes with the information he had at the time, it becomes clearer why he did what he did.

Ammianus says that the Goths moved slowly over the next three days. Encumbered by wagons and a train of non-combatants, this is probably the time it took them to negotiate the difficult road along the east bank of the Tundzha before emerging into the more open ground about 20km north of Adrianople. It is possible that the Greuthungi and Alans were approaching the rendezvous from a different direction, possibly along the west bank of the Tundzha which is easily fordable in several places.

The Goths had intended to head for Nike, bypassing Adrianople to the north, and then cut the road running south-east towards Constantinople. This plan presumed that

MOVEMENT OF GOTHS ACROSS EUROPE

Valens would have been further to the west, rather than occupying a fortified position outside Adrianople. Valens could no longer be bypassed and the Goths on the move with their wagons and families would have been very vulnerable to attack. Fritigern now had to either find a good position to fight from, or withdraw back to the north. If he delayed too long there was a risk that Valens would be reinforced and become too strong to defeat in battle.

This leads to the matter of how many men Fritigern actually had. Valens' scouts reported the force as 10,000 fighting men, which Ammianus says was erroneous, but unfortunately he does not say by how much. Numbers as high as 200,000 men are quoted by some historians but even the most incompetent of scouts could not mistake

200,000 men for 10,000. It seems more likely that Fritigern probably had something like 10,000 men, maybe a few thousand more, directly with him, but that some other bands, such as Alatheus' and Saphrax' Greuthungi and Alans, were close by but not in the immediate vicinity and therefore were missed by the Roman scouts. Had the Goths vastly outnumbered the Romans, it would have been noticed as the armies were deploying and some officers would have urged a withdrawal. However there is no indication that this happened, and although Valens was blamed by his contemporaries for attacking rashly and not waiting for Gratian, there is no indication that the Goths had an overwhelming numerical superiority. Had this been the case it would have been immediately seized on by the Romans to explain the defeat.

However many Goths there were, Valens believed they numbered 10,000, and he called a council of war to decide the next move. Sebastian and a number of like-minded officers urged him to attack at once. No doubt they were influenced by their recent success on the Maritsa and felt that victory was within their grasp. Others, led by Victor, the *magister equitum*, whom Ammianus says 'though a Sarmatian, was a prudent and cautious man' (*The Later Roman Empire AD 353–378*, 31.12.6) argued that they should wait for Gratian's reinforcements. This view was shared by Richomeres who had just arrived at Adrianople, in advance of the western reinforcements, carrying a letter from the Western Emperor, urging Valens to wait for reinforcements, and not attempt battle on his own.

The fact that the issue was debated at all indicates that if Valens believed the Goths numbered 10,000 men, his army cannot have been substantially larger. If the estimate of 15,000–20,000 Romans is correct, then it was probably on the lower side, since if Valens thought he had odds of 2:1 in his favour, he probably would not have hesitated. If he had 15,000 to the Goths' supposed 10,000 he needed to weigh the advantage Gratian's reinforcements would give him against the disadvantage of sharing the credit. In the end, 'the fatal obstinacy of the Emperor and the flattery of some of his courtiers prevailed. They urged immediate action to prevent Gratian sharing in a victory which in their opinion was already as good as won.'

As the council concluded and the Romans began to prepare for battle, Fritigern sent a Christian priest to the Roman camp with an offer of terms. He asked for the reinstatement of the original agreement made at the time of their crossing of the Danube two years earlier: land to settle in Thrace, in return for perpetual peace. Fritigern also sent a private note to Valens in which he hinted that he really wanted peace and that all Valens needed to do was make a show of force to cower the Goths, after which Fritigern would be able to persuade them to come to terms. Fritigern possibly believed he could defeat the Romans and hoped to draw Valens out rather than risk being besieged in his camp when hunger and disease would have been even deadlier enemies.

THE OPENING MOVES

In any event, the peace overtures were rejected and at dawn on 9 August 378, Valens left his baggage, the imperial treasury and his civilian councillors inside the city, guarded by legions, and marched from Adrianople at the head of the rest of his army. The day was blisteringly hot and the terrain was rough and hilly. After a march of 13km the Romans came in sight of the Gothic position which was probably along a dominating ridge immediately south of the modern hamlet of Muratçali which is 16km north of the centre of Adrianople and 5km east of the Tundzha River. The actual Gothic camp was probably centred on Muratçali which has a small stream running through it and is well protected by high ridges on three sides.

This location of the Gothic camp is not certain. The only other battlefield analysis was done by F. Runkel (*Die Schlacht bei Adrianople*, Berlin, 1903) in which he identifies the ridge at Demirhanli (which he calls Demeranliga) as the location of the Gothic position. This is exactly the same distance from Adrianople as Muratçali, but to the east rather than the north. Such a location presumes the Goths made further progress towards Nike. While the Demirhanli ridge provides a good defensive position to attack from the west, it would be easily outflanked to the south (where the main Roman road lay) and more importantly it has no water source behind the ridge for the encamped Goths to use. The ravines are also more open with a much smaller chance of the Gothic cavalry escaping detection. In contrast the Muratçali site offers a watered, protected camp location easily defensible on three sides and close to the Tundzha for forage and ample water. The shape of the ridge and its gullies also makes it easy to lose sight of troops if to the south, as the Romans were, but the high points of the ridge, where the Goths were positioned, offer clear views in all directions.

Although contemporary accounts constantly refer to the Romans encountering a circle of wagons (not only here but also at Ad Salices), it would be wrong to think that they would have been formed in a single large circle. The Goths were a whole people on the move, and even if some families and baggage had been left behind at Cabyle, it is quite likely that there were at least 30,000 people including women, children, invalids, captives and slaves with probably about 2,000–5,000 wagons. Even at the lower estimate, this would have resulted in a line of wagons about 15km long in single file (a full day's march) which, if drawn into a circle, even when the animals were released and brought into the middle, would have resulted in a massive 2–3km diameter circle that would have taken an entire day to form. It is much more likely that clan and family groupings formed several smaller groupings of a few wagons close to the water supply while some wagons would have been used as a barricade to guard the vulnerable approaches to the main camp area.

At about 2.00pm the Romans began to deploy. The right-wing cavalry formed the head of the column and moved forward to screen the deployment while the infantry began

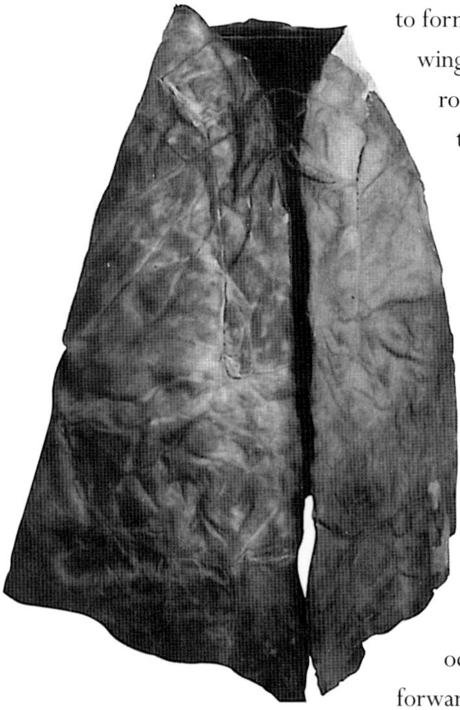

Front view of a remarkably well-preserved leather cloak dating from the Roman period, found at Sogaards Mose, Denmark. Finds like these provide clues to the types of clothing worn along the frontiers of the empire, which would ultimately find their way into the imperial armies. (Skive Museum, Denmark; photograph by Niels Thomsen, Stockholm)

to form up behind them, facing the Goths, in their customary two lines. The left-wing cavalry, forming the rear of the march column, were strung out along the road a long way back and hastened to move up, probably swinging off the ridge to the west to move up the relatively flat ground of the wide Tundzha Valley.

It is often assumed that the Goths remained inside their wagon laager and fought from behind the barricade, but this is highly unlikely. Usual practice was to engage the enemy in the open and only fall back on the camp if defeated. Had the Goths remained behind the wagons they would have not only surrendered initiative to the Romans but they would have been unable to use their preferred tactic of charging into hand-to-hand combat and engaging the enemy with spears, swords and shields. It is far more likely that the Goths formed up on the dominating ridge just south of Muratçali while the majority of the wagons were tucked away behind the ridge.

It is also clear from the descriptions of the battle by Ammianus that the conflict took place in the open, not amongst the wagons. In fact on one occasion he says that one part of the Roman line managed to fight its way forward as far as the wagons, clearly indicating that the fighting took place outside the wagon laager. This occurred on the Gothic right flank where the wagons were probably used to block the open approach to the camp from the Tundzha Valley.

As the Romans began to deploy, Fritigern played for time. Although he had sent out a summons for all his troops to converge, not all of his forces were in the immediate vicinity. In particular, the Greuthungi and Alans, who were foraging along the Tundzha further north, had not yet joined up. Therefore, he again sent envoys to Valens ostensibly to try to negotiate peace but in reality to buy time. According to Ammianus:

> The enemy deliberately wasted time so that their own cavalry, which was expected at any moment, might have a chance to get back while this sham armistice lasted, and also to ensure that our men, who were already exhausted by the summer heat should be parched with thirst. With this in view they fired the countryside over a wide area, feeding the flames with wood and other dry material. A further fatal circumstance was that both men and beasts were tormented by severe hunger.
>
> (Ammianus, *The Later Roman Empire AD 353–378*, 31.12.12)

Negotiations went back and forth, hung up on technicalities and protocol. At first the Romans rejected the Gothic envoys as being too lowly in rank. Then Fritigern offered to negotiate in person if some high-ranking Romans were sent as hostages. Valens proposed sending his kinsman, the tribune Equitus, but Equitus objected on the grounds that he had previously escaped as a prisoner of war from Dibaltum and he feared the Goths would take revenge on him. Eventually Richomeres volunteered to go.

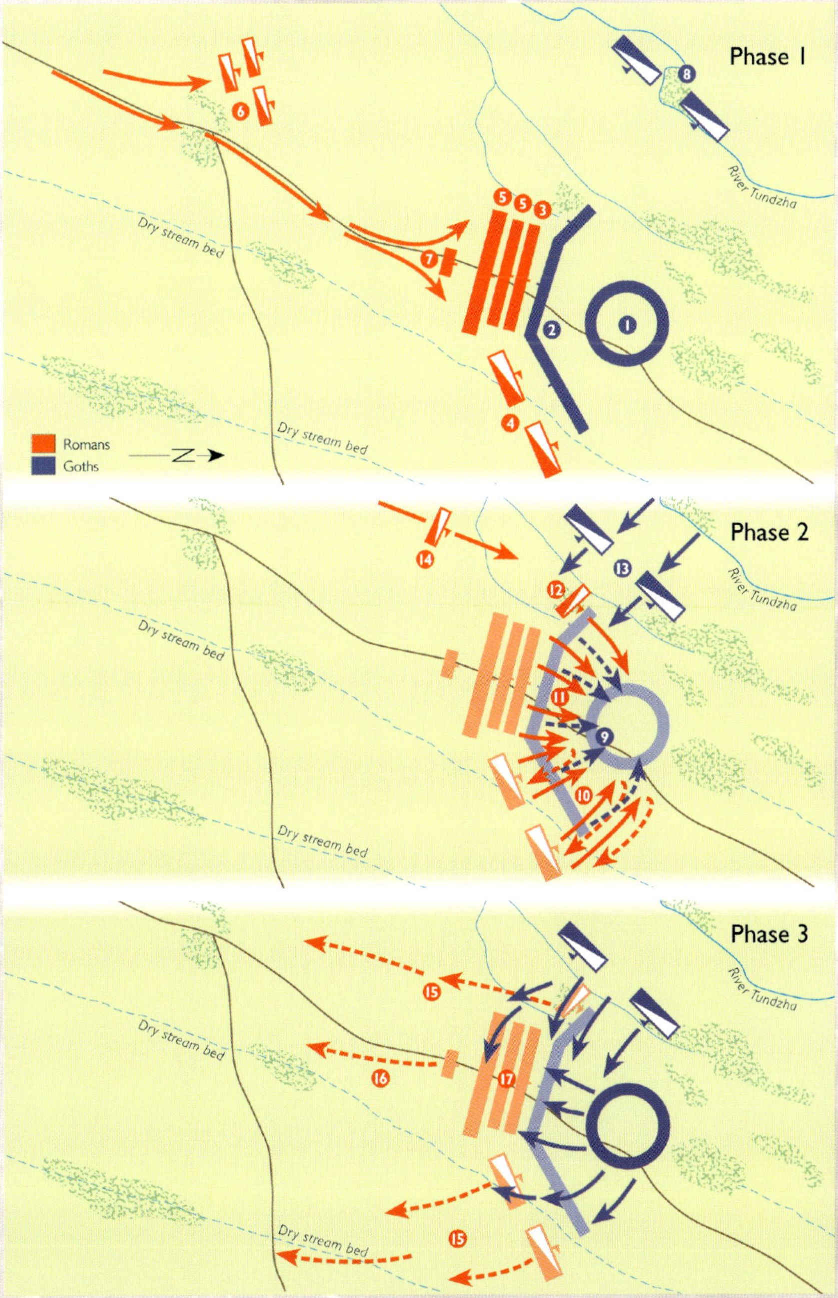

BATTLE OF ADRIANOPLE, AD 378

Phase 1: Roman Army deploys from front line of march with cavalry on the right wing and light infantry in lead. 1) Gothic wagon circle defended by infantry; 2) Gothic light infantry; 3) Roman light infantry; 4) Roman cavalry on right wing (*sagitatti* and *scutarii*); 5) Roman heavy infantry; 6) Roman cavalry on left wing; 7) Roman reserves (Batavi); 8) Gothic cavalry (arriving late).

Phase 2: While the Goths try to delay the battle to allow their cavalry to return, the two armies come to blows. 9) Gothic infantry withdraws to laager during negotiations; 10) *Sagitatti* and *scutarii* repulsed; 11) Main Roman infantry force attacks laager; 12) Part of cavalry on Roman left wing attacks laager; 13) Gothic cavalry returns, shatters Roman left wing; 14) Roman cavalry on left still forming up.

Phase 3: 15) Most Roman cavalry driven from field; 16) Roman reserves withdraw; 17) Roman Army trapped between Goths counterattacking from laager and Gothic cavalry.

Fritigern's motivation here is obvious. He needed time for Alatheus and Saphrax to join him. But why Valens allowed these negotiations to go on is much less clear. If he had wanted a negotiated settlement he had the chance when the Gothic envoys first came to him back at Adrianople, but he had sent them away. Perhaps having seen the Gothic position, he was now less sure of victory. Perhaps he too realized that he did not have quite the superiority of numbers that he had counted on and therefore he was looking for a negotiated way out of battle, or perhaps to put off an engagement until Gratian could join him. Whatever the case, before Richomeres reached the Gothic camp on his diplomatic mission, the decision was taken out of Valens' hands by his subordinates.

BATTLE IS JOINED

The Roman skirmishers from the right wing, who were screening the deployment and keeping an eye on enemy movements, became engaged. What exactly happened is unclear. Ammianus says that a force of archers and *scutarii*, commanded by Cassio and Bacurius, 'impulsively launched a hot attack and engaged the enemy' (*The Later Roman Empire AD 353–378*, 31.12.14). The *scutarii* were probably one of the elite cavalry units

Detail of two soldiers from the mid-4th century Great Hunt mosaic at Piazza Armerina, Sicily.

of the *scholae*. The archers could have been either mounted or on foot, Ammianus does not specify. Since in an earlier incident he specifically mentions 'foot archers', his lack of precision here probably indicates they were a unit of horse archers.

It is highly unlikely that these troops launched an attack on the wagon laager. It is more likely that they were probing around to the left, looking for a weak point in the enemy defences and trying to see what lay beyond the ridge-line, which blocked all view to the west. Possibly they intercepted some other bands of Goths moving up to reinforce Fritigern's position, probably the scouts from the Greuthungi and Alans.

The job of skirmishers is to act as the eyes and ears of the army, keeping a watch on the enemy and preventing him from interfering with their own army's movements. They fight from a distance with missile weapons, using hit-and-run tactics. If they become embroiled in hand-to-hand fighting they will inevitably be destroyed. The Roman skirmishers in this case somehow got involved in more than they could handle. Possibly they only saw a few of the enemy and thought that they had a chance to inflict some real damage, but then the Goths threw in reinforcements that turned the tide. It might also have been arrogance on the part of the *scutarii*, who, as an elite, well-equipped cavalry unit, may have felt that they could defeat the enemy face-to-face.

Whatever caused the engagement, the result was predictable: 'their retreat was as cowardly as their advance had been rash' (Ammianus, *The Later Roman Empire AD 353–378*, 31.12.14). To make matters worse the retreating Roman cavalry were attacked by the Gothic cavalry, supported by the Alans.

As the Greuthungi and Alans chased off the Roman right-wing cavalry, the Tervingi launched an attack all along the line while the Romans were not yet fully deployed. The cavalry of the left wing was still not in position and they were struggling to move off to the left, down the steep hillside. It is also quite possible that some of the infantry were also not yet fully in position.

Ammianus provides a colourful account of what happened next:

> Our retreating troops rallied with shouts of mutual encouragement. But, as the fighting spread like fire and numbers of them were transfixed by arrows and whirling javelins, they lost heart. Then the opposing lines came into collision like ships of war and pushed each other to and fro... Our left wing penetrated as far as the very wagons and would have gone further if it had received any support, but it was abandoned by the rest of the cavalry, and under pressure of numbers gave way and collapsed like a broken dike. This left the infantry unprotected and so closely huddled that a man could hardly wield his sword or draw back his arm once he had stretched it out.
>
> (Ammianus, *The Later Roman Empire AD 353–378*, 31.13.1)

Probably what happened is that the retreating Roman right-wing cavalry rallied briefly but were hard pressed by the Gothic and Alan cavalry and chased from the field. They fled back past the Roman left-wing cavalry who were trying to move forward and deploy. The lead elements of the left wing probably engaged the pursuing Gothic cavalry and had some initial success, driving them back to the wagon laager. This success was no doubt a result of catching the pursuers in a state of disorder. The rearmost units of the Roman cavalry, however, were infected with the panic brought on by the routing *scutarii* and horse archers and, rather than supporting the lead units, turned and fled as well. As this was going on, Fritigern's main body charged down the hillside on foot, to engage the Roman infantry. This move resulted in the typical see-saw action that occurred when two battlelines collided and each side tried to push the other back. Meanwhile, however, the handful of Roman cavalry on the left wing were overwhelmed by the Goths and Alans and were routed. This exposed the left flank of the Roman infantry line and the Gothic cavalry charged into this open flank.

THE LAST STAND

The Roman infantry, now abandoned by the cavalry, were being pressed together from all sides. Ammianus' description of the confusion brings the battle to life:

> Dust rose in such clouds as to hide the sky, which rang with fearful shouts. In consequence it was impossible to see the enemy's missiles in flight and dodge them; all found their mark and dealt death on every side. The barbarians poured on in huge columns, trampling down horse and man and crushing our ranks so as to make orderly retreat impossible.
>
> In this scene of total confusion the infantry, worn out by toil and danger, had no strength left to form a plan. Most had their spears shattered in the constant collisions… The ground was so drenched with blood that they slipped and fell … some perished at the hands of their own comrades… The sun, which was high in the sky scorched the Romans, who were weak from hunger, parched with thirst, and weighed down by the burden of their armour. Finally our line gave way under the overpowering pressure of the barbarians, and as a last resort our men took to their heels in a general rout.

(Ammianus, *The Later Roman Empire AD. 353–378*, 31.13.3)

While many of those who could fled the scene, some elite units held their ground. Two of the army's senior *legiones palatina*, the Lanciarii and the Matiarii, held firm, unshaken in the midst of the confusion. Valens, apparently on foot and abandoned by most of his bodyguard, managed to make his way over to them and from the temporary refuge of their ranks, he ordered Trajan and Victor to bring up the reserves. But the reserves were no longer there. Victor sought out the Batavi, who had been placed in reserve nearby, but they had already fled. Victor did the same, as did Richomeres and Saturninus, leaving the Emperor to his fate.

We do not know much about shield designs from the 3rd century, but finds from Dura Europos indicate that mythical scenes were popular. They could well have been individual designs painted on a background of a common unit colour. This conjectural reconstruction shows that the owner was a follower of Mithras, the most popular soldiers' religion until well into the Christian period. (Simon MacDowell)

There are two stories of Valens' death. The first is that he was killed by an arrow and fell amongst the ranks of the few remaining soldiers of the Lanciarii and Matiarii and his body was never found. The other is that, although wounded by the arrow, he did not die immediately, but was taken by his guards and some eunuchs to a nearby farm house which had a fortified second storey. The house was attacked by the Goths who did not know that the Emperor was inside. The defenders managed initially to drive back the Goths with archery but they returned and piled up brushwood and straw against the house and set fire to it. One man jumped from a window and was taken prisoner by the Goths but the others, including Valens, died in the blaze. The prisoner later escaped and told the story.

Ammianus says that two-thirds of the Roman Army died at Adrianople. Amongst them were Trajan and Sebastian as well as 35 tribunes. Ammianus compares the slaughter to Cannae and the comparison is apt because in both battles the Roman cavalry were driven from the field leaving the infantry to be hemmed in on all sides and destroyed.

THE DIVISION OF EMPIRE AND ARMY

FROM THE MID-4TH CENTURY, the story of Rome is a tale of two halves – east and west. In general, the Eastern half of the Roman Empire was, by the mid-4th century AD, economically stronger than the west, and there was no real evidence to indicate that Eastern 'Greek' soldiers were inferior to Western 'Roman' soldiers. Various military reforms had, however, been based upon Hellenistic Greek rather than Roman concepts, and also reflected Germanic or Iranian influences from beyond the frontier. Meanwhile the military importance of frontier peoples grew. Nor should the fact that half the Roman Empire fell to barbarian assault hide the remarkable effectiveness of this late Roman defence structure, given the weakened foundations on which it was built. A watertight frontier was now impossible, so the late Roman Army

Justinianic defences at Martyropolis (modern Silvan, Turkey) built when the city became the base for the new general of Armenia. (Michael Whitby)

relied on a screen of garrisons backed by mobile field armies. Garrisons were to hold back minor enemy incursions and, by forcing an invader to disperse in search of food, they also made him vulnerable to counterattack by the nearest army.

The weakness of this system lay in the slow speed even of field armies, which also had to be spread over a wide area, decreasing the emperor's control. The Roman Army also failed to achieve a decisive superiority in cavalry, while troops tied down its static garrison duties declined in quality. Meanwhile, late Roman emperors generally owed their position to the army; power often lay in the hands of competing generals, while civil wars were more of a threat to ordinary people than were foreign invasions.

The Byzantine Empire was, of course, merely the eastern part of the old Roman Empire under a new name – the disappearance of the western half in the 5th century generally being regarded as the moment of transition. Though deeply Christian, Byzantium was very militarized and as cruel as any of its foes, with religious strife being almost as common as religious debate. Although the Byzantine Empire was a continuation of the Roman Empire and faced similar military problems, its solutions were very different. In North Africa, for example, Rome's large army concentrated on

The ruined walls of Dura Europos by the River Euphrates. (Ancient Art and Architecture)

HUNNIC RAIDS AND DISINTEGRATION OF THE WEST

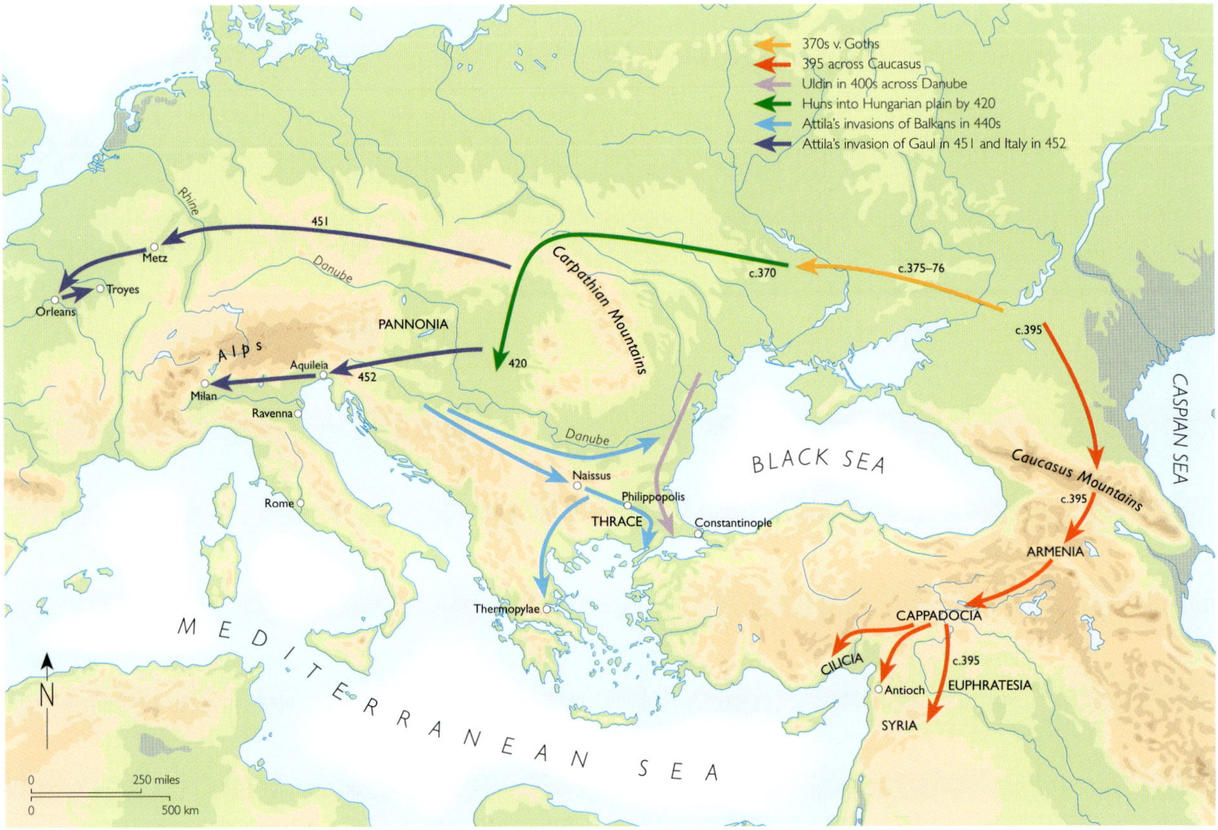

securing main roads and urban centres. Byzantium's small army built more fortifications and took a defensive stance.

By the late 5th century, Roman troops were so demoralized that emperors feared to go to war because a gathering of armies so often led to unrest. The 5th and 6th centries were, in fact, the worst for military revolts, and many modifications to the command structure aimed at avoiding such trouble. The Eastern Empire often relied on bribery to turn one enemy against another and so defended shrunken frontiers. However, Justinian I (r. 527–65) reorganized the armies of the east or, as it could now be called, the Byzantine Empire, and regained large parts of what had been the Western Empire.

By Justinian's time the Empire's revived economy allowed it to field a small but highly trained and a well-equipped army. *Foederati* units now included both barbarian volunteers and indigenous Roman troops rather than consisting of barbarians enlisted as tribal groups. Yet the army remained essentially a mercenary force as the old class of citizens, the basis of ancient Roman armies, had all but disappeared. It was still divided between garrisons and field armies. Local forces consisted of *numerii* of 200 to 400 men under a *tribunus*, one or two being based in each provincial town. Mobile mercenary field forces consisted of light cavalry *foederati* plus heavy cavalry *cataphracti*. The *hippotoxatai* horse archers formed the fighting elite and proved devastating in North Africa and Italy. Hand-picked and highly trained armoured *cataphracti* were not new, but again proved effective, though expensive. On the other hand the empire now lacked many good horse-raising regions, though Justinian did try to reserve Cappadocia for the breeding of large cavalry mounts.

Central to the new military structure was the *comitatus*. Copied by Germanic kings from the Romans in the 3rd century, it was borrowed back by Justinian and his generals

JUSTINIAN'S ARMY, 6TH CENTURY AD
In the centre of the scene is a Thracian cavalryman of *Leones Clibanarii*, while to the left is an irregular soldier of the *Numerus Felicium Theodosiacus*. On the right of the scene is a Guards infantryman, armoured with a mail shirt and carrying a battle-axe and spear. (© Angus McBride, Osprey Publishing)

Excavations in the 1970s revealed the southern corner of the fortress at Exeter. The clay rampart was 6m wide but survived to a height of only 0.9m. About 8m in front lay a massive ditch, 3.8m deep and 4.2m wide (shown here). (Exeter City Council)

Belisarius and Narses. By swearing an oath to those who recruited them rather than to the state, they were naturally seen as a threat to the Emperor; nevertheless such professionals, enlisted on a long-term basis, formed a core around which large armies could be built.

Looking at the end of our period, in some ways the organization of 6th-century Byzantine armies seems remarkably modern. The units were divided into platoons or *dekarchia* which themselves consisted of small tactical sections led by NCOs. The old centurion had now become an *ekatontarch*, the most senior of whom served as second-in-command to the army's *comes* rather as the late Roman *vicarius* had done. An *ilarch* supervised the NCOs and junior officers, and also has command of half a regiment if this was split tactically. Junior officers included the *lochagoi* or *dekarchai*, the *pentarchai* and the *tetrarchai*, all being selected for bravery and intelligence.

By the early 6th century, cavalry were truly the dominant arm and still seem to have been divided between spear and archery specialists. Like the Sassanians, Byzantine horse archers shot to order by ranks, and were known for the power of their shots rather than their speed of shooting.

The tactics of the period were described in the earliest Byzantine *taktika* military treatise written by an unknown soldier, perhaps during the reign of Justinian. Most of this work deals with fortification, suggesting that the author was an engineer. It also referred to enemies capturing Byzantine outposts by 'wearing our equipment' and of the use of fires and smoke for signalling. In discussing open battle tactics the writer relied on ancient texts and archaic terms, though he did contrast these with his own day, e.g. when he stated that troops were drawn up in squares or oblongs instead of the old phalanx. The four front of ranks and those of the sides would be armed with long spears, those behind having javelins. Armour, he insisted, should be worn over a thickly padded garment, as should helmets. Cavalry formations were the same as the infantry, though in looser order. In battle, as our anonymous writer suggested, the elite should be the centre of the first and second lines, with the *Bucellari* guards held back as a reserve around the commander.

Horse armour, because of its weight and expense, was probably quite rare. Examples of full-scale horse armour have been found at Dura Europos, but their use was probably limited to the *clibanarii* of the eastern regions. Chamfrons like this one, although thought to be designed for cavalry games, may have been more widespread and used in combat by Western *cataphracti*. (National Museums of Scotland)

Amongst many interesting details were instructions on how infantry archers should defend themselves against cavalry attack. The first two ranks shot at the presumably unarmoured legs of the enemy's horses, while men further back shot high to drop arrows on a foe who, the writer stated, could not raise his shield while riding. Cavalry would not yet have had stirrups. As the enemy closed, the infantry picked up spears which until then had lain on the ground. At night, he suggested, men carrying lanterns should be fully armoured. Ambushes, he wrote almost regretfully, were a common tactic even amongst 'Romans' (Byzantines); and when making a feigned retreat non-essential equipment like sword scabbards could be dropped to add authenticity.

Where archery was concerned, a thumb draw was the strongest though other methods should also be used to avoid tiring the hand. Rapidity of shooting was, he declared, a matter of practice not technique, and it was also a good idea to shoot at an angle to the enemy's ranks so as to get around their shields.

DISINTEGRATION OF THE WEST

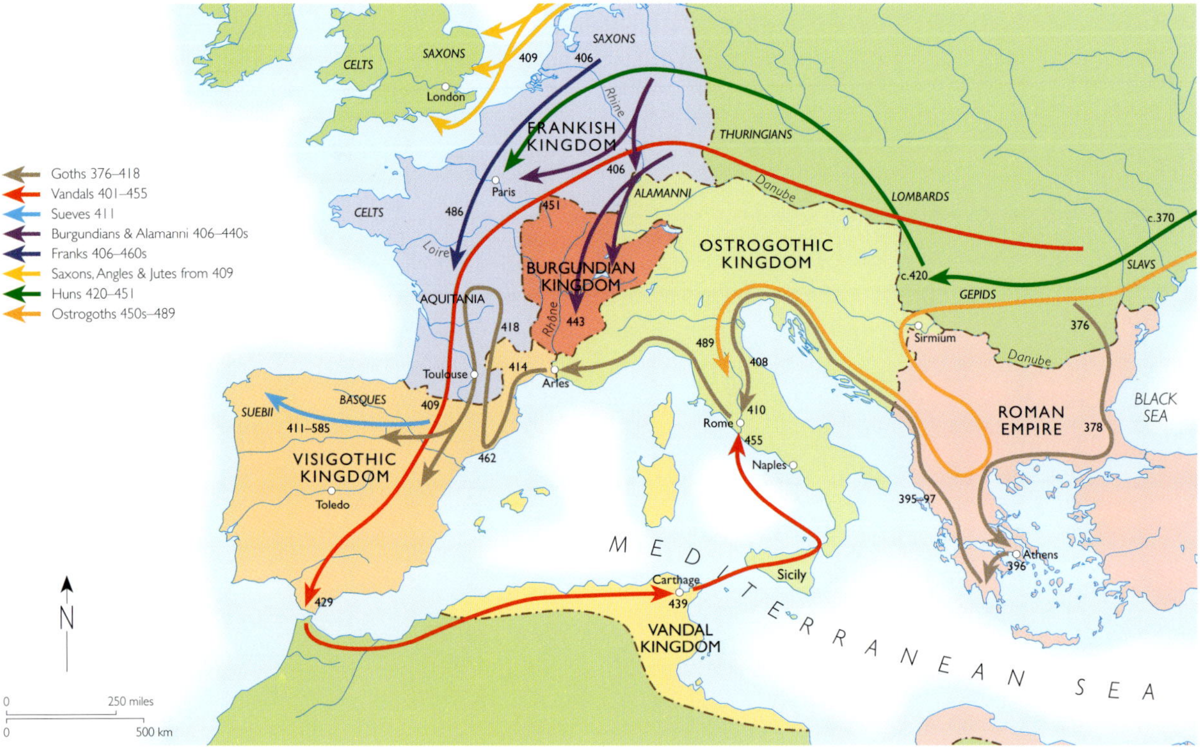

On the field of battle Byzantine commanders did use sophisticated tactics. At Taginae in 552, Narses placed dismounted *foederati* across the Flavian Way with infantry archers thrown forward on either side. Behind the archers and protecting them were Narses' elite cavalry, with a further force of archers and cavalry on high ground to the left ready for a counterattack. The Ostrogoth enemy charged the Byzantine centre several times, but were repulsed. Narses advanced, the Ostrogoths broke and the battle was won. Two years later at Capua the Byzantines again used a mixed force of infantry and horse archers to achieve victory. Analysis of such battles also suggests that spear-armed Byzantine infantry fought in close order behind their shields, whereas infantry archers operated in looser formation.

Byzantine heavy cavalry remained a once-only shock weapon, but during the 6th century large, densely packed formations of Byzantine and Sassanian horsemen both failed against steppe nomads. As a result, both armies divided their cavalry into smaller units with defensive, offensive and reserve sections. On the other hand, the Byzantines did have some advantages against nomadic peoples such as the Avars, particularly when fighting in the Balkans. During the winter months the nomads' horses were in poor condition while at night nomads were vulnerable because they did not generally make

COLLAPSE OF THE WEST, EARLY 5TH CENTURY
Here we see three soldiers from the late imperial period, as Rome's power collapsed. From left to right to see a *buccelarius* of a nobleman's household, a *limitani* frontier soldier plus an armoured *cataphract* of the *Sagitarii Juniores Orientalis.* (© Angus McBride, Osprey Publishing)

strongly fortified encampments. Against the Sassanians in the east, the Byzantines evolved a strategy of guerrilla warfare, tactics which lay behind the famous 'shadowing warfare' later used against Moslem Arabs. In such ways, the Byzantines lay the foundations of their future empire.

One of the most famous of the Dura Europos frescos is the so-called 'Ebenezer' scene. This detail includes figures wearing hooded mail or scale shirts (left), and various clothing styles seen in the Eastern theatre. The two unarmoured riders (centre & right) wear blue tunics and red trousers. (Yale University Art Gallery)

AFTERWORD

A PERIOD OF WAR LASTING four centuries and involving several different regional conflicts is unlikely to have a clear end, but three major developments can legitimately be considered to signal the conclusion of the campaigns of the late Roman period: in the Eastern Empire and North Africa the sweeping victories of Islamic Arabs; in the Balkans the progressive occupation of territory by Slav tribes, who eventually generated identifiable governing elites; and in the west the consolidation of tribal kingdoms in spite of Justinian's massive effort at reconquest.

In the east, while Heraclius had been locked in his desperate struggle with the Persians, events of enormous importance were unfolding in the Arabian peninsula. At Mecca a 40-year-old trader received a divine message from the angel Gabriel. For the next dozen years or so Muhammad stayed in Mecca, receiving more messages, and gradually built up a following, although this success increased tensions with the polytheists who remained the majority community. In 622 Muhammad and his followers moved north to Yathrib (Medina), an event (the *hijra*) which marked the start of the Islamic era.

By Muhammad's death in 632 he had asserted his control over Mecca as well as much of the northern part of the Arabian peninsula, and under his successors the Arabs pushed into Palestine and Syria. In 633 and 634 there was a series of limited victories, which permitted the Arabs to enter Damascus. In 636 a major Roman counter-offensive, commanded by the Emperor Heraclius' brother Theodore, who had assembled most of the military resources of the eastern provinces, ended in disaster at the River Yarmuk. Roman resistance was broken and over the next few years the major cities of Palestine and Syria surrendered, while in 640 the Arabs took over Roman Mesopotamia and campaigned into Armenia, Cilicia and Anatolia. In 639 attacks on Egypt began and by 642 this province too was captured; in less than a decade all the richest areas of the Roman Empire had fallen under Arab control.

What is most striking about this achievement – apart from its speed and complete surprise – is that at the same time Arab armies were dismantling the Persian Empire. Admittedly the Sassanid dynasty had been in turmoil since Khusro II's overthrow in 628, but the accession of Khusro's grandson Yazdgard III in 632 had brought some stability; however, Persian armies were unable to withstand this new challenge. By the early 640s Yazdgard had been forced to abandon all the royal cities in lower Mesopotamia and seek refuge in north-eastern Iran; in 651 Yazdgard was under pressure even there when his assassination terminated the Sassanid dynasty and confirmed Muslim rule over the whole of the Middle East.

By 700 the Arabs had wrested all of North Africa from Roman control, and had started to conquer the Visigoths in Spain. The one direction in which they failed to make lasting progress was in Anatolia, where Roman resistance gradually hardened. After capturing Alexandria the Arabs developed a powerful navy, which brought control of Cyprus and endangered the southern coastline of Asia Minor and the Aegean islands. On land the Arabs repeatedly raided large areas of impoverished Asia Minor, which resulted in the destruction and desertion of many of the major cities: refugees streamed away from the invaders in search of safety in the mountains, while repeated disasters challenged the stability of religious convictions. At Constantinople in the 670s however, the Arabs eventually stumbled decisively: the capital's substantial walls and the Roman Navy (with its secret weapon of Greek fire) were underpinned by the city's divine defenders, amongst whom the Virgin was prominent through the relics of her robe and girdle, and the Arabs were compelled to retreat.

Over the next generation a new order was created in Roman territory: the old social system based on the grand provincial cities had been swept away so that villages and rural markets came to the fore, while administrative organization was directed towards sustaining the military units responsible for frontier defence. Only Constantinople survived as a recognizable city, and even its population had probably shrunk to a tenth of what it had once been. Continued failure to reverse Arab successes contributed to religious upheaval: for much of the 8th century the rump of the Eastern Empire was riven by disputes about the validity of images in Christian worship, with iconoclast emperors supporting the Muslim view that images were idolatrous.

In the Balkans, the Romans experienced losses which, if less spectacular in terms of military action, were almost as complete as in the east. We have no detailed knowledge of the sequence of events after Maurice's death in 602, when Roman authority had been superficially restored over much of the peninsula. Phocas and Heraclius both gave precedence to eastern campaigns; troops were progressively removed from the Balkans, which permitted Slav groups to move unhindered across the countryside. The Avars occasionally invaded to extend their authority over the Slavs and surviving Romans, but even their humiliation outside Constantinople in 626 brought no lasting respite. As the Avar federation disintegrated, smaller tribal groups emerged to dominate particular areas, the Bulgars in the north-east, and Croats and Serbs in the north-west. By the latter part of the seventh century only the hinterland of Constantinople and isolated enclaves at Thessalonica, Athens, Corinth and other places accessible by sea remained under Roman authority.

In the western state, the deposition of the last Roman Emperor in 476 had brought one sort of end, with Vandals in control of Africa, Visigoths in Spain and southern Gaul, Merovingian Franks in northern Gaul and the Ostrogoths soon to arrive in Italy. Justinian's reconquest threatened to turn back the clock, but in the later 6th century it was the Romans who were being squeezed by the arrival of the Lombards in Italy and the reassertion of Visigothic power in Spain. The west was even lower down the list of imperial priorities than the Balkans, and little could be done to influence events: in 578 Emperor Tiberius had recognized this when he returned the gold which the Roman senate had sent as a gift for his accession with the advice that they should use this to purchase allies amongst the newly arrived Lombards. By the 590s Roman rule in Italy was confined to Ravenna in the north, which was precariously joined to another area around Rome, and from there to larger enclaves of the extreme south and Sicily. In the seventh century even the visit to Rome of Emperor Constans II did not conclusively re-establish Roman authority. Eventually a combination of religious hostility to iconoclast developments in the east, lack of respect for the absent and unsuccessful emperors, and resistance to tax demands terminated east Roman control over Rome and Ravenna; the Roman Empire survived in Sicily and parts of the south, but had ceased to be a significant element in Italian affairs.

The most important events for the future of the west occurred in France. By the early 6th century this had been largely united under the Merovingian Frankish dynasty, which had first suppressed Roman warlords in the north and then driven the Visigoths from the south. These victories were accompanied by the significant conversion of their king, Clovis, to Catholic Christianity rather than the Arian beliefs which other Germanic tribes espoused; but partitive inheritance between competing branches of the family then disrupted the kingdom's unity. During the sixth century Clovis' successors had on various occasions intervened in Italy, on both sides of the Roman reconquest, contemplated a grand alliance of tribes to challenge Constantinople, resisted Avar encroachments in southern Germany, and weathered attempts from Constantinople to destabilise the dynastic balance between different parts of the kingdom.

After the 630s Merovingian rulers wielded little real power, which increasingly slipped into the hands of the royal stewards, the most powerful being the family of Pippin. By the late 7th century the Pippinids had effectively displaced the Merovingians and it was the Pippinid Charles Martel who rolled back the Islamic invaders at Poitiers in 732. Thereafter his grandson Charles 'the Great' – Charlemagne – reunited Frankish Gaul and conquered the Lombards in Italy. Charlemagne's visit to Rome in 800 and his coronation in St Peter's sealed the creation of the Holy Roman Empire.

With new empires came new armies to fight their cause. Yet the Roman Army discussed in this book has left an enduring mark on military history. Not only are the campaigns and battles of Rome still studied in depth at universities and military colleges around the world, but the power of the Roman military machine makes it a perennial subject for Hollywood movies as well as publishers. The history of the Roman Army, after more than a millennium of study, shows no sign of losing its power.

FURTHER READING

PRIMARY SOURCES

Note: There are numerous translations of the Roman primary sources. The following are recommendations for further reading, not a definitive list of these translations.

Ammianus Marcellinus, *The Later Roman Empire AD 353–378*, ed. W. Hamilton, St Ives: Penguin, 1986

Anon, *De Rebus Bellicis*, tr. E. A. Thompson, Oxford: Clarendon Press, 1952

Appian, *The Civil Wars*, tr. J. Carter, Harmondsworth: Penguin, 1996

Arrian, *Array against the Alans*, tr. by Sander van Dorst: http://members.tripod.com/~S_van_Dorst/Ancient_Warfare/Rome/Sources/ektaxis.html

Athenaeus, *The Deipnosophists*, tr. Henry G. Bohn: http://digital.library.wisc.edu/1711.dl/Literature.AthV1

Caesar, *Caesar's Gallic Wars*, tr. W. A. McDevitte and W. S. Bohn, New York: Harper and Brothers, 1869

Caesar, *The Civil War*, tr. J. Gardner, Harmondsworth, Penguin, 1967

Caesar, *Commentaries*, tr. W. A. McDevitte and W. S. Bohn: http://etext.virginia.edu/toc/modeng/public/CaeComm.html

Caesar, *The Conquest of Gaul*, tr. J. Gardner, Harmondsworth: Penguin, 1982

Cassius Dio, *The Roman History: The Reign of Augustus*, ed. I. Scott-Kilvert, Harmondsworth: Penguin, 1987

Cassius Dio, *The Roman Histories*, tr. Earnest Cary: http://penelope.uchicago.edu/Thayer/E/Roman/Texts/Cassius_Dio/home.html

Cicero, *Selected Letters*, tr. D. R. Shackleton-Bailey, Cambridge: Cambridge University Press, 1986

Diodorus Siculus, *The Library of History* (various translators): http://penelope.uchicago.edu/Thayer/E/Roman/Texts/Diodorus_Siculus/home.html

Dionysius, *Roman Antiquities*, tr. Earnest Cary, Loeb Classical Library, 1964–78

Festus, *Epitome*, French translation: http://remacle.org/bloodwolf/erudits/Festus/index.htm

Florus, *Epitome of Roman History*, tr. E. S. Forster: http://penelope.uchicago.edu/Thayer/E/Roman/Texts/Florus/Epitome/home.html

Frontinus, *Strategemata*, tr. C. E. Bennett: http://penelope.uchicago.edu/Thayer/E/Roman/Texts/Frontinus/Strategemata/home.html

Granius Licinianus, passages based on translation of N. Criniti at: http://www.attalus.org/translate/granius.html

Herodian, *History of the Roman Empire from the Death of Marcus Aurelius to the Accession of Gordian III*, tr. Edward C. Echols, Berkeley and Los Angeles: University of California Press, 1961

Horace, *Odes*, tr. J. Conington: http://old.perseus.tufts.edu/cgi-bin/ptext?lookup=Hor.+Carm.+1.1.1

Hyginus, *De muntionibus castrorum*, Latin text at: http://www.thelatinlibrary.com/hyginus/hyginus6.shtml

Josephus, *The Jewish Wars*, tr. G. A. Williamson, New York: Penguin, 1981

Juvenal, *Satires*, Satires 1–3: http://www.fordham.edu/halsall/ancient/juv-sat1lateng.html

Lactantius, *De Mortibus Persecutorum*, ed. J. L. Creed, Oxford: Clarendon Press, 1984

Livy, *History of Rome*, ed. Rev. Canon Roberts, New York: E. P. Dutton & Co., 1912

Maurice, *Strategikon*, in Dennis, George T., *Maurice's Strategikon. Handbook of Byzantine Military Strategy*, Philadelphia, PA: University of Pennsylvania Press, 1984

Nixon, C. E. V., & Rodgers, B. S. (eds.), *In Praise of Later Roman Emperors: The Panegyrici Latini*, Berkeley: University of California Press, 1994

Onasander, *Stratêgikos* in *Aeneas, Tacitus, Asclepiodotus, and Onasander*, tr. Illinois Greek Club, Cambridge, Mass.: Harvard University Press, 1987

Ovid, *Ars amatoria*, tr. A. S. Kline: http://www.poetryintranslation.com/PITBR/Latin/ArtofLoveBkI.htm

Ovid, *Fasti*, tr. A. S. Kline: http://www.poetryintranslation.com/PITBR/Latin/Fastihome.htm

Pliny, *Historia Naturalis*, tr. J. Bostock and H. C. Riley: http://old.perseus.tufts.edu/cgi-bin/ptext?lookup=Plin.+Nat.+toc

Plutarch, *Fall of the Roman Republic*, tr. R. Warner, revised, New York: Penguin, 1972

Plutarch, *The Makers of Rome*, tr. I. Scott-Kilvert, Harmondsworth: Penguin, 1965

Polybius, *The Histories*, tr. W. R. Paton: http://penelope.uchicago.edu/thayer/e/roman/texts/polybius/home.html

Procopius, *The Secret History*, tr. G. A. Williamson, Middlesex: Penguin, 1966

Sallust, *Bellum Jugurthinum*: http://penelope.uchicago.edu/Thayer/E/Roman/Texts/Sallust/Bellum_Jugurthinum/1*.html

Suetonius, *The Twelve Caesars*, tr. R. Graves, revised, Harmondsworth: Penguin, 2003

Tacitus, *Agricola*, tr. by Alfred John Church and William Jackson Brodribb: http://www.fordham.edu/halsall/ancient/tacitus-agricola.html

Tacitus, *Annales*, tr. Alfred John Church et al.: http://old.perseus.tufts.edu/cgi-bin/ptext?lookup=Tac.+Ann.+1.1

Tacitus, *Germania*, tr. Thomas Gordon: http://www.fordham.edu/halsall/basis/tacitus-germanygord.html

Tacitus, *Histories*, tr. by Alfred John Church and William Jackson Brodribb: http://classics.mit.edu/Tacitus/histories.html

Theodosius, *Imperatoris Theodosii Codex* (The Theodosian Code): http://ancientrome.ru/ius/library/codex/theod/liber16.htm

Varro, *De Lingua Latina*: http://www.thelatinlibrary.com/varro.html

Vegetius, *De Rei Militari*, tr. John Clarke: http://www.pvv.ntnu.no/~madsb/home/war/vegetius/

Zosimius, *The New History*, tr. Ronald T. Ridley, Canberra: Australian Association for Byzantine Studies, 1982

SECONDARY SOURCES

Astin, A. E., 'Saguntum and the origins of the Second Punic War', *Latomus* 26, 1967, pp.577–96

Barker, P., (4th ed.), *Armies and Enemies of Imperial Rome*, Worthing: Wargames Research Group, 1981

Bath, T., *Hannibal's Campaigns*, Cambridge: Patrick Stephens, 1981

Bell, M. J. V., 'Tactical reform in the Roman republican army', *Historia* 14, 1965, pp.404–22

Bishop, M. C., and Coulston, J. C. N., *Roman Military Equipment from the Punic Wars to the Fall of Rome*, London: Batsford, 1993

Blockley, R.C. (ed.), *The Fragmentary Classicising Historians of the Later Roman Empire II*, Francis Cairns Publications Ltd., 1985

Blockley, R.C. (ed.), *The History of Menander the Guardsman*, Francis Cairns Publications Ltd., 1985

Bowman, A. K., *Life and Letters on the Roman Frontier: Vindolanda and its People*, London: British Museum Press, 1994

Breeze, D. J., 'The organization of the legion: the First cohort and the equites legionis', *Journal of Roman Studies* 59, 1969, pp.50–55

Brunt, P. A., *Italian Manpower 225 BC–AD 14*, Oxford: Oxford University Press, 1971

Campbell, J. B., *The Emperor and the Roman army, 31 BC–AD 235*, Oxford: Clarendon Press, 1984

Connolly, P., 'The Roman fighting technique deduced from armour and weaponry', in V. A. Maxfield and M. J. Dobson (eds.), *Roman Frontier Studies* (Proceedings of the Fifteenth International Congress of Roman Frontier Studies), Exeter: Exeter University Press, 1989, pp.358–63

Connolly, P., 'Pilum, gladius and pugio in the late Republic', *Journal of Roman Military Equipment Studies* 8, 1997, pp.41–57

Cornell, T. J., *The Beginnings of Rome*, London: Routledge, 1995

Cornell, T. J., Rankin, B., and Sabin, P. (eds.), *The Second Punic War: A Reappraisal*, London: University of London Press (Bulletin of the Institute of Classical Studies 67), 1996

Daly, G., *Cannae: The Experience of Battle in the Second Punic War*, London: Routledge, 2002

Davies, R. W., *Service in the Roman Army*, Edinburgh: Edinburgh University Press, 1989

de Beer, G., *Hannibal*, London: Thames & Hudson, 1969

de Beer, G., *Hannibal's March*, London: Sidgwick & Jackson, 1967

Dobson, B., 'Legionary centurion or equestrian officer? A comparison of pay and prospects', *Ancient Society* 3, 1972, pp.193–207

Du Picq, Charles-Ardant, *Battle Studies: Ancient and Modern,* Harrisburg: US Army War College, 1903 (trans. Col. J. Greely & Maj. R. Cotton, 1920)

Evans, R. J., *Gaius Marius: A Political Biography*, Pretoria: University of South Africa, 1994

Feugère, M., *Weapons of the Romans*, Stroud: Tempus, 1993 (trans. D. G. Smith 2002)

Fields, N., *Warlords of Republican Rome: Caesar versus Pompey*, Barnsley: Pen & Sword, 2008

Franzius, G., 'Die römischen Funde aus Kalkriese 1987–95', *Journal of Roman Military Equipment Studies* 6, 1995, pp.69–88

Frederiksen, M. W., *Campania*, London: British School at Rome, 1984

Gabba, E., *Republican Rome: the Army and Allies*, Oxford: Blackwell, 1973 (trans. P. J. Cuff 1976)

Goldsworthy, A. K., *Cannae*, London: Cassell, 2001

Goldsworthy, A. K., *The Complete Roman Army*, London: Thames & Hudson, 2003

Goldsworthy, A. K., *In the Name of Rome: The Men who Won the Roman Empire*, London: Phoenix, 2003

Goldsworthy, A. K., *The Punic Wars*, London: Cassell, 2000

Goldsworthy, A. K., *The Roman Army at War, 100 BC–AD 200*, Oxford: Clarendon Press, 1996

Goldsworthy, A. K., *Roman Warfare*, London: Cassell, 2000

Hanson, W. S., *Agricola and the Conquest of the North*, London: Batsford, 1991

Hopkins, K., *Conquerors and Slaves*, Cambridge: Cambridge University Press, 1978

Hyland, Ann, *Training the Roman Cavalry: From Arrian's Ars Tactica*, Stroud: Sutton, 1993

Keppie, L. J. F., *Colonisation and Veteran Settlement in Italy 47–14 BC*, London: British School at Rome, 1983

Keppie, L. J. F., *The Making of the Roman Army: From Republic to Empire*, London: Routledge, 1998

Keppie, L. J. F., 'Mons Graupius: the search for a battlefield', *Scottish Archaeological Forum* 12, 1980, pp.79–88

Lazenby, J. F., *Hannibal's War: A Military History of the Second Punic War*, Warminster: Aris & Phillips, 1978

Lazenby. J. F., *The First Punic War: A Military History*, London: University College London Press, 1996

Le Bohec, Y., *The Imperial Roman Army*, London: Routledge, 1994 (trans. R. Bate 2000)

Millar, F. G. B., *The Emperor in the Roman World*, London: Duckworth, 1977

Milner, N. P., (2nd ed.), *Vegetius: Epitome of Military Science*, Liverpool: Liverpool University Press, 1996

Nillson, M. P., 'The introduction of hoplite tactics at Rome', *Journal for Roman Studies* 19, 1929, pp.1–11

Oakley, S., 'The Roman conquest of Italy', in J. W Rich and G. Shipley (eds.), *War and Society in the Roman World*, London: Routledge, 1993, pp.9–37

Ogilvie, R. M., *Early Rome and the Etruscans*, Glasgow: Glasgow University Press, 1976,

Parker, H. M. D., *The Roman Legions*, Cambridge: Heffer & Sons, 1928

Patterson, J. R., 'Military organisation and social change in the later Roman Republic', in J. W. Rich and G. Shipley (eds.), *War and Society in the Roman World*, London: Routledge, 1993, pp.92–112

Rainbird, J. S., 'Tactics at Mons Graupius', *Classical Review* 19, 1969, pp.11–12

Rawlings, L., 'Condottieri and clansmen: early Italian raiding, warfare and the state', in K. Hopkins (ed.), *Organised Crime in Antiquity*, London: Duckworth, 1999, pp.97–127

Runkel, F., *Die Schlacht bei Adrianople*, Berlin, 1903

Sealey, P. R., *The Boudican Revolt against Rome*, Princes Risborough: Shire Publications, 1997

Smith, R. E., *Service in the Post-Marian Army*, Manchester: Manchester University Press, 1958

Speidel, M. A., 'Roman army pay scales', *Journal of Roman Studies* 82, 1992, pp.87–106

St Joseph, J. K. S., 'The camp at Durno, Aberdeenshire and the site of Mons Graupius', *Britannia* 9, 1978, pp.271–87

Sumner, G. V., 'The legion and the centuriate organization', *Journal of Roman Studies* 60, 1970, pp.61–78

Syme, R., 'Some notes on the legions under Augustus', *Journal of Roman Studies* 23, 1934, pp.14–33

Watson, G. R., *The Roman Soldier*, London: Thames & Hudson, 1969

Webster, G., *Boudicca: The British Revolt against Rome AD 60*, London: Batsford, 1993

Webster, G., (2nd ed.), *The Roman Imperial Army*, London: A & C Black, 1979

Wells, C. M., *The German Policy of Augustus*, Oxford: Clarendon Press, 1972

Wells, C. M., (2nd ed.), *The Roman Empire*, London: Fontana, 1992

Wells, P. S., *The Battle that Stopped Rome*, New York: Norton, 2003

Zhmodikov, A., 'Roman republican heavy infantryman in battle (IV–II centuries BC)', *Historia* 49, 2000, pp.67–78

INDEX

B

C

D

E

K

L

M

N

O

P

Q

R

S

T